SELECTED LETTERS OF E. E. CUMMINGS

EEC, 1952
(Marion Morehouse Cummings)

Selected Letters of

E. E. CUMMINGS

EDITED BY F. W. DUPEE AND GEORGE STADE

HARCOURT, BRACE & WORLD, INC. | NEW YORK

CONTENTS

1930–1939

1940–1949

1950–1954

1955–1962

ILLUSTRATIONS

FOREWORD

Here is a selection from the thousand or so letters of Edward Estlin Cummings which the editors of this volume have succeeded in recovering and examining. Many additional letters doubtless remain to be assembled and published in some future edition of a more definitive kind, with an editorial apparatus of corresponding dimensions. The present selection has been made and edited for the pleasure and instruction of the common reader, especially the reader who is familiar with Cummings' poems, plays, and prose narratives. For we do not suppose that Cummings' letters will be found to manifest an excellence wholly independent of the main body of his work — an excellence of the sort that would place them with the letters of those poets — they are very few, after all — who have been masters of the form.

On the whole, Cummings seems not to have regarded letter writing as either a conscious art or a vehicle for any urgent confessional impulse. He invariably and delightfully speaks his mind and is for the most part quite as candid in praising or censoring the minds, works, and actions of others. But he seldom soars to any heights of sustained introspection or plunges into any depths of mere personal scandal, about himself or anyone else. To be sure he is far from being a sloppy or vacuous correspondent; and the survival of the first and second drafts of a number of his letters testifies to the care he used when he wanted to. Insofar as conscious art is detectible in his letters it is recognizably akin to the art of his verse and prose, since he was as thoroughly all of a piece as any fine and celebrated poet has ever been.

To say this is not to minimize the supreme importance for his imaginative writing of acquired method and skill, that is, "technique." On this sometimes overinflated subject, no one has spoken more precisely than Cummings himself, in an early essay on T. S. Eliot: "By technique we do mean one thing: the alert hatred of normality which, through the lips of tactile and cohesive adventure, asserts that nobody in general and anybody in particular is incorrigibly and actively alive." Almost any Cummings poem is just such a tactile and cohesive adventure. Everything the mind can isolate for inspection in the poem, down to the seemingly arbitrary spaces between letters and the calculated misuses of capitalization, asserts that the poet is incorrigibly and actively alive. The reader may find that similar techniques are at work in many of his later letters and are possibly latent in the graphic and verbal exuberance of many of his earlier letters. The medium is notably different but the voice, with its disciplined spontaneity, is the same.

Being at once so gifted and so all of a piece Cummings was the delight, the wonder, and sometimes the despair of the several friends who have written about him in books of reminiscence. Among them John Dos Passos, his friend of many years, is the keenest observer. Writing in his superb memoir, *The Best Times,* Dos Passos brings Cummings alive in all his gay iconoclasm, his elegant courtesy, his quick generosities, his gleeful mischief, his brilliant talk, his sharp eye for the tender beauty of inconspicuous things and persons, his equally sharp eye for the vulgar absurdity of things and persons too conspicuous, his New England brahmin's unabashed pride in his own taste and judgment.

"Cummings was the hub," Dos Passos writes, meaning the center of the circle of young writers and artists (and their girls) who gathered in Greenwich Village in the early 1920's. Several of the group had known each other, slightly or intimately, at Harvard; and Cummings, on graduating with honors in 1915, had delivered a commencement oration in defense of "The New Art" (Matisse, Gertrude Stein, Stravinsky, etc.), which at that time was very new indeed. In addition, most members of Cummings' Village circle were connected in some way — as contributors, editors, owners — with the magazine which was the leading avant-garde publication throughout the 1920's — that is, of course, *The Dial.*

What impressed Dos Passos in his friend was not only the very original poetry which Cummings was publishing in *The Dial* and which, incidentally, led him to write to his father, in 1920, "It is a supreme pleasure to have done something FIRST." It was also his talk, or rather the relationship between his talk and his vocation as writer and painter. The artist's vocation and the man's conduct struck Dos Passos as wonderfully blended in the total personality of Cummings. The two friends spent hours exploring New York on foot together, as young people used to do at a date when walking in the big changeful city was pleasanter than it is now. And Cummings, always a busy note-taker and journal-keeper, combined wandering with the recording of impressions.

"As we walked," Dos Passos writes, "he would be noting down groups of words or little scribbly sketches on bits of paper. Both of us lived as much for the sights we saw as for the sound of words. Cummings had "all sorts of cryptic ways of talking. 'Dos d. your w.,' he would say when he thought I wasn't drinking fast enough." In those days they often dined in speakeasies with the great French-born sculptor Gaston Lachaise, his wife, and his wife's son, Edward Nagle, who had been at Harvard with Cummings and Dos Passos. "After a couple of brandies on top of the wine Cummings would deliver himself of geysers of talk. I've never heard anything that remotely approached it. It was comical ironical learned brilliantlycolored intricatelyca-denced damnably poetic and sometimes just naughty. It was as if he were spouting pages of prose and verse from an unwritten volume. Then suddenly he would go off to Patchin Place No. 4 to put some of it down before the fountain ceased to flow. His mind was essentially extemporaneous."

Just as Cummings had "all sorts of cryptic ways of talking," so he had all sorts of cryptic ways of writing. In his role as correspondent, these riddling maneuvers present the editors of his letters with certain problems of tact versus elucidation. To these problems we must now turn. We wouldn't for anything commit the impertinence of explicating (even where we *could* explicate, which isn't everywhere) his odd transliterations from the French and other languages, some of which he knew extremely well, or the tricks he plays with people's names. Three specimen explications should be enough to serve the reader as a guide for tackling the text on his own (where the text requires such tackling, which again isn't by any means everywhere). The first specimen is from a letter (No. 47) which is rich in multilingual wordplay. "La Shoot Dew Dough" = *la chute du dollar,* the alarming French phrase for the decline in value of American currency during the Great Depression. The two other examples are from letter No. 202, which, like many of the most elaborately stylized letters, is addressed to Ezra Pound: "poor shawn shay" = *pour changer,* "for a change." "O'Possum" = Old Possum, Pound's pet name for T. S. Eliot, a name which elsewhere in the letters undergoes various strange and significant deformations, for example, "Tears Eliot."

In his letters as in his poems EEC's way with punctuation, syntax, capitalization, and spacing is also very much his own, especially after 1918, when he began using a typewriter. The printed letters in this volume reproduce those singularities as closely as possible, except that spacing of the headings has in many cases been regularized. Only the more obvious mechanical errors in the originals have been corrected. In the vast majority of cases, moreover, deletions from the original text (indicated by three asterisks) occur only when the omitted material has been judged insignificant by the editors. *In not more than half a dozen instances has material been deleted for reasons of discretion,* although in a couple of cases initials have been substituted for full names. Among the omissions are, regrettably, many of the sketches with which Cummings often enlivened his letters. The presence of these in the originals is indicated by: [*sketch*]; and brackets are also used to enclose explanatory material too brief to require footnotes. The footnotes themselves have been kept at a minimum, our assumption being that most of the people and events referred to in the letters are likely to be known to most readers of this book. For certain identifications not provided in the footnotes, the reader should consult the section entitled "Events and Characters."

Cummings appears to have been a prolific correspondent from his childhood until his death, in 1962. Many of his letters have not survived or have not been available to us. These include letters written to his first and second wives, who have informed us that any communications he may have addressed to them have since disappeared. The principal sources from which we have made our selection are the following: 1) the letters of 1947–1962, a period during which he normally made and preserved carbons, which are in his widow's possession. 2) Letters addressed to Mr. or Mrs. J. Sibley Watson, large numbers of which survive. 3) Letters addressed to his mother, his father, his sister, Elizabeth, and other members of his family. These, which survive in still larger numbers, provide the fullest, most confiding, and most nearly continuous epistolary record of his life which we know to exist. His was the kind of New England family which not only encourages the writing of letters but solicitously preserves them.

For assistance in gathering, selecting, and editing these letters, we are chiefly indebted to the poet's widow, Marion Morehouse Cummings. Our next largest debt is to the poet's faithful friends, Mr. and Mrs. J. Sibley Watson of Rochester, New York, who have kindly assisted us with copy, funds, and hospitality. In addition we owe much to John Dos Passos and his book, *The Best Times: An Informal Memoir* (1966); and to Charles Norman and his biography, *The Magic-Maker: E. E. Cummings* (1958; revised edition 1964). For further assistance, financial, editorial, or secretarial, we are grateful to the following: Lewis Leary, formerly Chairman of the Department of English, Columbia University, Alan Lawrence Bateman, Gladys Weintraub, Susan Shaw, Joan Howard, and Michael Bavar. For permission to reprint letters in their collections, acknowledgments are due to the following: the Libraries of the University of Texas, and Mrs. Mary M. Huth, Librarian; the Library of the Boston Athenaeum, and Mr. Walter Muir Whitehall, Director and Librarian; the Yale University Library and Mr. Donald Gallup, Curator of the Collections of American Literature; the Princeton University Library; the Brown University Library, and Mrs. Christine D. Hathaway, Special Collections Librarian; the Houghton Library of Harvard University, and Mr. Rodney G. Dennis III, Curator of Manuscripts; the Lachaise Foundation, and Mr. John B. Pierce, Jr., Trustee.

EVENTS AND CHARACTERS

1894   EDWARD ESTLIN CUMMINGS ("Estlin") is born October 14 in family residence 104 Irving Street, Cambridge, Mass., the son of EDWARD and REBECCA CLARKE CUMMINGS. His energetic, versatile, and highly articulate father teaches sociology and political science at Harvard in the 1890's and in 1900 is ordained minister of the South Congregational Church, Unitarian, in Boston. The Irving Street household will include at various times Grandmother Cummings, MISS JANE CUMMINGS ("Aunt Jane"), EEC's maternal uncle, GEORGE CLARKE, and younger sister ELIZABETH ("Elos"), who eventually marries Carlton Qualey. EEC attends Cambridge public schools, vacations in Maine and at the family summer home, Joy Farm, in Silver Lake, N.H. "Ever since I can remember I've written; & painted or made drawings."

1911   Enters Harvard College, specializing in Greek and other languages. He contributes poems to Harvard periodicals, is exposed to the work of EZRA POUND and other modernist writers and painters, and forms lasting friendships with JOHN DOS PASSOS ("Dos"), R. STEWART MITCHELL ("The Great Awk"), EDWARD NAGLE (stepson of the sculptor Gaston Lachaise), SCOFIELD THAYER ("Sco"), JAMES SIBLEY WATSON ("Sib"), S. FOSTER DAMON, GILBERT SELDES, M. R. WERNER ("Morrie"), JOSEPH FERDINAND GOULD ("Joe"), ROBERT HILLYER.

1915   Graduates *magna cum laude;* delivers commencement address on "The New Art."

1916   Receives MA from Harvard Graduate School of Arts and Sciences.

1917   In New York. Lives at 21 East 15th Street with the painter ARTHUR WILSON ("Tex"). Works for P. F. Collier & Son. In April joins Norton-Harjes Ambulance Corps. Sails for France on *La Touraine,* meeting on board another Harjes-Norton recruit, WILLIAM SLATER BROWN, who will remain his lifelong friend. After several weeks in Paris EEC and Brown are assigned to ambulance duty on Noyon sector. Brown's letters home arouse suspicions of French army censor. On September 21, he is arrested together with Cummings, who refuses to dissociate himself from his friend. Both are sent to concentration camp at La Ferté Macé, where they submit to further interrogation. Following strenuous efforts on his father's part, EEC is released December 19. *Eight Harvard Poets* published, with EEC among contributors.

1918 Arrives in New York from France January 1. Moves with W. Slater Brown to 11 Christopher Street. Drafted during summer; stationed at Camp Devens until his discharge following Armistice. Moves with Brown to 9 West 14th Street, New York. Meets Elaine Orr, whom he will later marry and who is the mother of his only child, Nancy ("Mopsy"), now Mrs. Kevin Andrews. The marriage will end in divorce.

1920 In New York. Works seriously at his painting. Friendship with GASTON LACHAISE. First number of the new *Dial,* owned by Scofield Thayer and J. Sibley Watson, with R. Stewart Mitchell as managing editor, comes out in January. Other friends connected with *The Dial* at various times and in various capacities: PAUL ROSENFELD, music critic; HENRY McBRIDE, art critic; GILBERT SELDES, MARIANNE MOORE, KENNETH BURKE, EDMUND WILSON. On his father's urging, EEC begins, in September, to write *The Enormous Room,* an account of his and Brown's experiences in the La Ferté Macé prison.

1921 Travels to Portugal and Spain with Dos Passos, then to Paris, which remains his European headquarters for the next two years. Friends made during these years include EZRA POUND, HART CRANE, JOHN PEALE BISHOP, LEWIS GALANTIÈRE, GORHAM B. MUNSON, MALCOLM COWLEY, ARCHIBALD MacLEISH.

1922 In Rapallo and Rome during early summer; meets parents in Venice in late summer. *The Enormous Room* published in mutilated version by Boni and Liveright, New York.

1923   Summer at Guéthary, France. Back in New York in autumn, moves to 4 Patchin Place, which remains his New York address until his death. *Tulips and Chimneys* published.

1924   In Paris on first of several short trips he makes to Europe during the later twenties.

1925   Wins *Dial* Award. Begins to write and draw for *Vanity Fair. &* and *XLI Poems* published.

1926   His father killed in an accident. *is 5* published.

1927   Marries Anne Barton; this marriage also ends in divorce. *Him* published.

1928   *Him* produced in New York by Provincetown Players, April 18, James Light, director.

1930   [No Title] published.

1931   Trip to Russia. *CIOPW*, a book of pictures in Charcoal, Ink, Oil, Pastel, and Watercolors published. *Viva* published. First show of his paintings, in New York.

1932   Meets and soon marries Marion Morehouse, well known as model, actress, and photographer. Henceforth they are rarely apart. New York exhibition of his watercolors.

1933   Trip to Europe. Visit to Tunisia. Guggenheim Fellowship. *Eimi,* an account of his trip to Russia in 1931, published.

1935   Travels to Mexico in June and to California in July. *no thanks* and *Tom* published.

1936   ¹/₂₀ [One over twenty] published. A selection of twenty poems, the first volume of his poems to be published in England.

1937   Trip to France.

1938   *Collected Poems* published.

1940   *50 Poems* published.

1944 *1 × 1* published. Show of oils and watercolors at the American British Art Gallery in New York.

1945 Show of oils, watercolors, and sketches in Rochester.

1946 *Santa Claus* published. Special EEC number of *Harvard Wake*.

1947 His mother dies in January.

1948 Show of watercolors and oils at the American British Art Gallery.

1950 Academy of American Poets fellowship. Trip to France, Italy, and Greece. XAIPE published.

1951 Guggenheim fellowship. Death of Aunt Jane: a small inheritance.

1952–
1953 Charles Eliot Norton Lectures at Harvard. Lectures published in 1953 as *i:six nonlectures*.

1954 *Poems 1923–1954* published.

1956 Trip to Spain, Italy, and France.

1957 Gives Boston Arts Festival poetry reading in Public Gardens, June 23.

1958 Bollingen Prize in Poetry. *A Miscellany* (a collection of fugitive pieces) and *95 Poems* published.

1960 Trip to Italy, Greece, and France.

1962 Collapses of cerebral hemorrhage at Joy Farm and dies on September 3, at 1:15 A.M. *Adventures in Value,* photographs by Marion Morehouse with text by EEC, published.

1963 *73 Poems* published.

1965 *A Miscellany Revised* (an expanded edition of the 1958 volume) published. *Fairy Tales*, illustrated by John Eaton, published.

1899–1914

[104 Irving St., Cambridge, Mass.
November 27, 1899]

I AM SORRY
DEAR NANA
BUT I WILL
BE A GOOD BOY

2 / TO HIS FATHER

104 Irving St.
March 1st 1900

FATHER DEAR. BE, YOUR FATHER—GOOD AND GOOD,
HE IS GOOD NOW, IT IS NOT GOOD TO SEE IT RAIN,
FATHER DEAR IS, IT, DEAR, NO FATHER DEAR I,
LOVE, YOU DEAR,
ESTLIN.

3 / TO HIS MOTHER

[104 Irving St.]
March 23 1900

MOTHER DEAR I-AM VERY-VERY-SORRY YOU haVe The
BACK ACHE MoTher Dear. I-LOVE YoU VERY MUCh.
CaN I go oUT TO DAY. I HOPE I CaN go OUT TO DaY.
YOU DONT KNOW WHAT WE ARE GOING TO BUY.
YOUR LOVINg
SON-ESTLIN

104 Irving St.
[April 18, 1900]

DEAR FATHER. I SEND YOU THESE VIOLETS. TO
SMELL OF, ONE FOR MOTHER. I LOVE YOU BOTH
DEARLY AND MY AUNT JENNIE TOO, TELL HER I WILL
GO TO LYNN TO SEE HER

ESTLIN

5 | TO HIS PARENTS

135 Nahant St. Lynn [Mass.]
[December 16, 1901]

Dear Father and Mother,

I am well and I slept until six o'clock this morning. Grandpa
and Uncle John and I have been out and it is a very cold morning. We are all well. I would like to see you and baby sister, but
I like to stay here. The sea was high yesterday, and I went to the
beach a few minuets with Grandpa. i hope you are well. take
good care of Jack and Mack and Don. they were all much surprised and very glad to see me. i am going to take lunch with
aunt Jennie and Lawrence in the School-room at a quarter of
eleven. My cold is better and i can breathe through my nose
much better this morning. i have not had any trouble with my
ear. With love and kisses

Estlin.

6 | TO HIS PARENTS

135 Nahant St.
[December 19, 1901]

Dear Father and Mother,

I have received your letters and I hope you have received
mine. i will com home in a week. I went shopping yesterday with
aunt Jennie and I enjoyed it very much. I saw lots of toys there
and some very funny ons. I hav bought most of my Xmas pres-

ents and one for Mother. one of my presents was a bucking mule for Frederick. Daddy dear, I hope you are well. I think you will be glad to see me back will not you? Anyway i will be glad to see you. I am well.

[*sketch*]

> with love
> Daddy dear
>   Estlin

7 / TO HIS MOTHER

[135 Nahant St.
April 23, 1902]

Dear Mother

I hope that you and the baby are all very well are they? I will send a lion to you and I will send an elephant to baby sister. We have duck's eggs for   [*sketch*]   breakfast they are very good and I wish that you would have some. Wont we have a nice time up at the farm.

> With love
>   Estlin

My cold is better

8 / TO HIS GRANDMOTHER CUMMINGS

[104 Irving St.
May 3, 1902]

Dear nana,
     I hope that you are very well are you? I will come to see you soon and make you a nice little visit. Ask Uncle gorge how peterkin is. Wont we hav a nice time going up in the lift when I come to see you!!!

> With love
>   [*sketch*]   Estlin
Peterkin and his dog. E.E.C.

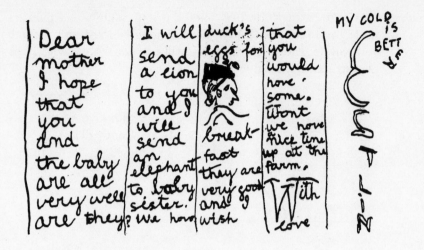

Dear mother I hope that you and the baby are all very well are they?

I will send a lion to you and I will send an elephant to baby sister. We have

duck's eggs for break-fast they are very good and wish

that you would have some. Wont we have nice time up at the farm.

With love

MY COLD IS BETTER

CHAPLIN

FACSIMILES OF LETTERS 7 AND 8

Dear nana, I hope that you are very well are you? I will come to see you soon and make you a nice little visit. Ask Uncle gorge how peterkin is. Wont we hav a nice time going up in the lift when I come to see you!!! With love
ESTLIN.

PETERKIN AND HIS DOG. E.E.C.

[Silver Lake, N.H.]
June 26, 1902

Dear daddy,

I hope you are very well. As long as you inquired about Spunk I will tell you something about him. On June 26, 1902 Spunk died we dont know why. It had been raining very hard all the morning. he was all right when I gave him his breakfast and I was just going to give him his dinner when Sandy said he was dad and the Crothers had just gone away from looking at him. sandy covered him with burlap in the morning and Nana thinks he may have smothered. The two Jacks are very well and so are mack and Don.

With love
E.E.C.

[135 Nahant St.]
April 17, 1903]

Dear Father and Mother.

I hope you and father are very well.

Are Mack and Don very well and happy? or do they miss me.

I miss you and father and the baby very much as I suppose you think.

I have looked out of the kitchen window and Uncle John's window and drawn and colored several pictures which I am going to take home when I come.

We are all pretty well down here. How are you too, and the baby besides, and the whole family up at your house? though I suppose the house belongs to me just as much as it does to you too.

Aunt Jennie says to tell you that she has enjoyed my visit very much and she has received your letter. Both she and Nana Cummings send their love.

I have not been able to go to the beach yet, except the day I came down here, and then Aunt Jennie had to put her golf cape on me because it was very cold and misty. It has been raining all the time down here. Aunt Jennie and I have read storys so even if I coulden't go out we had a nice time in the house. Today Ruth and Donald Goss played with me, that is they played part of the morning, and Donald was a regular little boaster, for when I made a battle ship he immediately said he could make one that could knock mine down. So he set to work and made a battle ship which was at the most not any better than mine, nana says, for she was present at that time.

This afternoon aunt Jennie took me up into the attic and stood me on a box. Then she opened the skylight and I put my head out and saw the ocean, and the houses, and the lighthouse, but not before she had put on me her coat, and she had put on a shawl herself.

Good by

With love

EEC.

[sketch of elephant]

11 / TO HIS PARENTS

Bear Spring Camp

[Oakland, Me.

July 15, 1914]

Dear Family —

Mr. & Mrs. C. [Churchward] & Mr. & Mrs. K. [Kreelans] took the Lozier, & J. [Jack Churchward] & I and Pearly (the C.'s man) took the Ford touring car. They went 1st most of the way and we kept up well. We ate a sea-food dinner & got in here about dark. We passed thru Brunswick, Augusta, Gardiner, etc. & had stunning views, esp. of Kenneybeck R. & Al sunset. Mr. K. is 27 & not bad; his wife is a well-meaning feather-headed boob-ess. The camp here is conventional but simple, & no sheets! Beautiful lake. I never hope to see such roads as we met. The Lozier rear wheel (left) went in so that it almost threw Mrs. K. out (in one place) & Mrs. C—who drove all way (130 m)— skidded & nearly scared life out of the Kreelans who are almost as innocent of motoring in a real car as a cat is of Xmas (they own a Metz!)

Going fishing now

Kennebunk River Club
Kennebunkport, Me.
Sunday [July 27, 1914]

Dear Mother—

Mr. & Mrs. Churchward are very anxious that I should stay on for next week here. Mr. C. wants us to go on a picnic in the larger motor boat Wednesday, and if I stay Mrs. C. will join Jack & me on a little trip in the Lozier to view the beauties of this place. There sure is no healthier ever invented—Mrs. C. says to tell you so. My noze is redder (she also adds, meaning not hers, but your devoted son's).

The ocean is the most wonderful thing in the world just now. As I never had ½ chance at it, believe me I'm taking full advantage. Assure Nana that nought could be safer! (Jack is an expert, & I a good swimmer) We went canoeing today & it was perfect. I'll probably get in my very first (1st) sea-fishing soon! Such names as they have (the fish)! There's a dead monkey-fish hard by the boat club in a bay and he looks like anything! Tell Elos he's shaped   [*sketch*]   so, no kidding!

The place itself is a quiet enough & very pretty little town,— not what I thought it [to] be. We're leading the simple and sober here—always outdoors. Tell Dad that Jack won a dollar from Mr. C. for chinning himself 15 times from a beam in the ceiling: then Mr. C. offered me an equal amt. of kale (mazuma, $) if I'd do it <u>20</u> times. I did. Jack's going to visit me just the same.

1916–1917

49 West 39 [New York, N.Y.]
Wednesday? [June 22, 1916]

Dear Family—

Yesterday I had a real experience—that of being called by an editor. After keeping me on edge for three days, [Frank] Crowinshield showed me in an hour and a half that my humour was not of the "Vanity Fair" variety, etc.—which I knew all the time. I sudored. A healthy humiliation, Estlin—as Sco [Scofield Thayer] might say. Afterward in the open air I was thankful as I was doubtful all along whether I could do ha has and poems at the same time. Sco entertained me magnificently while he was here. He has now left to be married, after expressing doubt on the advisability of "V. F." I shall write him that that danger is avoided!— also to thank him for his very wonderful letter—the most wonderful ever seen.

I am now on the trail of a livelihood thru Mrs. Roberts of "The Craftsman". Her husband edits the "Digest." If he has not work for me, she has promised "a strong letter" to every editor in N.Y. individually—most generous lady. Of course I have seen nearly all. But I shall get two or three letters to great unknowns from her, and stick to it for a while longer ✳ ✳ ✳

P. S. I feel like the "questing Beast" of Malory.

14 / TO HIS MOTHER

[21 East 15th St., New York
January 20, 1917]

Dear Mother

Dad's letter & yours arrived almost simultaneously. I surely had no idea I was calling down the wrath of Peleus' son in the hat matter—hope it was soon appeased. The watch arrived O.K.—I mean, of course, it wasn't running, and hasn't since, but its striker is immensely soothing on rough winter nights. Also the "comforter," tea-service, 2 gray blankets, etc. came duly. And yes, we ✳ have bought beds. They are very intellectual, not to say aesthetic; and with the proper treatment will

soon become emotional; but not over-emotional, you understand. Also mattresses. The pillows are an improvement, I
really think, over my improvisation, which was: To raise the
head-end of mattress, insert total no. soiled clothes, and allow
said end to fall, producing a parabola, which acted as a tobag-
gan, spiriting the human body toward the floor. ✳ ✳ ✳ I
am, by the way, returning the most generous check which accompanied Dad's letter, as: (a) We are alright and not really
in need of a single thing (in fact, the trouble is to find a repu-
table burglar to remove our superflous stuff) and, what is even
more important, (b) the "bet" which I consistently refused to
make I still and with equal consistency refuse to make—for the
very good reason that I have rarely been on time in the past,
and expect to be hardly more so in the future; that 1 shoe-shine
lasts me a week, and—but I spare your weeping blushes. In
short (as Mr. Micawber would say) I am "earning my own living," and as I find it excessively banal, I had rather not mix it
up with any more pleasant methods, such as accepting, borrow-
ing (etc.) that which is popularly known as "mazuma" from
source or sources other than this dear, beloved, sweet, bene-
ficient, spunky "office," or "firm" as some prefer to name it.
✳ ✳ ✳

* EEC and the painter Arthur "Tex" Wilson, with whom EEC shared an apartment
while he worked for P. F. Collier & Son, mail-order booksellers.

15 / TO HIS MOTHER

[21 East 15th St.
April 7, 1917]

Dear Mother—
    Forgive the PBO$_3$ (or whatever lead oxide is) as Willie
[Arthur Wilson] is at the armory scrutinizing a "10 inch gun"
(whatever may that be) and he has the pen that has the ink in
it.
    Now I see where the war spirit comes from! And a sicklier
war; a 99^{44}/$_{100}$%-er war; a sadder bluff—! Apparently N. E.
states are amusing themselves by themselves for themselves.
Very patriotic. A San Franciscan, friend of a friend of mine
(of Edward Nagle), arrived in NY a week ago, and seeing the
flags on 5th, asked: what holiday we had here that they didn't

celebrate in the west? Again: I went down to the "Curb" with excited anticipations 2 days before "war" was declared: nothing doing. 1 day before: dull. The day: fist-fights by muckers. Why? a guy asked a chap in a brown cap (one of the signallers). "Nothin' doin," he replied, "so we have to start somethin'". Very true!

I shan't go to war unless I go in a real one—or in the aeroplane squad. Thank god, the room is in Wilson's name—I wouldn't be a "resident of NY" for a good deal, as (you may know) any such is automatically conscripted (per act of legislature, last fall) as soon as the Mayor gets the grouch from Washington— 2nd hand.

I don't know why I talk of this pseudo "war" as I have no interest in it—and am painting and scribbling as ever . . . I read but one paragraph of [Woodrow] Wilson's speech, being taken with a dangerous fit of laughter. Sounded to me like Bliss Perry asking his exceptionally large class of 158 dubs to buy the poetical works of my friend Paul Shivell—just across the yard, gentlemen, at the cooperative   *   *   *

16 | *TO HIS SISTER*

[21 East 15th St.]
Apr. 17, 1917
Sat.

Dear Lulu—

*   *   *   Don't know how mother got the idea I needed an overcoat! Did you suggest it? Curses!! Why, I got a card about a year back, saying I didn't live where I was, and why not? I indignantly visited the nearest AE co office, suspecting pro germanism (of course). "Your package is at 10 Ave and 33," says an imbecile to whom I appealed after drooping on the counter 10 minutes. Up I go (87.9654 English miles by the alarmclock) I repeat, up I go. ((No elevator)). My delightful roommate nearly died too. "Your package is out, just now," says a lugubrious Swede to me. "Call up tomorrow morning, if convenient." Ah, Sweeden!

Let us now approach $\begin{Bmatrix} \text{modern} \\ \text{present} \end{Bmatrix}$ times. At the discourteous hour of 8:30 a crash at the door. I describe an elipse and land with a brush in my teeth, a canvas on one arm, and my pajamas knotted sumptuously about the Tropic of Capricorn. (See "History of Our Planet," chs I–V) "This is the 5th time" respires "driver Brown" (an Wop, by the way). "Merci beans, pattutu" I replique in my best Scandinavian. . . . . So that's over.

Remember the guy that went hunting llamas in his pajamas? That's me! The band will now render:

"Sister Susie's sewing shirts for soldiers" I thank you all and one!! —

Lots of Cats here, fed by maiden ladies
Oh for Bob

17 / *TO HIS MOTHER*

21 East 15
[April 18, 1917]

Dearest Mother

✳ ✳ ✳ After lengthy consideration, far exceeding that of some Greek (Socrates?) who often remained rapt for a day at a time, I signed up with Eliot Norton ✳ to go over (with several others) on the 28th of this month (i.e. week from next Saturday) to drive old Fords, Packards, Motorblocs, Renaults (in fact anything on wheels) "without animus" as your friend the President would say. Hope the war isn't over before I get there.

Shall drop around to see you all one of these days, after I've got the details of passport etc. off my mind ✳ ✳ ✳

° *Brother of Richard Norton, who with Henry H. Harjes organized the Norton-Harjes American Ambulance Corps to serve with the French Army.*

18 / *TO HIS PARENTS*

[21 East 15th St.]
April 19th [1917]

Dear Mother and Father,

✳ ✳ ✳ Today there is a very boring parade of all the walkable schoolchildren in the world, not to mention several mangy

O.D.s, with infinite ineffectiveness of plurality in flags, noise, and roughhouse, mostly latter. I am seated just now in the thick, with eleven bands, two biplanes, eight million boy scouts (or muckers, as we called them in Cambridge) and twenty seven varieties of tiredbusinessmenwomenanddogs to right to left behind and so forth (as Tennyson so beautifully said once). I got one corking letter from Sears, a perfect bird, right off. Plimpton [of P. F. Collier & Son] wrote haughtily that he wanted the pleasure of shaking hands with me first—believe me he got it. After recovering, he said dully: So you're the clergyman's son. Miss—, take a look at him. You don't want to go abroad. I have a 16 year old son. Do you draw comics for the papers? NO? (surprised) But it makes money. etc. I draw a curtain over the rest . . . but got the letter. These letters are a formality for identification. Today I wrote prof. Baker for one. So I'm well provided for.

Keep right on making trousers for French orphans, not to mention Daniel Webster orations before the City Club! ✳ ✳ ✳

19 / TO HIS MOTHER

[21 East 15th St.
April 27, 1917]

Dear Mother—

After waiting 1¾ hours I succeeded in seeing Eliot Norton, who gave me a list of what volunteers should have. "3 khaki flannel shirts" is included, so I shall get some. Today was spent in waiting for an interview with E. Norton Esq., who filled me with letters and cast me breathless forth—poor E! His brain is certainly failing.

Cabling is simple: about 15¢ a word—care of Richard Norton, 7 rue Francois Premier, should be alright. La Touraine sails "about 3," and Dillwyn [Parrish] (for whom may the gods serve ever!) took me to the French Consul and French Line today—so my passage is assured. I have a fine cabin—and pay only $78 and something—owing to reduction given Volunteers. I got $50 in French notes today—wonderful! I want to kiss them!!!

Excuse the pencil—

À bord de "Touraine"
le 4me mai 1917

Parentes carissimi!

I am pro-German henceforth. And why not? Yesterday I partially emerged into consciousness; last night I visited the salle à manger for the first time since Saturday: today I am sitting in the salon de conversation writing this — a feat unparalleled. Should you ask why, I must name names. O name fore'er accursed — thy sinister initials peek at me from every impossible corner: C. G. T. French Line, a murrain on thee! Should the blond captain of a U boat consent to waste a torpedo on thy torpid bowels, I'd grasp his Hunnish hand.

Understand that it's a beautifully calm day, warm, sunny, etc. — yet this thunder mug of a boat jabbers and jogs and gapes from side to side so as to make writing an achievement equal to the Pyramids. I refrain from describing its conduct during the "northeaster" which we have been having for the past 5 days. Nor will I — ah no! — give generalities, even, concerning my conduct. Suffice it to say that after the honest sickness of Sunday and Monday, plus the genteel misery of Tuesday and Wednesday, I am barely capable of making my respects to ye. I should, however, mention my blessings: (a) I have no cabin mate (God pity him had I had him) (b) Dillwyn Parrish gave me an enormous basket of fruits; (c) last night came an ungodly sunset; followed by moonlight and the amazing phenomenon of a mystical moon rainbow.

The cabins (or state-rooms, or something) are dependent for ventilation (as I might assume you know) on half a dozen, — nay, two or three, — "portholes." These, naturally, were shut during the N. E'er. Hence I dragged up and down, sleeping mostly on deck till the hoze-men tapped me on the leg at 5:30 A. M., or leaping from top to sides of my bunk with my stomach grinning at me from the mast-head (if there be one). To locate that stomach has taken me all this time. Even now, I tap on wood as I claim the distinction of "running down" one of the "most notorious criminals" of "the era."

My acquaintances are three: (1) a Mick from Cambridge, Mass. (2) a gentle thuglike person named "Edgar Guy Lemon" (3) a wholly possible boy from Worcester, the home of the Bartletts, whom I met on the strength of my brothership to

Lucy's playmate, "Elizabeth Cummings." His name is W. S. Brown. He suffered 'neath Talcott Williams at Columbia, incidentally.

The "boat" is a funny thing, made of wood and stone, with a few bricks loose in the hold. Everytime the rudder is moved a 2000 sack of Fords [?] is kicked down-stairs. When the "boat" wants to whistle, "she" shuts her eyes, stops her heart-beats, buttons her vest, and goes off with a heart-rending scream that reminds you of Cambridge policemen at busy traffic-corners. "She" has a way of dying in the grip of a fair-sized wave, which is heartily amusing.

I was very sick after my first bath. I wanted to take one today, but Hémon le garçon (of course 87 years old) went on a bat in the clothes-closet or somewhere and couldn't be found by "madame" the queen of the scullery maids, so I didn't. Hémon has only stolen 2 or 3 books, etc.; so I give him everything I can afford, trusting to his upright nature for the rest.

Should you ask of the passengers?—Perhaps. I am forgetting to enclose a memo or list. Brown & I are both "additionals". Notice lieutenant someone, who is "1st class", "additional", and "not on board". True military mind! 23 caterwauling Andover "boys", 3 or 4 anemic old gentlemen, a wine-agent, and me—such is the total. I forgot a count & countess. Latter very sick up to yesterday. Hair suspiciously moist. Count most amusing creation; very naïf and smokes a tentacular pipe.

The stern—or 2nd class—is sometimes amusing, with soldiers matching pennies and boasting about how "if you know how" it's easy to turn a 2 weeks leave into 6 months, and one fine child, father, and mother. Mother plays the "piano" in the 2nd class salle, and child sits as if very sick. I hope not—

The amazing vulgarity of the whole deal—I mean La Croix Rouge, Voluntier Cummings—keeps one from jubilations on one's successful escape from conscription, which, says wireless, has magnificently sailed through the "congress" of the Land of the "Free" and the Home of the "Brave". Tra-la, tra-la. All the beef-slobbering, soup-guzzling, khaki-breasted muckers on board will, I trust, someday be congressmen—or senators!

le 5ᵐᵉ mai 1917

Since writing the foregone—I have had a change of heart. Several incidents contributed thereto: first, and foremost, the immemorially delightful sententia of a pocket-size sailor in the stern of this charming "paquebot," i.e. — "submarines pooh-pooh." He stood beside one of the unwieldiest land-cannon ever known to exist, same being mounted on poop deck (or whatever it s'appelle) in such a manner as to fight submarines merely by its aspect. For service it would require the aid of 100 gigantic midshipmites to clear the creature for action and take off its suspenders for it, and then — supposing it ever went off — adios! The sea-eel would receive the education of his life as the "S.S. La Touraine", under the influence of the recoil, hid herself in the mud of 6000 fathoms (circa).

Deuxièmely, I had breakfast this morning, having adroitly connived at my awakening with the help of Mr. Brown. As it happened, it was well he woke me when he did. I was in a most peculiarly embarassing situation, to wit: arm in arm with Albert Latschar,(a society-moth, friend of Willie's [Brown's]), sliding on roller-skates down an enormous hall, past four patronesses, in my dress-suit, with our hats on! The language in the above sentence is not sufficiently twisted to express my bewildering demi-consciousness.

An Andover "boy" across the salle is having "Amerique" spelled out for him.

Finally: Hémon le garçon — whom I always suspected of being a scholar second only to Kitty, on account of a similar brusque self-consciousness and inability to answer when addressed, and whom for the said reason I had several times convicted of stealing whatever I happened not to have, (as book of poems given by Edward Nagle, tooth-brush, twilight-sleep, etc.) — Hémon the lily maid of Astolot patted me on the back the other day, [sketch] took me to a port-hole, and after showing me the fruit remaining in my basket of bon-voyage, tossed said fruit gaily overboard, saying in his frivolous way: "Stink"! I am sleeping comfortably now.

Tonight we enter the mythological danger-zone. This only means that we can't sit on boxes of Pathé (movie) film (the stern is heaped with them) and smoke, — hoping for something to happen, — as of yore. Also, all lights will automatically plunk into nihil.

But there will be a full moon — !

le 6me mai 1917

The steerage of the Touraine (that swanlike barque) is immense. Today I rose at 8 for breakfast, and progressed to the 2nd Classe Salon, where the Belgian Priest who has never been seen to sit down and who likes his cigar and is absolutely delightful, presided at the mass. I enjoyed this ceremony very much, not being able to see the pontiff or hear much he said, and having all the time in the world to remember the surrounding faces. Last night, I should have said, after multifarious warning by the gunner, by Hémon, and by the deck steward, the lights went out at onze heures. Immediately all the "college-fellows," alias Andover, began their sickening yaps, driving Thine Ever to bed at onzeheuresquart. Mr. Edgar Guy Lemon ("Red" Lemon) said yestreen that he had never seen so many people he hated so much — a sentiment of great value according to my humble "judgement."

I nearly suffocated during mass, because I got squeezed under a table while trying to kneel, and found the table to be stationary. It is amusing, by the way, to see people absent-mindedly drawing to them the chairs in the salon (which don't move, except when spoken to by the steward).

All life-boats are cleared; the rail is taken up and off all around the stern, and there's an esquimo in the Crow's-nest. People are threatening every night to sleep on deck, but nobody does. Perhaps they will tonight. My graciousness toward empirical submarines continues.

Having missed most of the ships, fish, drift-wood, et cetera, hitherto — I yesterday saw a 3 masted square-rigger under full sail. It was the best thing I ever saw.

Nothing favors excitement; or rather, Germany doesn't stand a chance of wasting valuable torpedos on this ship: for there's a deep, cold, inhospitable mist over all things that's to a T the colour of the Touraine's ancient complexion. [sketch]

Today at lunch one was instructed to wear his damugly button en plein air. Meaning (I guess) the herd is to be mustered into one train and thrown in a bunch on Paris. Rumour mentions a free-pass from Bordeaux for the Ambulance service (that's "we").

Every night, nowadays, Paul the Bomb-thrower and the Postman's-Uniform-Red-Fez-Cornell-Buttons-Cigar chewer-man lead a crowd of ardent passengers — steerage, soldiers, Premier classe, ladies, boys, girl — up and down the decks, in military formation, and to the strains of "Marquez le pas!" etc. — Everybody balling "Margarreatar." Mr. Brown and I, however, are content with "Le chat qui la regarda."

I lost my fountain pen; and Hémon didn't get my nomenclature; so I found a little assistant-steward and threatened me [*sic*] into informing my grievance — then, I said to Hémon — "ja'i perdu mon stilo." Instantly he pulled a drawer, which I knew not of, from the 8 in 1 washstand, and lo! — my stilo, and everything else I'd lost for the past week. While I stood in contemplation of the ruin⁄and romance which I'd built about Hémon's criminal head, that diminutive "garçon" smote me on the back so that I fell into the sink; such is his childish pleasure in deception.

le 7ᵐᵉ mai 1917

Nothing amusing happened yesterday — we sighted two or 3 harmless-looking craft; the captain paced the poop, and inquired of the cut-throat-crew in the stern — "which is the gunner?" — whereat a feeble old freight-handler committed an atrocious salute, and was commanded to "train her on the enemy," — the 35's cartridges (or shot, or whatever they are) were exposed to wondering comments of Andover; and the man who wants "you fellows" to "get together," and who remarked when we sighted a half-wrecked schooner several days since: "She's coming too near for comfort! I don't like it" — this man was excited; but noonelse.

Early tomorrow morning we'll probably go up the river Garonne 65 miles to Bordeaux — that is, if our present pleasantly stupid security continues.

Perhaps someonelse was excited: a number of "fellows" slept on deck — one man with a life preserver (or "gilet"!) under his doomèd dome. I just heard a gold-toothed "chap" say that there's a notice posted for everybody to sleep in their clothes tonight, and that he had most of his on last n . . . . How "we" are "temperamental" in "times of stress"!

I had a long talk with Hémon le garçon, (consisting in gutturals and nods by me, and streaming sentences by H.), which ended in his jumping toward the upper berth of my cabin and rotating his hands in mid-air like a ferry-boat. I smiled appreciatively (because I was and am fearful of Hémon), whereupon he swatted me gigantically on the nuque and disappeared. I have a bruise where his appreciation of my singular intelligence has lighted. He must have been a prize-fighter before he became my chamber-maid.

The boat took to bucking (but not squishing) last night, and

I feared for my mouton cresson, potage, and glacé pistache (which last was made of excelsior and tasted like brown-paper coloured green). "Red Lemon" (it is rumoured) lost his menu.

Did I recount the dictum of the fierce "boy" who's "coming back" "on the ice, through Russia" and who replied, when some-one said this would be unexciting, — "I've had excitement enough trying to hold down my lunch." — ?

No lights at all, yesterday. None tonight, of course. I shall have to read in bed — or, now, by day. By the way — there's a book here, of which I read 3 pages, which abslitively and posalutely soars deeper into undiluted putridity than any printed punk ever discovered by these watching eyes. The name is under fire (?) by "Sapper" (?) and where I took up "the thread," "the girl" 'moans:" "not lover and brother too, O God" — Again: "he died bravely, said the old man, choking down the tears." Also: The sunset was gone. There remained a faint light, touch-ing the poplars with silver. — Perhaps a rook cawed: I hope so. Some day I shall (not) write an "essay" on What War Did to Literature: A Chamber of Horrors, from the Sanskrit of [indecipherable], with notes and annotations by "Minor."

Should I be unable to write you for some time — as is likely — consider yourselves embraced by this unworthy bundle of ex-pression!

21 / *TO HIS MOTHER*

Hôtel du Palais [Paris]
11 mai 1917
4:30 (P. M.)

Dear Mother —

Till one-thirty I watched the lights along the coast, having come on deck from the steerage, where a seven-foot Arab danced, and a Turk played, and Greeks sang their songs — "to pass danger-time." At 3:30 Hémon cried something at me, and I took my place in the line of passengers, who, pass-port in hand, waited their turn with the authorities who had come on board from the pilot-boat two hours before. After getting through this, I went on deck — it was about 5 o'clock — and saw France. We docked at Bordeaux several hours later.

After checking their duffles, the N-H "bunch" alighted on terra f.; then squirmed into a bus and drove to the station. Suitcases were piled together, and everyone went off for an hour. At 10:30 the train for Paris pulled out. Hémon, Brown, and I got into a compartment with 2 Frenchmen and a sweet boy about 10. At 8:30 we arrived at Paris, having doubtfully dined on board. At the Gare d'Austerlitz the leader and everyone save B. and me got out—signals were badly crossed. The Gare D'Orleans gate-man, however, didn't notice our lack of tickets, as we squeezed thru with the American Field A. men, who travelled (like N.H.) en masse. Emerging on the quai from the tomb-like station void of cable-office, we lost ½ hr. waiting for some means of conveyance, and then a pieds started for 7 Rue François Premier. Everyone we asked said "Tout le droit—dix minutes." It was ¾ hr. before we reached 7, and there a magnificent scrub-lady (may she live for ever!!!) escorted us jokingly around the corner on the Cours la Reine to the Hôtel du Palais. The rest of our party had fortunately not turned up (they are at the Mont-Thabor Hotel). We couldn't get anything to eat at the Palais and were informed that every restaurant in Paris closes at 9:30. Supperless we circled the Ferris Wheel, and "turned in." It was also amusing to ask for the Palais Royal—which I did that night—and didn't get in till one A. M. The next few days were spent in walking, and waiting for our turn to "sign on!" We are now lost forever to the non-military world, and expect our uniforms momently. When we are to leave Paris is not known.

This is a delighting Hôtel, much like the Brevoort. You climb a flight, turn a corner, walk in pitch darkness down a hall with a ghostly mirror at the other end, turn a very bad corner, walk another 10 blocks, find your key-hold, and glide into luxurious bed. Candles are exclusively used after 9:30. Incidentally, the streets of Paris are pitchy at night, exaggerating the fragrance of the tremendous horse-chestnuts and their green confrères along the Seine.

We never get up for Petit Déjeuner, but stroll down the Avenue d'Antin to the Rond Point des Champs Elysées, on whose N. W. corner is the Alexander III Hotel. Under an awning we sit and drink our cafés, with Le Matin & Figaro to keep us company. Generally we eat away at noon, and sometimes again at supper. We've seen only 1 show, which was very, very poor, I am quite sure, tho' I only understood two phrases: "La jolie vache"—and—"Merci, M'sieur." We (B & I) intend to see Massine & the Ballet Russe Monday evening or Wednesday matinee. A monoplane flies over the Palais as I write this.

Hôtel du Palais
[May, 1917]

Dear Mother & Father—

* * * Today is Friday. 8 days from this writing my long
threatened uniform is to be. Not that I'll wear it till I actually
leave Paris; for the plenitude and penetration of war here leaves
in the mouth a taste resembling newly blacked shoes. But lest
M. l'Ascenseur (pun) disapprove—behold I will tell you that I
spent $12 already on Cézanne and Matisse photogravures, and
threaten daily to buy a painting outfit, which will cost as much
again. Also, that Brown and I never walk less than 10 miles a
day here, and never return without a small library between us.

I'm getting used to eating vegetables as a separate course
after the entrées, and of being waited on by one-eyed cross-
eyed-pop-eyed, wise-in-their-own-conceit garçons. Everyone
who isn't at war is a cripple of some variety: everyone who is in
Paris on leave is a cripple of some worse variety—with blatant
exceptions. "The Kings Music" (60 lousy Scotchmen and Irish-
men in hussar's hats) have profaned the Paris streets for 3 days
now, being escorted everywhere by great hugs—sickening.
Thank God the Parisians roar with them. One little girl, on the
arm of a French officer shrieked: "my hat's like that: that's why
I left it at home"—or words to same effect. The Englishmen anyway are a bunch of bums, only worsed by the Americans—who
are the most abhorrent human tripe ever spilled from the swill-
can, tout et seul. Willie's exception. How we dread meeting
them! How we flee them!

But we have been warned against the evils of Paris by an
English official at 7 R. F. P.,—so maybe that has something to do
with the noble way we spend our money. Not that we don't
(memories of ὁ πχρθενον) seek out the best and wildest of restaurants—wild, I would say, as regards food—for other wildness
there is none during the duration of this state of affairs known
as la guerre. Only last night B. & I visited the Sultana Cherqui,
Tournisseur Algérien, in a sweet court off the R. Montmartre.
Here we sat in emptiness, eating divine cous cous (the national
dish of Algeria as the Sultana says) and artichoke salade with
ripe olives in it. I wept. It was the best meal yet in Paris. AND
no one-eyed 1½ legged, ⅔ blown-to-hell, noseless, etc. etc. etc.

etc. etc. etc. etc. people intruded. Only one lively little M. who entered with a 5 foot bread-stick reading a newspaper (<u>not</u> the bread-stick). Bless him.

Aeroplanes & dirigibles are daily occurrences here. They all go over the du Palais by preference. As I write, a huge tractor biplane with silvery nose glistening in absolute sunlight (queery as to metaphor, as Briggs [Dean Briggs of Harvard] would say) thunders over my head, making it impossible to think. It's going very fast, not at all like an American machine. Last night I sat in the Champs (with my feet in a running gutter) for a half-hour, watching an éclairée aeroplane come from perhaps 50 miles off, through a night bursting with stars.

23 / TO HIS MOTHER

[Hôtel du Palais]
4 Juin [1917]

Dearest Mother

—all your delighting letters have arrived safely, and are generally brought to me by W. S. Brown as I progress toward breakfast. Since we deux gave up entirely eating in the Palais, life has been more. We now leave about 9:45, breakfast at the Rond Point, move to L'Etablissement Chartier, Rue du Louvre, for lunch, and after walking our 20 miles (or so) go to one of 3 Italian Restaurants, <u>or</u> to our Cous-Cous place, where a sultana slaps us on the backs and calls us good boys (or something equally innocuous). By failing to get up at the hour of 5:45 AM I escaped departing with the bums mutts and jeffs (not to say ginks, slobs, and punks) who came over with us. Where they went god knows, but they seem to be gone, mostly. Our (B's & my) uniforms have been promised for ages (but thank Heaven aren't ready yet). B. gets his today. Don't know when I shall get mine, and almost hope never. But—in a few days, a week at most, we twain shall probably leave Paris for our 3 mos. sojourn in little hungry. I think after 3 months I may switch over and go up to Satonik. The crowd couldn't possibly be worse. Food here is fine after you're used to it. Bread that would delight you! no meat—which suits me to a T. Monsieur Brown (his aunt is Miss Slater who owns Webster [Mass.], but he's very nice) & I have already participated in all the grèves of

Paris (She is practically, or has been, in a state of revolution) [deletion] the finest girls god ever allowed to pasture in the air of this fresh earth. So now to see about uniform — hope you got my enormous steamer-letter.

24 / TO HIS MOTHER

[Camp at Ham, Noyon sector, France]
July 2, 1917

Dear Mother

I got your letter of June 1 only today! but don't be surprised — it's quite in keeping with the delightful inefficiency of 7 Rue François 1er — Hereafter, you'd better address me at Convois Automobiles, S. S. U. XXI, Paris. As it happened, the letter of yours travelled to Sandricourt, and not finding me there, trickled casually about Paris for a while, till its arrival here.

No excitements whatever so far — I have been technically "under fire" twice — very dull. Not one air-duel. Every day a dozen or less planes shot at by anti-aircraft bosch guns without results.

The "camp" here is divided into 5 sections (Brown & I are in no. 2). Once every 3 days the cars of a section leave this place and go "in post" — this meaning simply that the conducteur and aide of each take their bedding and canned cold food and leave at 10 A M, then go a few miles, park the car, and fall asleep waiting for malades, of whom none exist at present in our sector. At 11, 12 or 1 the next day they are "relieved" by their "comrades," and go "home." "My" conducteur is the most despicable, perhaps, "fellow" in the "camp." He's a tight-fisted, pull-for-special-privilege, turd, about 5 feet high, with a voice in b natural upper. I shall also tell you that nothing but pull got him "his" car or enables him to keep it. The other day he ran into a "comrade" who was standing quite still on the opposite side of a broad good road. I learned a day or so since that he is the man who poured essence in his radiator and water in his gasoline-tank — this is a fact. He has not "let" me drive for 3 days now. About the tent in which Brown and I sleep his nomen is "Pansy."

Much worse, still "perhaps," is the "chef" of the section, "Mister Phillips." He is so _____y [sic] that I shall say nothing of him. His "assistant" Mister "Andy" who keeps doing nothing to the cars, which consequently run well, has the benefit of a <u>complete</u> lack of education plus a <u>perfe</u>ct absence of inherent intelligence. Today, e.g., "Mr." Donalson ("my" conducteur) backed his car in crooked, for which, of course, I was heartily censured by same assistant. I lost Mr. D's P[oison] gas mask, however, and enjoyed seeing him "get hell" for it, so I am feeling comparatively peaceful at present.

The "men" are, as you would expect, "average" Americans, sans taste, imagination, etc. but easy (by contrast) to put up with.

I may send you souvenirs later, if I ever get near enough to "the front," or if the "front" ever wakes up.

We are to "move" in a few days for — I don't know which — complete "repos" or a more "spirited" atmosphere. ✳ ✳ ✳

I omitted to say that on day no. 2 "you" are "on call," which means that you can't leave the grounds. On day no 3 (day after tomorrow for Brown and me, as it falls) you have nought to do. We (B. et moi) shall I guess wander all day as far as possible from this forsaken out-house — if we're not driving in convoy along dusty roads.

One fine thing — I never have to wash. I changed my socks the other day because it rained hard. It was the première fois.

25 / TO HIS MOTHER

[Camp at Ham, Noyon sector]
July 7 [1917]

Dearest Mother —

In this, my fourth letter to you since arriving on French soil, or my fifth including the steamer one, I'm at a loss to know what to say, inasmuch as M. le Censor has seen fit to withhold my past effusions — to judge by your last letter, which I got yesterday. I shall, accordingly, do my best to say nothing at all, trusting that you will understand, given the above circumstances, that any other course would prove futile.

I am in good health, in S.S. U. XXI, Convois Automobiles, Par B.C.M. Paris. I don't know what all this means, but it's my present address. To continue my prudence: the food here is not remarkable, nor is the chef of the section, nor is his assistant, nor are the "men." In short, I look forward to my permission of

7 or 8 days as a lonely splendor in a life of boredom. Same permission will take place, God willing, in either 5 or 8 weeks, I don't know which.

I hope M. le Censor won't mind my saying that nothing exciting is going on where I am. It's true, anyway. In case you did not get my last letter, let me repeat that every day French aeroplanes are shot at by German anti-aircraft guns, without the slightest effect, that once in 3 days everyman is supposed to take his bedding and go "on post," i.e., wait at a specified place for malades or blessés. As I have just day before yesterday ceased to be on a car, this ceases to interest me any more. Up to that time, I was "aid" to a "driver," who couldn't stand me and complained; so I got off and am now doing nothing. My case is not unique. There are 20 cars here and 46 men. New ones arrive daily. But perhaps it is indiscreet to express any opinion of this state of affairs, so I abstain.

My only real friend here, but a fine one, is W. Slater Brown of Webster, Mass., of whom I spoke in the steamer-letter.

There may be a change soon. It is rumoured that we are to move, to go into "repos" for a time and then to tackle something really interesting.

On the 4th of July, 10 men out of the 40 odd here went to Paris for 48 hours permission. The selection was by lot. Neither Brown nor I were given a chance to be selected, altho' I particularly asked the Chef to be written among those who wished to go. After the selection, I asked him why my name wasn't in the hat. "Because," he replied, "that was left to my personal jurisdiction. You came out here later than the others." As a matter of fact, 3 of us, Brown, I and another, came on the same day from Paris to this section here. The 3rd, an 18 year old boy had his name in the hat, and he drew a yes. I said only: "That was not my fault. I was waiting in Paris for them to send me out." "I appreciate that," says M. le Chef, "but your conduct has been lacking in sticktuitiveness and enthusiasm." It had been my lot to have an intermittent diarrhea, due to the "food" (so-called) and especially to the dirtiness of the "cook." I had fared better than 2 men who went to neighboring hospitals. I had done whatever was asked of me, and been the goat for the "driver" on occasion, latter having a "pull" with the Chef. Of this I did not speak, but replied: "I suppose the same holds true of my friend Brown. I noticed that his name was not in the hat." M. le Chef started, and stammered: "Not at all, not at all. He got out here later." "I beg to differ," says I, "he got out here the same day I did." "I believe in giving preference to the older men," said the Chef haughtily.

This made me angry. I took a mouthful of cigarette-smoke and blew it flat in his face.

Things may improve. M. le Chef, due to frequent complaints against him by others than myself, has been given the sack, as I learned when he and the 10 got back from Paris yesterday.

Night before last, owing to scarcity of men, I went on post with a driver as aid. We had just turned in, when klaxons shrieked all over the sector, meaning "Gas — attack." We took 2 blessés, couchés, and got no sleep. There was a wondrous moon.

26 / TO HIS FATHER

[Camp at Ham, Noyon sector
July 20, 1917]

Dear Dad—

It was very good to hear from you—even though mother has kept you well under espionage judging from frequent reports received via mail. It seems that your sermons are getting more and more (if possible) patriotic, that Lowell (who previously talked only with the Creator) has come down off his high horse and is asking all sorts of favors of you, that Taft, Roosevelt, McKinley, and Admiral Dewey call on you hourly, and that Wilson keeps the wires in a continual state of apoplexy whenever you arrive chez-vous from your almost nightly diplomatic visits to Lisbon, Bruxelles, Westminster Abbey, and New South Greenland (Arkansaw). All I have to say is: keep them waiting. Some days since I received a telegraphic sans fil from Tokio, forwarded from Africa, in a code which I managed to intercept as follows: "Rev. C. busy bee crowned heads of Urope afraid of he." I repeat, it's necessary that you keep your feet in this mélé. I suggest an hourly discipline on the Ford, drinking plenty of orangeade, and a frequent application of spirits of ammonia. Be careful that your stenographer doesn't overhear anything unimportant, and don't, please don't trust Pershing ❊ ❊ ❊

Just to give you air, D. D., I'll tell you all the news from Nowhere in France. First I have writ some member of family about weekly. If letters do not arrive, blame ye not this dusky earth-worm. Second, having had nothing to do since I joined "my section," save carry "malades," who (according to camp humorist) have mumps — certainly nothing worse — I am now in répos in a neighboring town, expecting daily to leave for another larger town, where it is said that "we" will rest for perhaps a year, doing absolutely nothing, seeing no service, anchored to our Fords or Fiats, and generally miserable. In all of which the little finger of God the lord may be plainly seen with the aid of an 8 billion sun-power telescope. Same humorist says we are "sleeping for France." It's a lie. The "comrades" snore too much for me, at any rate. We are, however, eating for France, eating much of 3rd class food.

I will recount the sole piece of "service" I have seen. It will probably be my last. A man from Minnesota named O'Sullivan and I were in a Ford sleeping at a "post." 11:30 P.M. 6 obus dropped by Bosch all around us, sans warning. In stocking feet (I haven't undressed for weeks) with our casques on our heads, we lit in a little hole, one on top of other, while no. 2 landed, just 53 metres away, making (as we saw next day) a hole 5 feet deep, 12 feet long, 6 feet wide. We cranked up, & as we turned around, no. 3 burst hard by, which hastened our speed. The others pursued us down the road. After a few minutes we came back and I slept very well the rest of the night at the same "post;" in fact, I never awaked when a second fusillade came off at 3 AM.

I will send a snap of me in uniform as soon as I can. The casque is very becoming to anybody.

27 / *TO HIS MOTHER*

> [Camp at Ham, Noyon sector]
> 2nd August [1917]

Dear Mother —

Your letter dated "July 13, 1917" reporting the receipt of my letter of June 18th "from the Front" is "at hand," as they might say at "Colliers the Nat'l Weakly." The tooth-kit will be welcome, as also the handkefs, of which I have only 4 dozen left, I believe or perhaps 8, I forget which. As I have already tried to indicate in foregoing letter, I have received 3 socks & their contents.

Since that letter, I have moved three times, and am now in répos not far from the "base" you hypotheticize. My car was taken away from me the other day, and Brown (who was on it with me) was put on a Fiat with a crank ex-chauffeur, while I drew the place of aid on a Fiat with a "typical" American. As it happened, I drew the better place, for the only time Mr. Typical went out, he was in a hurry to get back here before moon-set, and an interesting trip resulted, as follows: I drove for ½ hour at average of 35 miles, thru villages, round corners, over holes, perspiration dripping from my hands, capless, intent — splended picture? — then Mr. T. took the wheel, putting my driving in the shade, averaging about 40, corners, turns, etc. — this being perfectly all right till we arrived at a bridge leading into the afore-said "base," when a faint light (no lantern allowed), set on a pole, abruptly indicated Eternity. With a fine presence of mind, Mr. T. A. swerved, took off part of central island (of wood) which halves these little wooden affairs, also his entire tool box, hit other side of bridge & lost his other box, and on we went for 500 feet. When we got out to look at the Fiat, the rear axle looked like a mosquito's beak, and there were 2 shoes blown, plus a ruined carrossière and total lack of tools etc. As there is no water in the river, the latter were found later under the bridge. The car was abandoned there, and we drove home on luxurious cushions in the lieutenant's Renault, which, by a peculiar co-incidence, met us just after the accident. Of course Mr. T. A. being a true T. A. (at least true to type hereabouts) announced himself as a martyr to the negligence of the French gov't which failed to put <u>any</u> light on the bridge! Very very droll.

Do you wonder at my love for Americans? Please, please, PLEASE don't get the idea that I am <u>ever</u> in danger of my life, or that I <u>ever</u> carry wounded soldiers, or that I am <u>ever</u> anything but grateful for the little incidents which serve to puncture the desperate situation of being quartered in the Divine Country with a bunch of _____s, [sic] incapable of escape, action or anything else.

I wrote father an account of a polite conversation with an obus. Not nearly as exciting, perhaps, as the accident above-told. The only other amusing thing happened at what might truly be called a <u>Juicy</u> place, whence we arrived here. Id est: the Bosch daily used to drop obus into an ex-aviation field an eighth of a mile away. Very droll to see the dirt fly and the poilus beat it. Of course the shell-song sounds right in line with your nose. Cheer up! They say after 2 weeks here in répos we may follow the division of the French army (to which we were attached at first) to the great ex-battlefield of the North, or the Road of Sweet Ladies. I hope, God knows, we get some excitement.

I received a letter from Sib [James Sibley Watson], who is in Paris, waiting to be signed up, waiting because, as he says, "all the organizations are changing hands"—that's as much as I know, save that 'tis reported Richard N. is hanging on by his eye teeth. God keep us from being taken over by the American Army!!!!!! I shall not come back after my 6 months is up under any circumstances. I wear a khaki uniform like this: with a nice fleecy-insided over-coat, which makes you very abstract [sketch] indeed. The sweater of Nana's will be fine. I am glad AW got his commission, but can't say I'm thunderstruck! He's a great boy.

The belt and pseudo-leather puttees cost me a pretty penny —the latter were supposed to be furnished with the uniform, but Brown & I never got them owing to the fine system at the tailors, "Messrs Sleater & Carter, Avenue de l'Opera, Paris," Leather here is immensely dear. The cloth puttees, which at this moment I wear, & which I also bought, look like this. [sketch] The uniform material is very heavy and well-wearing.

Hope Dad ne s'en fache pas with my 4th of July-ish Declaration of Undipendence! Give him my best love, and keep some for Yourself.

For your schedule, would state my different locations as follows:
1   Paris—1 month (May 8, on)
2   "Front" (a place hardly germain to my malcontent nature)—Letter of June 18th.
3   "Semi-Répos" (a place SO quiet that Dickens' "little Nell" might well be read as daily work)
4   "Front," really almost interesting (the juicy place aforesaid)
5   "Répos" pure and (very) simple (from which I write you this)
                                                      Au revoir!
Will try to get photos to send you, but have had hard luck in that respect so far.   P. S. the quiet life here has already driven 2 "comrades" home to the militant U. S. with shattered spleens.

[Camp at Ham, Noyon sector]
9me août [1917]
jeudi

Ma chère maman,

bien que je sache que vous vous attendez à des lettres chaleureuses pleines d'épreuves indiscutables de la nobilité de l'âme américaine, éclatant de contes héroïques, brillant d'une aversion monumentale pour l'ogre Guillaume et son fils dégénéré, je me trouve encore assez tranquille et calme, moins que jamais l'héros, malgré les effusions poètiques dont Amérique est la mère, et qui sentent, comme il me semble, le parfum sinon de la prémeditation, au moins de l'enthousiasme forcée. Il vous faut absolument croire que personne ne peut savoir, à moins de l'avoir constaté soi-même, ce que peut être la misère de la France, c'est dire, du peuple français, privé du jour au lendemain, de la nation misérable anéantie, dont la gloire révelés est déja fleurtrie. Et maintenant on va demander, en parlant à la Russie vacillante: "Quel ideal dressera-t-on devant lui assez haut pour qu'il reconnaisse nécessaire de lui sacrifier librement la vie?" Et tous les jours on n'est pas sans nouvelles d'une autre nation qui va se jeter sur "the traitors" et, coûte que coûte, les couper en deux — je vous le dis, ma mère, ça donne réflechir. Quant aux allemands, il y a qui les imaginaient aussi barbares que le sentiment de la pitié leur est complètement inconnu. Je dis a l'oreille, maman: ne comptes pour rien ces blagues-là. Le peuple français, ce qui a tout souffert pendant trois ans, ne garde, la plupart, que des sentiments les plus respecteuses pour ces bosches. Mais la Guerre — c'est pour eux, les français, une chimère abominable, qui a mangé leur amis et leur amies, tout ce qu'ils aimaient et pour lequel ils vivaient. Par exemple: un méchanique qui s'est associé avec la section sanitaire, me disait qu'au cours de quinze jours de la guerre il a perdu son père et ses deux frères. Sa mère est morte. "Je suis patriot," me disait-il, "mais pas comme ça. La guerre — non, non." Pensez-vous que je lui disais: Monsieur, vos sentiments vous déshonorent — ? Ma mère, je lui prenais la main, en disant: camarade, vous avez raison.

Mais nous ne parlerons plus de cette guerre. Ici, on est bien. Pendant huit ou neuf jours il pleut à sceaux. Par ici, pas un coup de cannon n'est tiré, parcequ'il n'y en a point. Comme disent

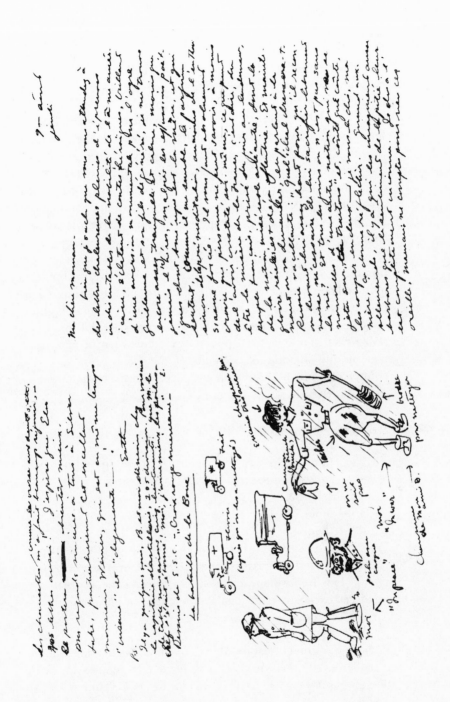

FACSIMILE OF LETTER 28

toujours les "communiqués"—Rien a signaler en dehors d'une activité assez marquée—en ce cas—des chaussures contre la boue. Oui, c'est vrai: on oublie presque l'appétit, tellement qu'il fait mauvais temps. Il faut nettoyer journellement les voitures, en nageant dans la fange jusqu'au genoux. Rien d'étonnant que je suis enrhumé depuis quelques jours.

Le présent chef de la section, avant, sous-chef, est un homme assez stupide, sans éducation, et qui se fache toujours, comme son prédécesseur méchant, de mon ami et particulière-ment de moi: "Autre cloche, même son." Comme je vous disais dans une autre lettre, il a donné notre voiture à un autre. Mais croyez-moi, ça m'est absolument égal, tellement que j'ai pour cet homme, et pour tous, excepté mon ami Brun, un mépris complet.

Il y a quelques jours, M. Norton nous a visité. C'est un homme maigre, plutôt grand, qui cause sans mouvoir la bouche, à un oeil obscurci par le monocle; dans un mot, un âne agréable et sans raison d'être. Il nous a dit que ça lui était une chose épouvantable, que nous n'aimions pas notre chef défunt, notre noble chef, qui était parti pour entrer dans l'armée; que nous n'étions que des enfants méchants, et que si nous sommes restés comme ça, nous n'avions rien à espèrer. Merde pour lui.

Le carnet de nos journées lirait comme ça—

7:15 reveille
7:30 "setting up exercises"
8— petit déjeuner
      (quelques jours, on fait une tournée en voiture, n'en
      trouvant personne malade, croyez-bien)
12: déjeuner
18— dîner
22— "bed"

Les chausettes comme la brosse aux dents, etc. m'a fait beaucoup réjouir—vos lettres aussi! J'espère que Elos se portera bientôt mieux. Mes regards sincères à tous à Silver Lake, particulière-ment cet excellent monsieur Weiner, qui est en même temps, "insane" et "degenerate"———!

P. S. Il y a quelques soirs, B. et moi dînions chez le capitaine d'artillerie, 205 division. Pour voisins de table nous avions cinq lieutenants. Que M. le Chef s'était etonné! Moi, j'aime mieux les poilus—

[Sketch]

[La Ferté Macé, Orne, France
October 1, 1917]

Dearest of Mothers!

At 11 A. M. Monsieur le Ministre de Sûreté plus 2 or 3 gendarmes convoyed my friend and me in separate voitures to his abode in N. [Noyon] Here we dined, each with his gendarme, still apart, and later were examined. Then removed to separate cells where we spent the night. My friend must have left the following day: I spent another night in my cell (sans sortir) having enjoyed a piece of bread, a piece of chocolate (thanks to friend) a small pail (or marmite) of grease-meat soup, more bread, ditto of beans, ditto soup & bread. This sounds like a lot. At 10 A.M. I left in the company of 2 gendarmes for the station of N. A distance of almost ½ mile. Had some trouble with a gendarme, who told me if I didn't want to carry my bagge I could leave it (I had a duffle-bag, chuck full, a long ambulance coat, a fur coat, a bed-roll, & blankets, total — 150 lbs.) by the wayside — which I naturally refused to do. We finally compromised by my hiring a sweet kid to lug the bed-roll (which he did with greatest difficulty). Chemin-de-fer till 5 o'clock when landed at G. where supped on grease-meat-soup in a better cell, and slept on planks in blankets (other baggage forbidden) till 4 A. M., when another pair of gendarmes took me to the station of G. (I with baggage) where we boarded c. de f. for Paris, arriving at 6 A. M. Wait till 12 noon. In interval coffee & newspapers. At 1 train left for B., where we arrived at 9:30 P M. I having dined on bread. All this time, my friend was 1 day ahead of me. Arrived at B., we checked big duffle bag & roll in gare, and set off on foot for La Ferté Macé, I carrying this time merely a small bag of letters, n. books, & souvenirs, which a gendarme had always carried hitherto. Douze kilomètres. Arrived midnight. Given straw pallet & slept on floor sans blankets. In morning found self in hugely long room with my long-lost friend and about 30 others as I guess — very cosmopolite group.

The following program is ours now till 15th October, when a commission comes to examine us for pacifism or something of the sort: 6-up. Coffee. 7 down to yard. 9:30 up. 10 down to salle à manger. 10:30–3:45 yard. 3:45 up. 4 down to salle à manger. 4:30–7 yard. 7 up. 9-lights out. I am having the time of my life. Never so healthy. Our meals are both soup, but we are allowed a spoon, which is better than eating with fingers, as we did in prison. By the way, a gendarme assured me this is not prison.

By the time this reaches you I shall have been out for some time. It's been a great experience. Monsieur le Surveillant is a fine man. We (my friend & I) have instituted "3 Old Cat" which we all play in the yard when it's fair. I couldn't possibly want anything better in the way of keep, tho' you have to get used to the snores, and they don't allow you a knife, so you can't cut the air at night which is pretty thick, all windows being shut.

Elos's letter I got before leaving the "front" and please thank her & give her my much love, as to all.

You can't imagine, Mother mine, how interesting a time I'm having. Not for anything in the world would I change it! It's like working — you must experience it to comprendre — but how infinitely superior to Colliers! If I thought you would excite yourself I wouldn't write from this place, but I know you will believe me when I reiterate that I am having the time of my life!

P.S. My bagge has been given back. I have my bed and am finely off! No more floor-sleeping.
P.P.S. arrested a week ago today.

30 / TO HIS MOTHER

La Ferté Macé, Orne
[October 14, 1917]

Mère bien chère!

Je t'écris ce quatorze octobre en attendant l'appel de descendre me promener avec les autres dans la petite cour. C'est ici un camp de concentration, il y a peut-être une huitaine d'hommes, agés de vingt à quarante ans qui se couchent ensemble dans une seule grande chambre. A six heures café; sept, promenade; dix, la soupe; une heure, promenade encore; quatre heure, la soupe; neuf heure, lumières s'eteignent jusqu'au jour. J'y suis avec mon ami, M. le ministre de sûreté de Noyons se méfiant des sentiments qui se sont trouvés dans quelques lettres écrites par mon ami à ses amis ou à sa famille en Amerique, et, quant à moi, parce que je suis son ami. C'est un peu drôle, n'est-ce pas? que l'unique fils d'une famille qui n'a jamais gardé que des opinions les plus pro-alliés qu'il sait possible de rêver serait le sujet de soupcons! D'ailleurs, un volontaire qui est venu avant que les Etats Unis nous sont entrés en guerre. Mais je n'ai aucune doute que dans l'agitation bien justifiée de la presse contre l'espionage épouvantable ici en France, avec l'arrestation presque journellement des véritables espions, se trouve l'explication de notre séquestration. Mon ami et moi avions juste fait notre application pour entre dans aviation français; et c'est peut-être donc qu'il faut être certain de la fidelité de ceux qui voudraient devenir soldats dans l'armée française. Courage! "C'est la guerre!"

Tu m'écrit, ma mère, que tu m'as envoyé, comme ma grandmère, un "sweater" que tu faisais toi-même. Je ne les ai pas encore reçu; mais les chausettes etc. envoyées par ma grandmère, et tes lettres, comme la lettre que m'a écrit mon père m'ont donné très beaucoup de plaisir, inutile d'insister! Le moment où je peux te dire qu'est-ce que je vais faire dans l'avenir crois-bien que je l'écrirai tout. Sois tranquille comme toujours—

31 / TO HIS MOTHER

[La Ferté Macé, Orne
November ?, 1917]

Dearest of All Mothers!
If you could see my "clumps" newly purchased for two francs, with warm slippers therein; my fur-coat sewed to a state of propriety by an "inmate;" my (formerly A. W.'s [Arthur Wilson's]) scarf bounding my manly thighs; and, last and best, my August's (Harvard Sq.) hat assumingly propped over my brow of alabaster—you'd not be surprised to know how happy I am. Add coffee served in bed, days spent with an inimitable friend in soul-stretching probings of aesthetics, 10 hour nights (9 PM–6:45 AM) and fine folk to converse in five or six languages beside you—perfection attained at last.

A few days since, the pleasure of this existence was triflingly ruffled by the "passing" of a "commission" of 3, which decide upon the question whether the passee shall be turned [over] to a camp de concentration, or regain his leisure—id est, return to the trenches, usine, ship, etc. whence he came. The C .

"passed" my friend 1st. After a long wait I entered the chamber. One of 3 people asked me a lot of questions, proving from collected translations of passages censored in the letters of my friend that the latter was not a hater of Germans or a lover of war. I assured them that I hated ("détesté" was their delicious word) nobody in the world, laying this breadth of view to my father's weekly occupation. Whether this made a hit or not I don't know, nor care a white ostrich plume, inasmuch as it happens to be true of me. My friend demanded an interpreter, yet I decided to sick [*sic*] the great in their own way, and launched thunders of American-French eloquence over the terrified trio.

The plupart of the gentlemen ensconced with us at this depot are aliens roused from their beds of ease and led here, often with wife and children. They are splendid comrades. I mean it. To compare them for a fly's thought (= moment) with the nefarious rulers from whom French justice, thank God, has finally, after 3 months of slavery, completely delivered us, would be not only assinine but hugely unjust. You can't begin to imagine our unimaginable glee at living safe and sound out of the nagging reach of our former owners. I say what I mean, as ever.

As to nourriture, my slight sickness of a few days ago suggested a new article of diet for the Menu, which now reads (irrespecting the free rations accorded à tout le monde):

eggs — sept sous per	
beurre — un franc	fish
vin rouge ordinaire — deux francs (le litre)	milk
tabac Maryland — un franc dix/le paquet	every
papiers (cigarette) — trois sous	day free
bougie — dix sous	to malades

My friend, who is the chef of unparalleled goodness & greatness, cooks me dropped eggs, scrambled, omelets, boiled, etc. etc. etc. Our expenditures touch five francs par jour pour tous les deux. My friend's long awaited money arrives regularly now, by the way.

I omitted to say that the commission will tender a proposition to M. le Ministre de l'Intérieur relative to the passees, whereat the M le M de l'I will do as he thinks advisable. My resolution is inéventable. I see the thing thru, alone, without any monocled Richards, American ambassadors, or anything else. Nothing under H. can change my resolve, and everybody but me, i.e. Gods, men, women & children had best keep butted out!!!!

Thank my best beloved Nana for the Rameses & socks! Mille fois. Thank D. Dad for his letter! Thank you for the sweater I've not received but eagerly expect (not that I am in need) Love to Aunt J., best to Elos, Bob, Sandy, & the new Irish maid (there's one, I'm sure).

1918–1919

104 Irving St.
22 janvier [1918]

mon chèr Dos—

crois bien que nous sommes heureux, ma mère et moi,
d'avoir de tes nouvelles. Tu va m'excuser si je te raconte quelque
choses de suite: à cause de quelques lettres "compromettantes"
qu'il avait écrit à ses amis et à ses parents en Amérique, mon bon
ami et excellent camarade William Slater Brown, habitant Webster Mass. est arrêté le 23 Septembre 1917 à la section sanitaire
(qui se trouvait à ce moment-là à Ollezy, une tout petite village
pas loin de St. Quentin) par Monsieur le ministre de Sûreté de
Noyon. En même temps j'étais pris, parce que nous étions
toujours ensemble, B. et moi. Arrivé à Noyon, nous avons reçu
le "3rd degree," et après sommes mis au cachet, toujours isolés
et séparés vous savez, chacun sa cellule. De Noyon en chemin de
fer jusqu'à une petite prison pas loin de Paris, je ne rappelle
pas à ce moment comment elle s'appelle. Après une journée
entière en voyage, je me suis trouvé au Camp de Triage de la
Ferté Macé(Orne) où j'ai retrouvé mon ami. Nous sommes
restés ensemble là-bas onze semaines. Nous avons passé une
commission. Enfin, mon ami est parti pour un autre camp—on
dit que ça veut dire pour la durée de la guerre—Moi je reste;
mais quelques jours après on m'a dit "Vous êtes libres. Il faut
choisir tout de suite: où est-ce que vous vous allez?" J'ai dit: Je
veux bien aller à Oloron St. Marie, Basse Pyrénés, pour finir
mes études, comme je faisais la peinture en Amérique. Bon.
Mais quelques jours après cela, on a telégraphié de Paris, et je
suis parti moi tout seul me présenter chez l'ambassadeur américain. Là bas je trouve un jeune homme qui s'appelle Monsieur
Wily, c'est lui qui m'avait trouvé, après quelques mois, et je lui
dois ma liberté complète. Il m'a demandé quant à Brown, pourquoi qu'il a écrit des bêtises? Moi j'ai répondé: Monsieur, ce
Brown c'est un tout jeune homme, il a juste 21 ans, c'est un bon
garçon, une caractère noble et sans peur. Mais il faut que vous
compreniez que tout le monde l'a embêté à la Section Sanitaire,
alors, s'il a fait des indiscrétions ca c'est pas grande chose,
comme je pense.

Monsieur Wily (c'est un américain) a fait l'impossible pour
me donner les papiers nécessaires de partir en Amérique, et en
fait je pars par le paquebot "Espagne" arrivant à New York le

1e Janvier, 1918. Ce monsieur s'est montré bien intéressé: et j'espère qu'il pourra faire quelque chose pour mon ami aussi.

Mon pauvre Dos! Vous êtes tout a fait ennuyé de cette histoire, je le sais bien. Je m'excuse en assurant que c'est pour mon camarade à ce moment enfermé à un camp de concentration que je raconte tout ca — si vous voulez lui envoyer des cigarettes, ou même une carte postale, en lui disant que vous êtes un mien ami, et que je t'ai écrit que sa famille en Amérique et tout le monde là bas va faire son possible pour lui, je te remercierai pour toujours. Parce que, vous savez, c'est un brave garçon, et — comme je sais bien — on est souvent ennuyé en des circumstances pareilles.

Moi j'ai été malade depuis quelques semaines, mais maintenant ça va un peu. Tout le monde dit que t'es un héros, un conducteur "sans peur et sans réproche" que tu joues "base-ball" avec les cent cinqs, et patati et patata. Ah, mon Dos, que je me gêne, que je m'ennuie pour la Ville Lumineuse, la Ville Réale, la Femme Superbe et subtile qui s'appelle — tu le sais — Paris.

33 / TO HIS SISTER

11 Crist [Christopher St.]
New York, N. Y.
April 9, 1918

Dear Lulu —

W. Slater Brown, Edward P. Nagle, and I. O. U. were traversing la sixième avenue, entre la dixième et la onzième rue, a la côté ouest, quand nous avons découvert un tout petit chien gris-blanc, un peu sale, et beaucoup timide, qui chancelait entre les ash-cans "— Comme il avait faim!" Monsieur Victor Hugo, en "Les Miserables" fait parler Gavroche (à propos d'un chien comme ça) "The poor little chap — look, he's swallowed a barrel!" Nous avons demandé à manger pour le petit, en causant avec le "night-waiter" du "Hudson Lunch," et ce bon garçon dit: Faites-le entrer! Brown a appellé monsieur chien, et le garçon lui a donné à manger de viande ancienne. A ce moment le chef du "Lunch" se fait visible, en criant d'une mine effrayante — "est-ce qu'il est un Mut?" En recevant une réponse affirmative, le chef dit de suite — "Il faut le laver dans le sink" (ce qui était donc plein des assiettes et tout cela). Mais nous sommes échappés ensemble sans dégâts matériels; ou "pertes terribles" comme disent les communiqués anglaises toujours de l'armée bosche victorieuse.

Enfin, ce chien se tient tout près de Brown et marchait toujours avec nous, causant souvent avec les "police-mans" en route.

La nuit, il dort chez nous, et nous allons l'appeller "Bes," parce que son nom doit être "Asbestos."

C'est interessant, nous avons trouvé ce matin que notre petit est une Elle.

34 / TO HIS FATHER

[11 Christopher St.]
July 1 [1918]

Dear Dad,

* * * This is a perfectly patriotic community. Little children mouth the bloody-thirstily-inspiring words of "over there over there" "so what are you going to do to win the war" etc ad infin-. Moovies show reels where ex-soldiers about-to-commit-traitery are so moved by the patriotic appeal of babies in nightgowns that they weep bitter tears — and go out and kill Mexicans! A grim looking bunch of dames sits collectively in a booth on 14th shrieking faintly at everyone "buy a stamp",while o'er their sacred heads ring the printed words "Help to make the Kaiser's coffin" or some such reference to the "BabyKiller". How fierce we are. I enclose the a propos clipping,underlining being my sole attempt at comment. Ethically it may interest you;aesthetically the whole business has long since ceased to interest truly yours. Who builds misrepresentative unrepresentations of traffic,bridges,green-haired females, — by the way,if I should land Thursday in jail,you may be wired by God's Own Representatives to confirm a report which I shall promptly spread concerning my future occupation as farmer on my paternal parent's 100acre farm in New Hampshire. That being,of course,a "useful occupation",like baseball.

Tell mother I've dined twice with J. of the Dial,to whom Scofield introduced me before dashing for dentist. He will take some stuff,he says,tho' what stuff troubles him,or rather his Georgian anatomy. Another man dead — if not from the neck upward,at least downward. Scofield had his number and gave it to me,and I briefly expressed:not very deep. All the Dial's editors have been camping out here at odd times. How popular we are.

If or when I do come on,I'll try to bring with me in manu Sco's picture and the one I'm just now working on. The pastels will fit nicely in your suit-case * * *

35 / TO HIS MOTHER

[11 Christopher St.
July 4, 1918]

Dear Mother,

I had dinner tonight with le sculpteur Lachaise of whom I remember speaking before. I told Lachaise I'd lunched at eleven or so,sat down on a chair and painted till seven,on "Brooklyn Bridge". After dinner(costing for me plus he 50 cents)I went up to see a thing on which he's now working. He's hampered,as he says freely,with the ununderstanding public(the most selling statue of his show on 5th Avenue was a prettiish "Pudeur",as the gallery-man Bourgeois christened it to Lachaise's woe) — "Ai don lai kit ai hay tit 'pudeur' dat mean someting to me Dirty" — I assure you there's a superb (naturally unsellable)statue in his room,its "Big-niss in li-tel-nis" massive,tho 8 inches high,pose supreme,divine. Not mentioning his 6 foot plaster nude which it took him 3 years,says Edward Nagle,to build,which he twice complètement demolished. Bourgeois thought the show would be pinched on her account. Then he came down to Eleven C. Street. I had "on show" the thing Dad contracted for,plus 2 new things(Scofield's picture and the Dessin I just wrote you of,and which I meant by B Bridge[)]. There were four other things,but to my joy Lachaise had no use for them,no more'n me,they being ancients if not honorables comparatively——Lachaise liked these three very much. DD's thing suggests to him an Interieur,where the air is Close,he uses the word Soul(-tristesse)for it,and says it is Seelawnt;fine word. Says it contrasts nicely with S's,which gives him the playing of joyous Kids — by the way the forms are exclusively inorganic! — which pleases me ever so. I called it "Traffic." Healthy,says he. (the first,Poetic)

As for 3rd,Lachaise is Restricted by my previous "catch-phrase" as the right hon Blissful Perry might term. Liked it very much. Suggested to him a woman,Perhaps Astec Woman. barbaric colours. These forms are beoot'fool — he honoured me by seeing a fitness of form-to-color in it. I gotno breedg,he says softly — then "in payn teeng,I think te(the)title al WAYZ bad,in payn teeng like diss,worde ttan bad" and he explained on and forth,to my taste. Saw "so leede" in it which I must have mistaken for a bridge! Etcetera.

I write all this nonsensich because you desire to know what my friends think about . . . and really because I wanted Lachaise and his reaction. Valuing both,and partly as french I suspect.

Dont let Dad get wild over my jail quips. Talked the situation with Lachaise,and he says it's all smooth sailing in all probability as long as I keep from "poo-lhawlz". A danger not likely to be incurred mayby by the Joyous Kid's begetter. The dimensions of this day's painting I thought might also interest. In lumière of Loafing charges! * * *

36 / TO HIS MOTHER

[Camp Devens, Fitchburg, Mass.
August 14, 1918]

Dear Mother,

I am afraid the response to ὦ πατρί was even singularly incoherent. My head is less achishly inclined today,and the offending member has been bumped by neighborly ones till it has lost its painful individuality. Continuing the bon mots column:

By the 2 lieutenants,antiphonally; — "Don't forget you men want to have guts at <u>both</u> ends of your guns"."Yes, we don't want any <u>helmets</u> as souvenirs, we want <u>guts</u>,we prefer 'em,we can use 'em for <u>fertilizer</u>."

bon appetit! mes lieutenants,quant à moi,je me sent malade à l'estomac.

Today too the greatest misfortune happened. A number of privates were pulled out of the ranks to "go to school" for noncommissioned officers,drill squads,etc. I was unhappily 1.

After 10 minutes argument with the captain,I was told to continue "schooling" and if necessary,drop out when the time

for promotion came. I told the captain about my temperament,my occupation,my equivocal behavior under fire,etc.—no
impression whatever,as I expected. The bullshit(to use a forte
and accurate expression-du-peuple)of such quality as above
quoted I doubt if I stand very long.

As to France. If there is anything in a lieutenant's statements one will have 3 months training here,then partir,then 2
months training in France. This should put us in the trenches
by January,I hope.

Vive la merde

P.S. appointed acting corporal on basis of "very high psychological examination".

VLM

P.P.S. The other day:man shoots breakfast,(6 AM)man breaks
leg(3 PM)man faints in ranks(5 PM). Hellelouyah.

37 / *TO HIS FATHER*

[Camp Devens
August 19, 1918]

Dear Dad—
Thanks for your enthousiastic letter! I should be more
happy still if I felt certain you completely understood—tho' by
no means agreeing with—my übermench and totally original
and disgusting attitude. So you'll excuse if I reiterate a few
characterless ferocities of my own invention:
(1)The fact that the army is generous enough to give me a new
body(there is no doubt about this,and I should be the last to
blink the appalling facts)does not sufficiently dazzle these cool
and perpetual eyes to make their brain forget that(except for
such minor obscurities as love,art & cie.)every "gift" is <u>A SWOP</u>.
If I should use the clause "at the expense of my soul" I should
be guilty of at once treason and(what is worse)banality. I
shall therefore,in my own unerringly erroneous manner,let it
stand.
(2)If I die tonight(from the effects,probably,of a semi-liquid
demiviscous pudding-of-rubber-heels which I did Not eat)I
shall be glad of everything which I <u>once could do</u> which "the

army" has forbidden my doing. I shall <u>not</u> <u>be</u> <u>even</u> <u>cheerful</u> <u>about a single other thing</u>.

(3)The question naturally arises:why,then,Detester of "Discipline",didst thou not pick-and-choose,instead of letting them put something distinctly over on thee,whence even now thou dost uplift thy pale shrill accents like unto a drowning rat held under the boisterous faucet of Freedom?

My answer:because I am he who would drink beer and eat shit if he saw somebody else doing it,especially if that somebody were compelled to do it. And I would think myself partially cheated of the expensive adventure of the universe did I not take a chance with Tim, [obscure]. And their kin and kith.

BUT

(4)I reiterate(in my coyly paradoxical style)I should think myself equally cheated if I allowed my humanly-sentimental-mind to interfere,<u>one iota</u>,with the sealed letters of sensation brought to my soul by these eyes,these ears,this nose & tongue.

So noone would be allowed to take my place? And come here in my stead? And enjoy the privilege of "dying"(or more correctly,living)for democracy?—very well;by the Iaveh,noone shall come out of the valley and the mountain with the same music in his eyes as me. Nor shall that music please,nor shall it exalt the old ideals,but it shall discover a hideous ecstasy whereat the players of other musics shall fall into the gummy latrine of destiny;and the last note of my song shall pull the chain upon them,and they shall be perfectly swallowed,and god help the sea anyway.

In other words,to cease Pindaric pleasantries,I commend you,pater patrum,to the worship of the cute and fastidious billikin of Silence,who sits on cushions of thistledown in the humorous throne-room of Imagination;

by god. Mine is the perspiration of my own existence,and that's all I give a proper and bloody damn for. As for the "results","fruits",and other painful-and necessary etceteras,be they unto whomsoever may want'em. They are no concern of mine—but the SWEAT is! and I would not change it for anyone else's sweat under heaven.

[Camp Devens
September 11, 1918]

Dear Mother—

* * * I was very glad to get Dad's letter. Sorry he found an effusive phrase in it—he'd better steel his worthy being for the unuttered future,I must say!

Incidentally,the roi de la royaume de l'avenir was a neatly ironic touch. I cannot but own that before I came to "war" I was furiously socialistic(in my placid,nonchalant,assinine,luxuriously inimitable way). From the day of my coming,dates an always crescendoing love of the aristocratic,of Scofield,for instance,of limousines and Debussy,of S.W. [Sibley Watson]— coinciding with a despising,hearty & unique,of slip-slop(vocal & dish-water)feet,smells,and in general,the functions of a οἱ πολλοι en sardine.

It must be comprehended,however,that I have my own unique & furiously placid way in this,which differs from the ordinary—that is,accepted—manner of dealing with an "unpleasant" situation. John Doe says I hate to sleep en bloc,dine à la merde,breathe per ordens and die en masse. Therefore I,(having inherited <u>intelligence</u> + a <u>Pull</u>,[)]will go see,or have papa go write to,Major A.,or Secretary X,which gentleman or -men will be most likely to advance me to a more decent—&— respectable-and-lovely footing.

I say—to hell with John Doe. Pensez vous que j'ai souffert pour rien la conscription obligatoire et tous des maux qui se viennent avec une séparation complète from all which I hold to be life? Not on your tintype;as Uncle George ecstatically would remark. I say:the artist is merely the earth's most acute and wiley observer of everything-under-the-sun. Mankind intrudes itself. (Draft) Does the artist duck? Nix. Does he let Major Abbot,KCB,EZ,etc. come between him and the new angle on destiny? Like fun he does. Nor President W,nor Napoléon Buonaparte. The artist keeps his eyes,ears,& above all his NOSE wide open,he watches,while others merely execute orders he <u>does</u> <u>things</u>. By things I do <u>not</u> mean wearing gold bars or pulling wires or swallowing rot-in-general or nonsense-in-particular. I mean the sustaining of his invisible acquaintance with that life which,taken from his eyes,makes itself a house in his very-brain-itself.   On the pergolas of that house his soul will lounge gorgeously while his arms & legs do squads right.

But why then wouldn't his soul lounge better in a pleasanter environment? it is asked.   —That is not for anyone but the artist himself to answer.   In a rude manner of speaking,at which I trust nobody will take offense,it is nobody else's dambusiness. To personalize the abstraction—if my prodigal family wants to keep on best terms with its fatted calf,it will lease the calf the pasture the calf wants to graze in.   For even a calf has a will of its own,they say!

If my attitude of being-left-absolutely-alone is incomprehensible to you,I daresay I am sorry,but not for all the lead pipe in Solomon's mines would I dare negate the invisible,and derail my destiny by [not] swerving from the polished and trite tracks on which my "neighbors" have so generously placed my unoffending cow-catcher.   Talk about verbum saps!   This is an earfull indeed of them   *   *   *

39 / TO HIS MOTHER

[Camp Devens
September 25, 1918]

Chère Maman—
Aujourd'hui il faisait voir une pluie tombait à travers le scène distinctive et mediocre et tout à fait misérable.   Alors,c'est un lieutenant(pas un sous-lieutenant)qui nous a donné de conseil en ces mots   *   *   *
" . . . . the word Kamarade doesn't mean anything to an american any more . . . Of course when they have ammunition they fight,and when they run out of it,they throw up their hands . . . . don't stick it in the chest,it's hard to pull out.   Stick it in the bellies,And Don't Stick It In Deep,stick it in A Little Way.   There's nothing better than to see a Bosch die.   They make more noise than the american army,bawling . . . and another thing.   Some of the boys when they've got one,stop,to finish it up good.   I don't blame 'em,but don't do it.   Let them die slowly . . . . Give the boys(young Germans)a square meal & they'll tell everything they know.   But you can't get anything out of the old Germans,from 25 to 50.   They've had their old Kaiser all their life and couldn't get on without him.   So don't take any prisoners among them."   (Pas de néants,je crois)

Au commencement:"We don't take any German Prisoners. We only have to Feed 'Em if we do. So we stick 'em.

Il a raconté une petite histoire délicate:un prisonnier bosche a réussi de trouver une grenade américaine,ce qu'il a jeté,mais la grenade en frappant la casque d'un soldat américain à travers s'est tombé à coté,sans aucun mal. Alors les américains ont pris ce bosche,ont mis une autre grenade dans sa poche,et l'ont jeté par terre,en faisant marcher la grenade qui a tout à fait demolli la victime misérable. Cf.(un oeil pour un oeil,un dent pour un dent. . . .)

Plus tard,un autre lieutenant nous a commandé en expliquant la manière correcte de jouer a la bayonette—"Look Ugly. Grit your teeth." Personne n'a rigolé. (Dis je personne? C'est pas vrai. Moi,je m'amusais beaucoup.—) ❋ ❋ ❋

40 / TO HIS FATHER

[Camp Devens]
Dec. 14 '18]

Dear Dad,

The lieutenant-inspector of whose general soldierliness I think I have spoken to you once or twice this morning addressed the men who go on guard today-and-tomorrow. I took down, while he was speaking,certain things which I thought would particularly interest you.

"I have a home in Georgia. My father owns 500 acres and works 15 to 20 niggers. I don't have to be here. I was discharged three times. They can't get rid of me.

"I went to school 3 years.

"I wished they'd sign a bill that every man in uniform would be here five years."

Even more interesting are the following:

"There is a feller up there(at the guardhouse)named Cox(?) he wrote his girl:the first time a guard's back was turned he'd come back to her . . . I got the letter. She didn't . . . I got 2 broken fingers now from Cox(?)and I'll have 2 more.

"You men ought to take a look at what they do to a man at the military prisons,Jay,New York;Leavenworth,Kansas;Fort Angel(?)California. I've been to all of 'em. When a man comes to Fort Jay,the first thing they do is give him a g. d. fine beating. They black his eyes for him. They do that on principle down there. All I ever wore at Jay was a pair of pants and a shirt with the sleeves tore out at the arms,winter and summer,that and my boots leggings and hat. All they do is fight from morning till night there."

He added:"When you men get out of this army you'll be so lonesome for the life you won't know what ails you. Some day you'll hear a military band and the shivers'll go up your spine and you won't know what for,and the next morning you'll wake up in an army bunk and say 'How did I get here?'"—at this point private D. laughed heartily for a whole minute,rocking to and fro with mirth.—"What are you laughing at?" the L.asked.—"I can't help it" was the answer. "I know you can't,I don't mind your laughing,but what are you laughing at?" When private D. responded "at what you said" the laughter became uproarious all over the audience.

I should be pleased to have this letter,which it will be noticed is a verbatim account at first hand,follow the Dial,which it so aptly backs up,to its destination.

Yours for patriotism-of-the-world

41 / TO HIS FATHER

Camp Devens
13 jany, 1919.

Dear Father.

The Captain had me in today before his lieutenants. He began with "Private Cummings,I've read this application for a discharge on grounds—er—and find no reasons whatever for accepting it on the basis of the order as received by us." I countered doggedly. After much mental fisticuffs,in which "sir" and "private" disappeared,he asked: "Cummings,do you consider that you've got as good a right to apply as the other men who put in?" "As far as dependency goes I am not qualified to say"—quoth I. "But for the occupational part I consider that I have as good a right as anybody in this company." I added that I was probably the most ill-fitted man to be here,and most un-at-home. "The army wasn't made to suit temperaments," he remarked. I was shaking in every muscle by this time. He ended with:"I understand this affects you only." "Certainly," I said. "That for temperamental reasons etc. you want to be discharged." "I support myself," I said simply and clearly. "The army supports you," he replied wearily . . . . etc etc etc.

Lieutenant Noonan—qu'il soit béni avec les anges à jamais! —interrupted the fire works once with apt questions as to my services in France.

Not once did I mention Charles [Eliot Norton?],or the sources of my superior information. (Nor did I retreat a millimeter.) Perhaps my best card was the contract with Mr. [Scofield] Thayer of New York for 4 pictures,$600 to be paid me on completion of the 4th and how the call-to-arms left me with 3 only completed. Perhaps you know of Mr. Thayer's agreeing to keep the contract open,while I tried for my discharge,i. e. promising me(in case I could get one at once)that the terms would still hold;altho' of course the time was long since up.

Anyway,the clerk in the orderly room told me that the list "recommended-for-discharge" had my name on it. (It is by this time at Headquarters. Heaven knows what they'll say or do.)

C'est extraordinaire:vraiment,le capitaine était immensement faché à propos de l'ex-major A. J'ai vu cela très clair. Et pour moi—quelle bataille!—vous pouvez vous figurer l'intensité,l'acidité—! ✳ ✳ ✳

42 / *TO HIS MOTHER*

[80 Washington Square, New York
February 9, 1919]

Dear Mother

✳ ✳ ✳ A curious con-catination of circumstances has kept Brown & me in a condition of insanity pendant the last week:

Brown's father & sister & Bessie's Black Puppy all arrived. No rooms anywhere in New York. Sister takes this room(80 Washington Sq)Brown & father sleep at Columbia,I sleep with Lachaise in his studio. Then only 1 room is vacant in Columbia; consequently Brown & I(rather than go to a charitable home) decide to move & sleep in our newly devised habitat at 9 West 14th St. (Room 16,top floor,studio). We had paid in advance

$18(it is 20 per)for the studio,but there was as yet <u>no</u> gas,nor had we coal for the grate. (We have no gas-jets,a sky-light,an open fire,2 closets). So we slept strangely(having just bought 2 beds & matresses to match)and in the morning I undressed(peeling down to street clothes)and visited coal people. Nobody in. At length I rang at Elaine's. She wasn't up. Her maid came to the door. "Bergét"—she's great!! "Give me a lump of coal" I said. She was slightly surprised,but did up 5 huge lumps(a foot-cube each)which I carried from Washington Square to 14th St. Nor did they ever break out of the paper. Nor did the string break!

Now we have(all night)an open fire to undress & dress by,& gas for cold weather,cooking,etc.

All sorts of things(tea-things,extra-army blankets;draperies etc etc)are en route from Wanamakers. Elaine Thayer came up this morning as we were drinking our first cup of coffee—best I ever tasted—and left,threatening innumerable luxuries for us,same to arrive in some hours. She thought the place was great,you may be interested to know.

Every day Brown & I buy pails,hammers,brooms,pans,pots, etc. * * *

43 / TO HIS MOTHER

[9 West 14th St., New York
April 7, 1919]

Dearest Mother,

* * * A little tin geezi of MR.Pound 's coining,one Horace Brodsky,was in charge of the Penguin [Gallery] (or thought he was)and gave me and likewise Nagle a lot of trouble. Among other things,he failed in persuading me to give him $4 entrance fee twice. Meeting Lachaise that evening,I explored Mr. Brodsky's personality in forceful phrases—to which Lachaise said "Yes?" Next morning Nagle,who was mostly asleep,heard Lachaise say,"I called up Trotsky." "You called up Trotsky?" said Nagle,somewhat amazed. "Sure." "Well,"said Nagle resignedly,"How's Lenine?" "What you mean?"cried Lachaise —and thus it came about that he meant Brodsky. Lachaise had told Brodsky that:"You know those two fel-low-es which came

to see you? I wish you shall be very nice to them" — and Trotsky-Brodsky certainly was — after that. Not that he can be,but he did somewhat better;contenting himself with asking me if I minded his asking which side up my pictures went? Subsequently Mrs. Lachaise told him how fine they were etc. as she is very enthusiastic,or if not,makes an embarrassingly good imitation of it — such as asking me "How does it feel to be the sensation of the Independent? That's what everyone is telling me" . . . . and Brodsky exploded: "Waste of time and material" "that sort of art is something I cant see anything at all in" "anyone can do it" etc.   He is also supposed to have "ground his teeth" on an occasion when we failed to notice his august presence.   I am afraid Mr. Burly-sun [Albert Burleson, Postmaster General] wouldn't let go through the mails the remark which [Joseph] Stella the painter made à propos Brodsky — in English that is — so I give it in the original French

  "je sais shier des tableaux plus beaux que ce que dessine ce Brodsky" * * *

44 / TO HIS MOTHER

9 West 14th St.
April 24, 1919

Dearest Mother,

* * * You may be glad to know that Gleizes(the "first cubist" — probably the most individual,though somewhat cold, abstract painter in America,and — after Picasso — best known among painters of a type — was(to use Lachaise's phrase) "TAKEN OUT OF HIS FEET" by the two things of mine at the Independent.   According to Nagle,he said later on that they were the "best things in oil" that he had seen "in America". Mr. [Walter] Pach,the director,was(as you may imagine)highly pleased;and said very pleasant things à propos when Nagle and I came to take away our things. (Pach,you may be amused to know,came within an ace of selling "Sound.") Since,I have been asked to exhibit,free of charge,at a small pseudo-gallery in Washington Square,run by a man who looks like Vachel Lindsay plus Alfred Tennyson plus Bull Durham plus — X. I don't know whether or not I'll do it yet. You know how I hate Greenwitch Village.

I hope Dad got my congratulations on Easter. Brown's got a kitten,its eyes just open,which he found the other night in a grave-yard on 2nd avenue. He and Nagel were attracted by its crying. Its neck's almost half bitten,or cut,off,but under a rub-ber-nipple treatment he's apparently getting on finely. Wish Elos could see it — it's so tiny!

45 / TO HIS SISTER

[9 West 14th St.
May 6, 1919]

Dear Lulu,

* * * I sing a saga — the Kat the Kat the Kat which was found in a 2nd avenue graveyard requires desires inspires at-tentions from morn until night from one who perspires. Brown feeds it with a nipple in which we — [J. Sibley] Watson,Brown, and myself — succeeded in punching a minute hole. We did it with a redhot pin,oh it was hot and oh we were red. So now you lift the Kat the Kat by the shoulders and squirt a thin stream of superlac into its melodious little tummie. This is called the Willie-Nillie method of feeding,after its inventor,W.Brown of Webster.

It has weak hind legs,and when it walks it rushes forward a couple of millimeters and sits down frontwards. Watson said "it has a fine tail" which is shaped like a lombardy poplar and used by the Kat in locomotion to steady itself,as I think. We are spending our youth,the inventor and myself,in alternately smothering and freezing the Kat. Three times it has been found on the limen mortis by jove — so now we're getting expert at finding out and ministering to its wants. The main thing is to "cook" the cat,every night,hot or cold,about 4 A.M. over a gas-stove. After all what is sleep?as Ovid said.

The inchlong scar on its neck has,I think,healed;which is hopeful. The floor occasionally shows other signi esperanti — when the Kat's box doesn't. O the box the box.

and so i end my song of woe and dole * * *

[9 West 14th St.
May 6, 1919]

Dear Dad,

* * * My faith in humanity,as you call it,was somewhat
battered by the kaki(khaki?)clad hoodlums of our well-known
Uncle and their lightsome badinage on May Day. I witnessed
one lovely scene myself—the attack on The People's House,
which is just a block up. The helpless and worsethanhelpless
if not conniving,gendarmes did,however,nobly redeem themselves that night—a spectacle of interest which Nagle and I attended at Madison Square Garden—i.e.prevented uniforms
from entering to attack the Mooney Protest Meeting. The
mounted Police rode again and again at the inspired naval and
army patriots. One cop rushed clear up the steps of the Latham
Hotel to get his man. I suppose you know that one woman is
blind and many people injured from the attack on The [Socialist]
Call office,May 1. If not,read the Times for May 2. The Lib-
er[ty] Loan Campaign is somehow mixed up in all the roughhouse,which,to my personal observation,was led in two cases—
and papers say in all cases—by a canadian hero,who apparently
was "put wise". Cave Censeur—je ne parle plus . . . there is a
peerade here every afternoon. More or less.

Lucky my abstract talents do not exert themselves toward
realism. Sailors are so easy to draw.

READ THE NATION MAY THIRD PAGES 682 and 684.
The latter is superb.
(ps—the New York "Nation" is the only thing worth reading
today about Russia)

47 / TO R. STEWART MITCHELL

Silver Lake, N.H.
[August 18, 1919]

dear Stewart—

* * * My wardrobe is somewhat negative at the moment,ow-
ing to my recent visit of some weeks. I fear Gloucester would

disdain my sole and paint-stained suit of clothes. Here however
one wears what one bally pleases. Incidentally I wired Brown
to meet me in Boston and haven't heard—unless the occult
message was from him;which I greatly fear. I'd hoped he'd
stay with me till Columbia opens. Now I don't know where he
may be in God's green gruesome world. On the whole,would
you care to come up here for a while?

Think,my dear Stewart,of all these glorious advantages—
quelle merveille! however,God knows it's simple here. Should
you prefer more sophistication,I advise Cave Canem. At any
rate the mosquitoes seem to be largely dead * * *

PS
There was a young lady named Bundy
who was fucked by a Belgium on Sunday
on Tuesday a Uhlan
to her twat put his tool in.
(SIC TRANSIT GLORIA MUNDI)

48 / *TO R. STEWART MITCHELL*

[Silver Lake, N.H.]
Sunday [August 25, 1919]

Dear Stewart—
By all means cogitate your 1st-week-in-September. Au-
tumn,you know,is the most beautiful part of the year,or as Bob-
bie Hillyer Browning says:
"See God nor be afraid"
(Rabbi Ben Ezra)
(Maybe it's not "see god").—"Gods" is incorrect,but ah! I do
not know what I wrote,or as Al Jolson Tennyson says:
"I pipe but as the linnet must"
(In Memoriam)
But many thanks for the jock-strap offer. A true gentleman
never balks at anything. As Perk Reniers Shelley says:
"What if its leaves are falling like my own (leaves)?"
(Ode to the West Wind)
Thanks also for the manly explanation of the mysterious
φωνή-Χολλ. Butlers are bad business anyway,especially when
they try,insolently enough,to talk with the deafanddumb. As
Julia Arthur Howe says:

"They have trampled out the vintage
Where the grapes of wrath are stored"
(Battle Hymn of the Republic)
Brown located himself by writing me the other day;and I asked him to come up. Haven't heard in reply. Let me know where your σερεβέλλυμ fixes on a final date,in order that you may not sit on a cracker-barrel playing whist with the selectmen,waiting for me to meet you. Or as John Figleaf Whittier says:
"then too, we did the nightly chores"
(Snowbound)

* * *

49 / TO HIS FATHER

[9 West 14th St.]
November 7th 1919

Dear Father —

* * * Permit me to note,à propos today's papers:
1/ Your friend Elihu Root is counsel for the brewers
2/ Taft(as usual)fires his face off in the wrong direction by saying Coolidge's landslide will make "bolsheviki" strikers "pause" all over this country. (Contrast the at least intelligent editorial enclosed from N. Y. Call [enclosure missing]
3/ The "Globe" which as you know is a trust-owned paper of ultrastupidity is running daily front page articles by a man just back from Soviet Russia,proclaiming the "anarchy" fake(i.e. allied propaganda)that order has never been so universal in Russia,that Lenin & Trotsky have expressed for the 1st time in history the long-enslaved spirit of true Russia,that Kolchak's retreat(his latest)cost him is it 336,000?prisoners and god knows how many hundred miles—and that,in short,IRON CANNOT KILL TRUTH.
4/ Today(Nov. 7)all N. Y.'s radicals are throwing up their hats in celebration of the anniversary of Sovietism:there are big meetings everywhere—I expect to enjoy myself hugely
and finally
5/ that my last possible inclination to "give" to "Harvard" was shattered by arrival of the "National Bulletin, No. 11"—an unparalleled piece of pure bunk and bombast, e. g. —

"Where the call of conflict is,there will my sons be found. Where victories are men,my sons will be triumphant. And where great causes for a time go crashing to defeat,my sons will take their medicine like men."

O yes,
6/ and in the House of Commons they're kicking that skunk Churchill in the place Paddy smote the tympanum for his expenditures against Soviet Russia—his "defense" being that America is just as much at fault.
7/ Omsk being abandoned by Kolchak(Retreat number 1, 111, 111, 111). says N. Y. World,a godhonest conservative organ of illimitable light * * *

50 / TO HIS MOTHER

[9 West 14th St.
November 25, 1919]

Dearest Mother,

* * * You will be glad to know that Sibley Watson and Scofield Thayer are now respectively(1)owner and publisher. and(2)editor,of The Dial;which will change its format,drop political and take on literary characteristics. Last night Brown and I had coffee with Nagle and his mama at the latter's apartment(which is also Lachaise's,though he works as you know in his studio at Fourteenth Street)and,at Sco's suggestion,I borrowed a photograph of a relief of Lachaise for the new Dial. Not that Sco limited my judgement. He merely asked me to get any "drawings" by Lachaise which I could. Everyone was much pleased to learn of the news. It's great fun to be purveyor of such tidings to a man whom I like so much as Lachaise. Also to act as agent not to mention publisher for someone who,like Lachaise,is a good deal my senior! As always,I am peculiarly lucky to have such friends.

As for the Story Of The Great War Seen From The Windows Of Nowhere,please don't expect a speedy conclusion or rather completion of this narrative [*The Enormous Room*];for this reason:that in consenting(it almost amounted to that)to "do the thing up" I did not forego my prerogative as artist,to wit—the making of every paragraph a thing which seemed good to me,in the same way that a "crazy-quilt" is made so that every inch of it seems good to me. And so that if you put your hand over one inch,the other inches lose in force. And so that in every inch there is a binding rhythm which integrates the whole thing and makes it a single moving ThingInItself.—Not that I am held up in my story,but simply that progress is slow. I am sure the result will say(eventually that is)that no other method was possible or to be considered. It is not a question of cold facts per se. That is merely a fabric:to put this fabric at the mercy of An Everlasting Rhythm is somethingelse.

Very nice of you all to include me in the liberty bond dona-tion! Vive La Liberté. Or as the minute vendeur de journals in rue de Louvre said every day at déjeuner time,"la li-ber-té un sou . . . ."

1920–1926

[9 West 14th St.
January 9, 1920]

Dear Mother,

Herewith apologies for the long delay in writing you! I
have only just completed my essay [on Lachaise] for The Dial
[February, 1920],which as you remember I had begun while
with you in Cambridge. Alas,all that rather intent concentration
was due to be torn up. Then I began again — but not being
satisfied,tore up essay number two. By that time I was hard up
for time. So I did a good deal of distinctly difficult labor,mostly
between the hours of ten PM and seven A.M.,using the day as a
place to sleep in. I happened to notice that once it took two
hours and three quarters to write exactly three sentences — not
that I wanted three in particular. I only mention this to show
how more-than-carefully I worked it,over and then over,using
enough paper for what turned out to be thirteen and one-half
pages to fill a rag man's contract. The Corona bore up bravely
till the last word was written and promptly refused to write
figures,which mattered nothing at all. Expert-Machinist W.S.
Brown is due to fix it today.

But my reward was greater than I ever could have hoped
for. Lachaise wanted to read it before I sent it in,in order to
correct any technicalities — e.g. french spelling,notes on exhibi-
tions,etc. So I brought it down to his house. Some hours later
I found this note in the keyhole —

Couming.
    That great very great — may I just say that now I will
say as I can fully when I see you —
        We all say the same at home —
            Lachaise

And hardly had Brown and I finished reading it when in came
Lachaise,to whom the is it seventy four stairs — I forget what you
told me — were apparently as nothing — or I should say two times
seventy four,since this was the second time he'd climbed to see
me. He was appreciative as only Lachaise can be appreciative —
you who met him at Joe's can imagine how [much] that means to
anyone. Then he produced the essay,showed me some terribly
obvious blunders,with the words

"I have shoost find Come-ing some vay-ry lit-tel ting"
and then we three drank tea and ate buttered toast,discussing the

critical world in general and,with the essay as a basis,in particular. Then Lachaise said "I should run",and we wished oneanother good night.   I plead guilty to feeling excessively happy. * * *

    The other night Brown and I went by a vacant lot on Fifth and Twelfth where some leftover Christmas Trees were lying. They had been sold at wholesale there,but many were left. We took up,at his suggestion,five,arriving almost breathless after the seventy four famous stairs.   Now we have what we call a Forest. When Watson and his wife came to tea last sunday they were considerably astonished,but Brown passed it off with the remark

        "We're going to give Wagner here,Watson."
Everyone admires our Forest extremely.   The man next door wanted a tree but I told him where he got off.   You can't imagine how sweetly the studio smells !

[9 West 14th St.]
Saturday [Jan. 10, 1920]

Dear Father,

* * * Allow me to inform you that Mrs. Watson(senior) — High Church Episcopal—or is it something else?—raised such a cry over the "Jesus" in <u>Buffalo Bill</u> * that J.S. [Watson] Junior arrived in New York the day after he left it for Rochester! That one of Sco's oldest(in age as well as acquaintance)friends;an Englishman of the ancient regime,begged Scofield "to resume his gift"(The Dial)and has never recovered from—as Mitchell and I think—the Christian Hymn Article especially,and the ensemble in general. We are due to wake up some(Stoopid)^{n} th power people,croyez-moi! Attendez till you peruse the Lachaise Article,about which I have already written Mother,and watch out in the meantime for the Boolsheweekee,who have by to-day's Tribune,mind you,captured 3 armies,60000men,400guns, 1000 mitrailleuses,11000 rifles,18 armoured trains,200 locomotives,10000 wagons,"and large stores of food and munitions" — — —...!!!

      Aurevoir,Monsieur Koldfeetchack

° One of the seven poems published by EEC in the first issue of the new Dial (January, 1920).

53 / TO HIS MOTHER

[9 West 14th St.
January 20, 1920]

Dearest Mother —

* * * I have certainly been following the news(not "news" this time)about Russia. Naturally overjoyedment is nothing. The poor old dead defunct putrid New York Times is all up in the air — and nos amis italiens at the Cafe Wonderful are in extase! The Times supplement had,today,a cartoon(wouldbe, that is)of "Uncle Sam" striking a "Reds" — One of the italiens showed it to B with a swear:placidly B cancelled with his pencil the word Reds and wrote beside:"Prohibizione" — at which the i. was very happy. Father would be pleased to hear them curse out D'Annunzio,top to bottom. Only tonight came a huge argument redhot — subject,Fiume. The propatrialst had his block metaphorically knocked off,by sheer facts. Socialism and Antidannuncioism are one in this finest of cafés,as among all the italians of America and Italy. But don't think we are wholly political in our lives — au contraire,the main and only interest is(as always)painting,poetry,etc. A propos the completion of the Lachaise essai,one of my "Crazy Quilts" came forth from hiding. I was pretty glad to see him again! * * *

54 / TO HIS MOTHER

9 West 14th [St.]
[May 9, 1920]

Dearest Mother!
    It's a long time since I've written you — in which time various things have occurred,such as the finishing of my Eliot essay,the taking of five(if not more)pictures for the Dial(by Thayer and Watson),etc. I had a terrific time with the essay. It went thru 9(nine)writings;and finally boiled itself down to a couple of pages. Then the Gods of the Dial decided it needed altering here and there. So last,after consultations and rewrit-

ings,ad infin. it seems to be approaching the form in which it is due to appear in the June number.

I hope,speaking of Dialism,that the poems in the new(May) number amuse you * * *

It was very sweet of Elos to write explaining what an enjoyable time Peggy Gay [a friend of Elizabeth's] really had at the Bronx! I hope to have time to answer it soon—the rendition of the drawings(from pencil to thin complicated final ink state)is a slow and troublesome,but extraordinarily interesting,thing.

I was much pleased to hear you'd voted <u>pro</u> Liberator. Please note the superb cartoon in the latest—"The Child of Old Men". The Lib. certainly has "pep",if noone else has!

It was tremendously funny—May Day! Cops,Bulls,Stool Pigeons,Fixers,etc. etc. lined 5th Avenue in preparation for the "Vast Red Plot" fostered <u>for public consumption</u> by that charming person & <u>protegé of Wilson</u>—Mr. Palmer [Attorney General]. Not only that,—the government of this great city had a parade of all patriots—taxi drivers,tough guys,gangs,parochial school boys,<u>down</u> the Avenue to prevent the granting of a parade-permit to any "Reds" who might want to march <u>up</u> it!!! Ave,Ave.Hail Magy.

50 warships now drowse in the waters hereabout. Stewart [Mitchell] tells me some are going to Mexico in all probability. Well well,glad we're not on one!

                                        Amen!!

55 / TO HIS FATHER

                                        [9 West 14th St.
                                        May 22, 1920]

Dear Father,

I was tremendously pleased to hear from you in regard to the latest poetic installment in the Dial [May, 1920]—as well as interested in your critique thereof.

As far as the word "slobber" ["spring omnipotent goddess"] goes,I'm afraid I don't in the least agree with you. That,however,does not by any means necessitate a diminution of the gaiety of nations—whatever the latter may be!(it would seem to be rather obsolete just at present.) Your judgement to the effect that the Baloonman ["in Just-spring"] is a hint of youth and

Norton's Woods is, I take great pleasure in assuring you,entirely and illimitably correct. I consider it a compliment to this particular production that yourself deduced the precise milieu,as I guessed it would!

My own favorite among the "poems" is,as perhaps you have also guessed,number 1 ["little tree"]. This poem is later in composition than the other 4,and to my mind more perfectly organised. I am confident that its technique approaches uniqueness.

After all,sans blague and Howells,it is a supreme pleasure to have done something FIRST—and "roses & hello" also the comma after "and" ("and,ashes")are Firsts.

I need not say that I am extraordinarily that is as usual lucky in having what amounts to my own printing-press in Thayer and Watson—by which I refer to the attention which such minutiae as commas and small i's,in which minutiae my Firstness thrives, get at the hands of these utterly unique gentlemen ⁎ ⁎ ⁎

56 / *TO HIS FATHER*

[9 West 14th St.]
Tuesday
June 22, '20

Dear Dad!

You will,as a sensitive and(needless to say!)intelligent critic of my present,aorist and future(not to mention the well-known Imperfect,and omitting the non-existent or at best little used future-Perfect tense)be much pleased to know that my sometime oratory à propos South America,travel,boa-constrictors,sea-captains etc. had behind it a profound conviction—that in brief I have taken the advice of many followers of what I know to be one of your favorite professions,The Sea,including the counsel of a sea-captain with whom Brown is personally acquainted,— that we(Brown and myself)went today to a shipping office and inquired concerning jobs on Boats,to learn that there were many in the wind,that we should report tomorrow morning to inquire further,and that(inasmuch as we didn't give a good g.d. what they gave us to do,were both over 21,and O.K. physically) the chances were(apparently)pretty good. I consider that the working-for-one's-daily along with what one of your preferred singers has happily called "The divine average" (at least I think

Walt said it)is in itself a priceless bit of humanly documentary experience—but when you add:plus a change of habitat(which made France,in my case,—brief glimpse though it was,—invaluable as a mental stimulus)I have the one certain irrevocable hunch that this is for me to do without loss of time.   The proposition,you see,being not in the least"romantic"—the American Army cured yours devotedly of that—but extremely considered,pondered,and otherwise weighed to the point where nothing can budge the scales!   I—or rather we—are doing nothing hasty.   We are mousing keenly and keeping our eyes ears and the rest of the sensory paraphernalia wide-opened.   I feel,as I know you do,that I am exceptionally lucky in having a friend like Brown to stick with—and be stuck by,as La Ferté Macé proved beyond dictum.   Take it all in all,There is nothing like Now—there is also nothing like trying!   *   *   *

There are several ways of ending this letter—but the way I prefer is this:I wish very respectfully to state

(1)that I do not need money!!

(2) "   "   "   "   "   sympathy!—because,being a good(if innocuous)Leninnite or Trotskyite or what-you-like-it I should be very considerably hampered in my aims by a superfluity of the former(whereof I have plenty)and being a person of tolerable taste and intelligence I really cannot conscientiously accept or find a place for the latter.   Therefore! if you wish to help me excessively and extensively,you will agree to my wisdom and ambition in making an effort to subdue my environment, and in disregarding "the comforts of life" for a while—in short, you will let me go my own way in my flannel shirt and my ideas *
*   *   *

* EEC and Brown did not go to sea.   Instead EEC's father persuaded them to go to Silver Lake and work on The Enormous Room.

57 / TO R. STEWART MITCHELL

[Silver Lake, N.H.
October 6, 1920]

Dear Stewart!

A long time having elapsed since I wrote you it is about proper that I apologise—but what on earth good are apologies? especially between 2 members of the Mezza Barbera Club,Inc.

Here I've been working(as worked the sons of Egypt to build the pyramids,you understand—in other words,like H.) upon a little historical treatise [*The Enormous Room*] of vast import to my Family and Nobody In General—comprising my experiences in France,or more accurately <u>en prison</u>. Honestly to say,I haven't done nawthing else. Strenuous is no name therefore—3 pages a day,since my family left,on an average 2 hours to a page. Id Est,a six hour day,spended for the good of humanity,and of so,and of forth.

For de Lawdzake,as my Father's negro,Sandy Hardy,would say,allow me the pleasure to hear from yourself! Tu comprends that a six hour(sometimes 12)working day has its boring aspect— even in an environment as alpha prima as hither,where from day to day sunsets come,mornings are,trees become orange and vermilion—

Have you seen Elaine lately? I hear from her that every one is having a cold,& that she escaped pneumonia—as she says "softly". I should like to see her kid. Give her & <u>her</u> my love when you see her,please * * *

58 / TO R. STEWART MITCHELL

[Silver Lake, N.H.]
October 14, 1920

Dear Stewart—

Many not to say most thanks for yours which I got yester-day. Tu te trompes occasionally,or(precisely to speak)when you say that you suppose I'll ask why you're going to Paris; that you suppose I'll censure this move—

<u>I</u> ask why anyone is going to <u>Paris</u>??

My god do you think I am a creature insensible and with-out desire? You must not forget that I spent a month in Paris . . .

Also you are mistaken in supposing that every one considers you a perfect example of pompous self-satisfaction. I know of noone who does.

Again,mon petit sérieux,why—"as I think"?—coming after "I could do all things"—as if,even tho' the billions of putrescent nonentities which do wear pants upon this surreptitious planet lacked a perfect confidence in you,their limitations—which you so absurdly invent,so delightfully invent—could might or will alter(the one-twentie^th of a hair)your own sureness in the mobile accident of self-sufficiency.

But I am <u>not</u> self-sufficient do I hear you say? Merde! <u>Gardez-moi à ce moment</u>. In the 26th year of my age,without a book published,without a meticulous molecule of worship or confidence outside of those whom I $\begin{Bmatrix} can \\ cannot \end{Bmatrix}$ that is to say $\begin{Bmatrix} have \\ haven't \end{Bmatrix}$ drunk under the table—id est,my friends(of whom I count and shall count,always,your-<u>Self</u> as a thrilling member)—I,then,totally unworshipped and completely un- trusted with those tinyly profound exceptions,do on my 26th birthday(aujourd'hui)accept dollars two hundred and sixty from an enthusiastic father;also a fur-coat;also a charge-account at "The Continental Clothing House" also(sequitur)a pair or two of shoes and maybe a hat,also(it is on the way)a pair of corduroy trousers—! If I had <u>Sand</u>,"my God",I'd be on a boat now work- ing my indescribable way to Africa—but I haven't—

Therefore,mon petit auk douloureux,be goddam careful how you throw your <u>sand</u> about!!

only,I quietly insist,my worship of and my confidence in my<u>Self</u> is unmitigated in the face of these <u>paltry</u>(our word, Monsieur)Thermopolae—then,in the name of the tall and beautiful Dionysius whose hair is the Spring and whose feet are the Summer,do not let the covering of August with shoes and the hiding of May with a hat trouble you or me * * *

59 / *TO HIS MOTHER*

Pension Don Marcos,
Abades 6,
Sevilla
22 abril [1921]

Dear Mother,

It seems to me that a great deal has happened since I sent you and everyone post-cards from Salamanca. As a matter of fact,we [E.E.C and John Dos Passos] have seen three towns since Thurs;Plasencia,Carcares,Sevilla. The first is a tiny one,full of storks,where there was a procession on Sunday morning with candles. In Carcares there are Roman ruins which we saw after climbing a hill—the train waiting there for nearly an hour. But Sevilla is the finest—never have I seen so many,so intricate,and so delicate streets. We arrived just at lamplight,in the midst of the feria.

The feria is—or has been,since it ended yesterday—a double happening. There were the grounds—acres enormously illuminated,where people strolled and danced and went to sideshows and sat in the open air drinking coffee and cerveza,eating buñuelos—and there were the torros. We saw two bull-fights; one Tuesday,and one on the last day,yesterday. The first was with six black bulls,the second with eight.

It was for me an extraordinary experience. As you probably know,the procedure is this:2 gentlemen in cockades ride in,bow to the royal box,ride back to the entrance gate,and come out again heading a procession of quadrillas,bandilleros,and espadas,all of whom bow. The bull is admitted:the quadrillas— each matador has his own group—try him with cloaks:meanwhile the oldest and weariest and most bony horses are prodded on,each strided by an enormously padded man,with a spear that looks like a stomach-pump. The bull very excited,the horses are brought toward him one by one,beaten from behind. Each is bandaged over the eye which would normally see the bull. The picador points and yells at the bull—the torro charges,up and over goes horse and rider—the cloak-men rush in and get the bull away. The padded picador is lugged out of the mess and the horse is beaten and pulled to his feet,where he stands trembling,a big wad of intestines hanging from his stomach and slowly nearing the ground.

The bandilleros—several horses having been gored—now advance into the ring with little goads,two each. One at a time they distract the bull's attention,get him to charge,and at the proper instant very beautifully impale him with the goads. After he's received four or six,the trumpet—which separates the various stages—sounds,and the espada advances;having just bowed,then handed his hat to his best friend in the audience.

Holding a scarlet cloak by a little stiffening stick which makes about 18 inches of the edge rigid,he shapes the rest over an amazingly slender rapier,so that the cloak falls solidly,presenting a smooth surface of attraction. He engages the bull with as little foot-work as possible—merely moving his body backward as the rushes come. Then he faces the bull,aims, squinting along the sword,and—reaching forward between the lowered horns—plunges the rapier in at the shoulder.

The best espada,named Belmonte,was injured the day we arrived. They brought in Rafael Yallo—as the other espadas were rotten—and he completed his duties with a tremendous ovation yesterday. He is a beautiful swordsman,very nimble, fearless—and certainly fifty years old. The seventh bull,yesterday,received about eight swords,so rotten was Chicuelo the Espada,before being stabbed with a short dagger and folding up suddenly.

Day before yesterday(I think it was)I drew £25 on my letter of credit,finding that Dos had been paying for me,in Dosian fashion—and not wishing him to go broke on my account. The Crédit Lyonnais was extremely courteous,and handed me over 703 pesatas with a pleasant bow.

You will be glad to hear that a Spanish dentist,recommended through Dos's telegraphing to a friend in Madrid(which he did on his own suggestion,being(as ever)tremendously kindly)opened or lanced or cut my abcess,and thereby rendered Sevilla possible. The only thing left is an examination in Paris, and perhaps the removal of part of the root—O. K.! I'm now happy once more. Dos as interpreter for dentists has acted in an extremely valuable capacity,let me assure you!

This room,at D. Marcos,is a sort of chapel—where we were put,through good luck;instead of being refused,as might well have been,so big was the feria crowd in Sevilla. But Dos having telegraphed ahead for a room,and having stopped here two years ago,we were provided for. Three enormous beds—tile floor—stately ceiling—such our chambre. The pension has a beautiful court,and the service is excellent.

Today we visited the Alcazar—infinite marvellous gardens. Also acres of pseudo-Moorish arches and palaces.

I wish you could have seen the feria;the streets crammed with carriages in which the most exquisite girls rode,each with her mantilla,superb scarlet and vermillion—such shawls you never imagined—such huge combs,such amazing dresses. At night the various clubs gave dances in the open,in little pavillions side by side along certain streets. Men and girls stood up with castanets,swaying,twisting,stamping;spectators seated in a ring clapped in time;there was music and often singing. Millions of lanterns—streets full of toys—groups of bright balloons —victorias,laughter,andora hats,harmonicas,and a splendid merry-go-round on which Dos suggested we ride as a parting achievement—so we sat our pigs(wonderful pigs,with a triple sea-sick motion)in the light of the lanterns and the laughter of thousands of people.

60 / TO HIS MOTHER

[2 rue Perronet, Paris]
17 mai [1921]

Dear Mother!

* * * from Madrid Dos and I had come up to St. Jean de Luz,thence(joined by "Jack" [John Howard] Lawson)proceeded to Oloron,where Lawson left us for Toulouse,taking 1 of my valises. We shipped the other and Dos's "hippo"(vast bag). Then Dos and I took train to Bidono,thence to Aidiouse(Aidiu — can't spell it!)thence climbed onto the Pyrenees!

The climb began at Aidioux(new way to spell it!)a village up fairly high:we went on by sheep and mule paths to the snow-line,making for the Col(pass)de Siesta. An ancient sheepheard told us how to go;told us to keep in the rocks,off the snow. (Everyone but 2 or 3 had told us we couldn't make it at all,"la neige est mauvaise:elle est douce;vous savez" — so we made for the rocks:but a shorter way,behold! over snow — we started up,sinking in sometimes to our hips;otherwise to our knees. About 2 we ate a Dos-brought lunch of sausage,chocolate,bread — on a little island of snowless fuzzy moss,on the tip top of the ridge,in a mist which completely held us from the earth:then we suddenly looked left — and behold a huge snowdressed peak:"This must be the pass,"Dos said. We peaked over the back-side of our environment,and saw thru the mist a huge drop,snow and vagueness. Focussing,distances shrank;"Let's go over" somebody suggested. Dos went first,waist-deep;I lowered the baggage(his musette and an extraordinary bundle of mine — many things roped in my long overcoat,the rope going across my chest)then I followed "in his steps". Which was easier as I wore low shoes. A little way and I had to sit down and empty said shoes,because my feet burned with cold. From then on my said feet were all right,and we went rushing and tumbling downward in a tree-men-doos way,as Lachaise remarks. On and on and on. And on. No bottom. We hit a river,and Dos discovered its direction — so we followed. Always snow. But we had to keep it at a safe distance,because it had a way of keeping itself in a ravine which(in mist)looked at least 500 feet deep. Finally we came to patches of furze—finally again to trees—and it rained. My G. how it rained! After resting under a huge spruce and chocolating,we started down again, down a perpendicular meadow,in this position: [*sketch*] which we held to for nearly ¾ of an hour—my pants-seat disappearing rather rapidly. Never saw anything so slippery. Heard cow-bells—came out into a vista—houses. Slid along,waded our 2nd river,and approached a house—enter 2 ferocious dogs and very pleasant man who had nothing to drink or eat for us:which is reasonable,since the place was a mine. "How far is it to the nearest town?" Dos asked. "Trois kilomètres." On again,down a winding road. Here we ran into 2 men,a woman,and a cart with oxen. They wanted a complete story of our lives,and having received it told us we had about 12 k. to go. Would we ride? They were going there too in a few hours.

We thanked them. About an hour and a half later we came to Biel. We had started out for Larance!

That night we changed into dry apparel,and went to bed after a delicious supper ✳ ✳ ✳

61 / TO HIS PARENTS

[Paris]
samedi,23 juillet [1921]

Dear Father and Mother—

Since my last feeble epistletory,it(meaning le temps)has hottened tremendously;and many things have happened. For one,the Jardins des Tuileries are filled with the colour and rustle of fallen leaves—everywhere is the smell of autumn,this in midsummer is curiously potent. Again,I met(some days since)the train from Cherbourg at S. Lazare station—enter Brown(looking terribly tired)and Thayer(absolutely raw with sunburn)both fresh from the Aquitania that day. I escorted both to the Continental;then Brown and I crossed by taxi to 13 rue du Sommerard,where we obtained a very nice chambre from the bureau. Since,Brown has improved eight thousand per cent—I suspect Paris has a salubrious influence on everyone short of the inhabitants of the morgue!

I have been already four times to the theatre with S.T. [Thayer],which is to say the least a novelty,since the vie chère in Paris had kept me outside the doors of all save two shows therebefore.   And have dined(whisper)at Voisin,etc.   My new suit (looks pretty new still)and my wondrous blue shirts and my necktie and my startling socks all worked together for style and glory.   I am indeed some petit jeunesse dorée—when an American editor is concerned with the _addition_!

The other night,as we were walking back from the Rip revue "Ca Va" Pound disengaged himself from a pillar and bowed.   Thayer had previously threatened to allow me to meet the great one,I had demurred.   "Sooner than might have been expected" was P's remark:leaving the editor at that person's hotel I began an evening with the poet.   Which lasted until the croissement of the Boulevard S Germain with the rue des Saints Pères,where I tentatively promised to visit the great one and disappeared.   If it would amuse you:Mr. Ezra Pound is a man of my own height,reddish goatee and ear whiskers, heavier built,moves nicely,temperament very similar to J. Sibley Watson Jr.(as remarked by Thayer)—same timidity and subtlety,not nearly so inhibited.   Altogether,for me,a gymnastic personality.   Or in other words somebody,and intricate.

Our friend R.S.Mitchell has accompanied Mrs. Thomas his exmaiden aunt to London,whence Brown and I received last night each a cheerful postcard.   Poore left for England yesterday;Dos is(probably by this time)in Persia—but O Heavens "the gentle Adelaide" Lawson,has(rumor well substantiated)arrived to take the place of all three with her voluminously silly presence(making Brown and me two Superartful Dodgers). Fortunately my favorite restaurant(La Reine Blanche)is as yet uncontaminated by Americanism!

Whereupon I knock on wood alias ma tête de bois.

Elaine and I,just previous to B's arrival,went to two very fine races—Longchamps(prix du president de la République) and Auteuil(steeplechases).   We nor lost nor won,since neither of us know yet how to bet at a french race.   My horse came in first.   Je me suis egayé.   As you probably know,both these courses lie in the bois de Boulogne—a very fine place to wander, with enough trees to stagger all the sunlight in the universe. At the courses proper I will say that we were almost cooked alive.

Quel chaleur épouvantable.   Fantastique is possibly the word!   I see in New York it's cooking weather too,and rejoice I'm here—as always.

Our rooms,Brown's and mine,at the "Hotel Marignan", Sommerard,are extraordinarily cool.   Brown is working hard for S.T.,taking dictation chiefly—occasionally I am able to help him out.   The dictation occurs at T's hotel;then B rushes here, where he types it on whichever of our respective typewriters happens to work at the moment.   And one always does(work).

Not having received a letter at Morgan Harjes for a long time,I anticipate hearing from one of you about all of you and S.Lake—also concerning the famous Prison Tales Or Eleven Nights Without A Bar-Room.   Please give my love to Elos, Nana,Aunt Jennie,and all dogs bears dolls:never forgetting elephants.

62 / *TO EDWARD NAGLE*

Hotel Je ne Sais quoi,
rue Jamais de la Vie, Paris
Mardi pas gras [1921?]

Copain in excelsis
    having "vainly" attempted to "paint" and succeeded in tearing up a monstrous "aquarelle" after an hour's"labour"I feel in a sufficiently reduced or "humbled" condition to me plaigner to your "excellent" self.   I liked not only this letter from you and the one which preceded it(which I neglected to answer)but the letters,or parts of,which Brown has read me.   If I may say something vulgar,it strikes me that your style has changed.   And if I may utter a coarseness—for the better.   And to fart in ink,as it were,let me add—am delighted.

    The Marianne Moore-Snow Plough Simile in your last to Brown is as good as anything I've heard.   (P.S. I overhear myself invariably).   Salut et bis trois fois bis bis bis comme ca et puis un petit bravo messieumdamez.

    I didn't know the well known playmate,the other "Ed'ud", liked my poems and am therefore not only glad but surprised to hear so.   [*sketch of Cummings bowing*]   Hardly knew my own in last Dial:so strange,obscene,and lacerated not to whisper mutilated did same hors d'oeuvres graphiques appear.   Poems better known to me,tho' long erst forged. Think frontispiece "not wholly" "successful"(as S.T. [Thayer] would say,when the world was young),but quite gai quand même and almost identically,I imagine,your pose at the Stettheimer's barnstorming party. (NAGLE the windmill winder,the only spiral drunkard.)

☆ (I like Mopsy.) ☆

My teeth have killed me with immeasurable cubic agony and I am headed not to Vienna,therefore,but chez M. "Merril" of "Penn" 17 Avenue de l'Opéra. Incidentally,I think it's nearly over. To the chanson of 3-400 $ americains. The s o a b only makes 100–150 fr per working hour,being assistant hamstringer to a man aptly if not beautifully called Haze.

Thank you for your compliment on the animal book! If Mopsy agrees,it must really be good. Her decision is(naturally)final and supreme in such a matter.

For Christ's sake,don't tell me that Clark has sent the devil of destruction out of you into Brown—who smashes windows and chairs regularly nowadays,selecting only those over 60 fr. in value and peculiarly sturdy.

O Nagle:Nagle;Nagle,if you don't set fire to other people's rooms and knock down babies in 14th street any more sure there's no use in dying as Shaemus would say.

How is that old rickety knock-out-drop? Has he laid another 5000 putty dolls quick-as-guinea-pigs-and-twice-as-lifelike under Lachaise's bed lately?

Remember me in my best manner to G. L. [Gaston Lachaise].I congratulate Western and Union both on their goût. Expect to see millions of peacox blossoming on every W. U. T. and C. O. building the earth over.

Pen being full of bluish and dirty air,I stop. Sans blague—

A bientôt

Cummings

dit "le changé"

(P.S. am waiting for you to find me a studio,exhibit my work, and make me as famous in France as one "Nagle" is in the Etats Unis).

P.P.S. Elaine writes your painting is awfully good. Am jealous. Gr-RRR. You'll be walking on housetops you son of a bitch.

P.P.P.S. Enjoyed the Krazy [Kat] you sent B., very much!

[Paris]
Sunday
February 26 [1922]

Dearest Mother!

    it's at least two and perhaps three weeks since I've heard from you or the family—and as it happens I've been very regularly indeed to Morgan Harjes Cie. One reason for my—in fact daily—visits is:Dos,of Three Soldiers [pub. 1921] fame,shot through Paris(as I may have told you)on his way to America via England. "R. S. M."(otherwise Mitchell)arrived from Montpellier under the guidance of his,M.'s,aunt. Fortunately for all concerned,the a. fell ill,enabling her charge to disport himself a goodly deal with myself,Dos,and Brown. We had several really remarkable parties—and Dos(who paid left and right) borrowed 800 fr. from me to get home with—this being perhaps 2 weeks ago. Since then I've received a cable asking for a letter to Liveright authorizing inspection of my proofs by Dos;it having been agreed between us that his published-prestige should go to the general cause of uncensored MS.,and I having forgotten to give him a letter to Liveright there-à-propos. The cable was from England—I sent a letter in haste. Haven't received any answer. Talk about fame—Dos hadn't received one cent for all his Three Soldiers;that is,after a few days in Paris,he hadn't anything to get home on! Such are the tardinesses attendant upon écrivains. They always get it in the neck, apparently. Fortunately for us,Dos and I have our family backers! When all Brown's family have got through spending his inheritance he'll probably have his,too! (P.S. It seems Brown's uncle wrote to Brown's aunt Hope calling Brown a dangerous criminal,accusing Brown of continually begging for money(Brown had never suggested the subject)and of hounding his uncle over the world. So Brown's aunt Hope didn't send anything to the dan. crim.—until a week or so ago,when he received(I think)$50 with a hot admonitory note about unclehounding. She must think they cash air in Paris and take bites out of Notre Dame every few hours and drink the Seine out of old boots belonging to the city fathers.

    Dos was nicer than ever—told fine experiences,—attacks by Bedoins,wild-west style,shooting at Dos with rifles from pony-back,etc. While the fat merchants prayed and the camels kneeled down in sympathy. A great trip he must have had! He's been very sick though,fever 105½ in(I think)Syria,or Persia perhaps. Took it all very Dossianly! ✳ ✳ ✳

The cable suggesting that I and Brown return to read proof struck me as particularly liberal—I pondered the situation with great solemnity,and decided that it would be extremely foolish to leave just then,for the pays des libres et le chez-eux des braves. (Has the right twang,even in translation. Marvelous ditty). Especially as Dos happened to be entering America and with laurels and bells to say the least—and Dos's first words to me were a grim assurance that(Three Soldiers having,in his absence,been rendered Polyannish to some extent by the highly moral Doran Esquire K. C. B., C. O. D.,etc.)his possible would be done to save The Chambre énorme from any similar fate. (I believe Boni is much more liberal,incidentally,than Mr. George D.) Not only that—but Dos is seeing publishers to Hell in my behalf anent some poems. Meanwhile,in me quiet way(as Nagle would say)I've had scriptural correspondence with the editor of the Broom,a certain Reubenite named [Harold] Loeb,who (perhaps because his brain has only one) accepted seven out of 12 poems I sent to his consideration. The odd part is,that I sent the poems not to him at all,but to a very nice American poet named Alfred Kreymbourg whom I have met and who is one of the few genuine écrivains,personally speaking,whom I ever have run into. Now K. has fought L. and left The Broom—but Cummings' poems seem to have gone on serenely quand même. ✳ ✳ ✳

See Soviets going to the [Dawes?] conference! Bet they'll pusch the_____out of it,alone and without assistance! (Not that it won't collapse of its simple self).

O Briand,where are y-oooo? Ask poincaré he knows.

64 / *TO HIS SISTER*

Paris
3 mai 22

Personal

Dear Elos—

Thank you for the very long and extremely interesting letter. It discusses so many questions that the 26th volume of the Brittanica is a dilapidated nutshell against it. You will appreciate two or three answering generalities on my part:

#(1)for Christ's sake,this is utterly important — <u>it is the entire secret of being alive</u>:NEVER TAKE ANYONE'S WORD FOR ANYTHING.

(A)the chief significance of this command is readily seen, when you appreciate that it applies to the writer as well as to the rest of humanity. If I may remark:few theses advanced by "individuals" have this merit. Thus:the father of a family will found his philosophy on "the family law";a university professor will discuss life as an "educational possibility";a holder of Czarist bonds will be most sincere in his condemnation of the "Soviet menace". This latter illustration,and the tone of your letter,brings me to my second

(2)Sincerity — For the Holy Ghost's own sake,make no mistake here!!! THE ONLY SINCERITY IS PERSPICUITY. <u>There is no such thing</u> as "doing wrong" or "being right about something" — these are 4th hand absurdities invented by the aged in order to prevent the young from being alive. So,if two persons dispute with equal heat the Bolsheviki's right to exist,granted they both argue as they feel or think they feel, only <u>one</u> will be sincere;the <u>pro</u> Bolshevik;not because he is more genuine,but because(his mind being unclouded by "The N. Y. Times" and kindred bullshit)he is <u>more alive</u>,keener,has <u>more pep</u>,is not afraid,gives no ground to creeds,and NEVER takes anybody's word for anything — his perspicuity,therefore, is a self-sufficient intrinsic growth,a piece-of-thing-in-itself,irresponsible to anyone outside his ego,a joy forever,which all the policemen on 42nd street cannot kill!! Another illustration:I started,some years ago,against the continuous advice of my elders,to paint as I saw fit. Every day I "progress" — why? Because,thru being more or less true to the peppy thesis(1),I feel:more pep,pleasure in living,sensitiveness. Of course i was "right" — but that's nothing at all;the point is — <u>am I more full of pep than anyone else alive?</u> As a prostitute remarked,"<u>Ask yourself kid; ask yourself.</u>" Well — go ahead and ask!

(3)<u>TO DESTROY</u> IS ALWAYS THE FIRST STEP IN ANY CREATION. It is,for one so young as yourself,all-significant <u>TO DESTROY</u>. By all means,with every ounce of energy in whatever mind you've got,and putting aside all lackadaisical antique 5th hand notions about "Beauty" "Ugliness" "The Right" "The Art of Living" "Education" "The Best" etcetera ad infin.—Destroy,first of all!!! Of this i am sure: nothing "occurs" to anyone as an individual—nothing can possibly enter and be entertained by the mind of anyone except as somebody's tool(which you are at this minute,as i feel you realise finally,and am tickled to feel that above all in my "young sister")—except:the person or mind in question has FIRST OF ALL,FEARLESSLY wiped out,THROUGHLY AND UNSENTIMENTALLY defecated WHAT HAS BEEN TAUGHT HIM OR HER. In a nutshell;#THE MORE WE KNOW THE LESS WE FEEL !!!!!!!! put that in your pipe for Jesus' sake right away;subito!

(A)Example:I am told,by someone who is sure of it,that "we exist in the best possible world,"or that "all is for the best."

PROCEDURE

1)What does "the Best" mean! Can you eat it,like a beefsteak? Can you smoke it,like tobacco? Or is it a mere concept?

2)Is there any reason why another mere concept,e. g. "the worst" should be less acceptable to my or your intelligence than its fellows?

3)Are dogs,organ-grinders,mountains any the less alive for a complete ignorance of concepts?

4)Since the latter are as much a part of my pleasure in living as the former(=concepts. For me personally concepts do not exist;but I am going very slowly)by what right do I attempt to see indirectly? To,instead of admitting the smell and colour of a swill pail,attempt either to "enjoy" or "dislike" it or its multifarious contents?

5)Insofar as I am alive,I will be a son of a b. if anyone shall tell me "what life is" or "how to live." For,if anyone can tell me those items,then,pray,what use is there in my living?

(4)NEVER BE AFRAID. No matter who buldoses you,in however kindly or self-sacrificing a manner,NEVER take ANYONE'S word for ANYTHING. Find out for yourself!!!! Good God what else is in life?

A)e. g. I am taught to believe that prostitutes are to be looked down on. Before believing that,I will,unless I am afraid to do it,make the following experiment:I will talk with,meet on terms of perfect equality,without in the slightest attempting to persuade,a prostitute. Through my own eyes and ears a verdict will arrive,which is the only valid verdict for me in the entire world—unless I take somebody's word for something,which(because I desire to be alive)I do not.

B)To admit that i am,as an individual,a nonentity—that I breathe and move per someone else's social,political,moral, aesthetic,etc. ad infin.,"ideals",takes NERVE:—NOTHING IS SO DIFFICULT AS TO BE ALIVE!!!!!!! which is the ONLY THING WHICH YOU CANNOT LEARN ever,from anyone, anywhere:it must come out of you;and it never can,until you have KNOCKED DOWN AND CARRIED OUT all the teachable swill of Cambridge etc. And I'm the nigger that knows it and is sympathetic to you for that reason;because my mind has been there too.

C)My family,let us say,desire me to be an officer in the "War for Civilization."

Procedure

1)What is an "officer?"

Answer:one who leads men,thru an absolute power of life and death.

2)in becoming an "officer",then,I would be compelled to say to human beings:"die!" given a certain situation?

Answer:yes.

3)have I the slightest intention of dying if I can help it,let alone COMMANDING SOMEONE ELSE to die?

Answer:not on your hat. I never take anyone's word for "dying",and therefore noone shall be compelled to take mine if I know it;any more than I take anyone's word for "living."

4)Will the sorrowings of a devoted family who wanted me to be an officer(like all respectable Plattsburg boys of the upper bourgeoisie)affect my judgment in the slightest?

Answer:I AM NOT AFRAID. To Hell with everything which tries,no matter how kindly,to prevent me from LIVING MY OWN LIFE—KINDNESS,always,is MORE DANGEROUS than anything else! !

#(5)SEX IS EVERYTHING(as Freud says):You either know this or you don't. If you don't you don't. It's not what can be taught! J'espere,in your connection! By the way,when I see you I shall expect you to be conversant with two books:The Interpretation of Dreams,and WIT and the Unconscious. Both are by FREUD. ≡!! GET WISE TO YOURSELF!!≡

Conclusion:I write you in this way because,from your letter, it seems to me likely that you will begin to wake up! It is my

cherished hope,ma petite soeur! I have wanted you to wake up
for some time. WHEN YOU COME TO FRANCE,FOR GOD'S
SWEET SAKE LEAVE AMERICA !!!

65 / TO WHOM IT MAY CONCERN*

[Paris]
14 mai 1922

I desire that one of two things happen to "The Enormous
Room":either
    A)it be immediately supressed,thrown in a shitoir
    B)each and all of the below-noted errors be <u>immediately
    and completely</u> rectified without loss of time,fear of
    money,or any-thing-damned-else—
<u>Omissions</u> for which there is no reason and no excuse—
    1)portrait of Jan(not Jean)
    who is nevertheless mentioned,p134
    2)portrait of the Belgian Farmer,who is briefly described
    (with,I think,some others)in connection with an <u>omitted</u>
    incident—the Surveillant distributes mail,from a window,
    to men in the court beneath
    The Farmer is mentioned,p143
    3)portrait of The Young Skipper,who is described along
    with
    4)his Mate,in(I think)chapter VII of the original MS.
    They are mentioned together,p247
    The Young Skipper is further mentioned pp257,266

N.B.—Not having the MS with me,I cannot tell what other characters have been dropped out;but in the case of these four,any-
one who tries to make sense of the book as it stands can see that
their portraits have been omitted.
If the portraits omitted were in any way inferior,there might be
some(damned little by Jesus)excuse. They are NOT below,and
are—in fact—considerably ABOVE,the average in the mutilated book-as-it-stands.

I do not consider that the omission of certain explanatory matter
which should follow the "planton-cries" p79 is good for the
book;that matter should be put back in,with whatever else has

been dropped out,and put back in Goddamnquick. The appeal of the book is largely documentary;as a document let it appear complete or for Christ's Sweet Sake NOT AT ALL. As a piece of writing,I do not argue—I know how it should be,and if anyone thinks he knows better than I,let him F him-or her-self.

Misprints for which there is no excuse of the smallest variety —occur on,averagely,every other page. [*a list of misprints follows*] * * *

Translation of the French phrases is,at least half the time,very confusing to the reader—it being very important that he should understand that a certain character is speaking French and not English. I had this carefully regulated,and had translated myself as much as was good for the context,and in the MS THERE IS NONE OF THIS NEEDLESS AMBIGUITY. In addition,the translating is. . . .but I refrain. (P.S. AS IT STANDS the book is not merely an eye-sore but an insult.)

° *For John Dos Passos' account of this letter and of his part in the publishing of* The Enormous Room, *see his* The Best Times: An Informal Memoir (*New York, 1966*), 89.

66 / *TO WILLIAM SLATER BROWN*

Hotel Minirva
Rapallo
[Summer 1922]

Rapallo
    30 k from Genova   (in between,you broke your
    80 " " Spezzia   gamba di ferro)
Maybe you remember it was full of Inglesi. (Pound's here . . .) All of us are recovering from colds,don't know about Pound and Co.
    We'll go 2 Rome soon—in few days
    on the other side you see (certain inhabitants of the sala di pranzo. Item:
    The lira is around 20(=$1)
    The news is that the francesi are up to peace on earth et chetera(as it's pronounced in Liguria)alias the Ruhr
    for X· sake ask Dos to ask Boni to ask porka madonna

where's my check for the E.R.? [*Enormous Room*]   Have only got 1 so far—that was months late.

I am very tite — ½ chianti twice per giorno

N.B. did you get the aquarelles?

P.S.   Elaine and i sent RSM [R. Stewart Mitchell] a post card of a swan plus a very naked girl—wrote Elaine in protest.   He hasn't recovered yet!   Was very insulted etc. "O what a BOOTIFOOL death."

67 / TO WILLIAM SLATER BROWN

[Paris]
Sunday [Summer, 1922]

dear B.

Thanks for the(fortunately)incompletely incoherent letter written while urinating upside down,at 13 o'clock somewhere between Westminster Abbey and Baffin Land with the aid of a fountain pen improvised from the foreskin of a lascivious hippopotamus and ink drawn at intervals of 52.194 + or − seconds from the reluctant scrotum of a tame or pet squid,into an umbrella-stand.   As nearly as I can discover,N. Y. contains you with not inconsiderable difficulty;by "you" I refer to Joe Gould John Dos Passos The Angel Gabriel and G. Seldes.   The latter in a p.s. tells me what leads one to believe you are neither run over nor in the webster international bank.

A "natation" contest(from the first springboard ever seen in France;per pimply Gauls)has just happened across from this cafe(Notre Dame).   Le temps is muggy,hot,rainy.   My family are to be boxed and crated in few days by a Y. M. C. A. singleader and antiseptically shipped on the P. L. M. to an anti bolshevik stronghold in Venice,(Italy.)   A bung-hole of not unoriginal design permits the usual facilities to function,while food is injected through a disinfected periscope by spaded virgins in white gloves and chastity girdles.

They are,however,improving daily.   Last night we saw the Concert Mayol.

H Havane,Paris,seize septembre [1922]

Dear B

thanks for the Notables. thank you moreover for a Kat of indescribable beauty.

Having yestreen bought me a pair of calecons kaki with buttons on them,my navel is no longer afloat.

Which is why I can(though tight to an unusual degree for lunch) concentrate upon the tricky keyboard,thus:it has indeed proved a solace if not a positive comfort to discover that Slater Brown (recently released from an institution for the pieeyed)'s name and mug have burst into fame beside ditto of Gaston Lachaise (at present out on bail for having squandered 25 cents)and J. Ferdinand Glue,of Leslies Weekly.
                    paragraph.   large w
Whatever joy the writer may have experienced in this and all other similar connections were,it is to be confessed,dashed by the to say the least emphasis laid upon a it is to be assumed by any cleanminded mind undesirable member of and disgrace to the female sex. It is to be hoped that the temporary abberation at whose door or doors such criminal insinuations have or have not layed or lain is not permanent,but in fact a portion of that ephemeral transience of which those of us beneath the age of impotence are all too occasionally prone,or in the words of the immortal Mike Frost,Susceptible.
                    Paragraph   Small h
having returned recently from a tour of the woild in toytea days and expecting my family to leave me for Hinglint on Monday if not later,I am in no condition to do more than sell Bluejay Corn and Bunion Plasters among the poor whites.
                    O Thalassa
There is something rather touching in the status of the Greeks, don't you think? Your little mot must now read:Shine Shoes,Run Restaurants,and Retreat. Suppose a bigger better busier war for world peace and general castration of the individual is impending daily,but have an idea that your teeth will not be perfect

in time,so don't worry and drink more than usual if only in
memory of

Eldwood Eskalynn Comeinz,alias

yours for the vivisection of the Now

69 / *TO WILLIAM SLATER BROWN*

Grand Café Restaurant de l'Univers
Paris, le sais pas
4:30 (P M)
[December 5, 1922]

Dear B
many thank youzes for the more than apt strokes of if not
angelic genius small:miss a largeguess!
haven't seen Vanity All Is Fair in? but have extensively
partyed with Er former Heditor who more than fulfilled ex-
pectations excited by Daws's [Dos Passos'?] introduction—large
I refer to one Bishop whose wife also has caught a glimze of youze
at a strangetosaytheleastparty the details of which sounded like
somebody not being introduced to anybody by Johnathan The
Dos. Sorry. Was. Drank. Hence. Forget. Ting.
Am more than delighted that [*sketch of nude female*] etc.
has flourished under the millionaire treatment of the Cutter of
Angels. Also do i and I both trust in the recuperated health of
Edud'z [Nagle?] higlif cat(the seeker of thunderstorms). No
news is good news compared with Gould'z Gladdening Purchase
—congratulate him for me and notice how my emotion changes
the colour or color of the very fluid with which my pen pays
pussonul tribute to said mad miracle of postprestidigitatorial
presignificance.
A letter but now opened,from Dos,a letter registered,a letter of some or no little importance,has just yielded a check for
85$ from see [?] IS V.,fact seeming to confirm your optical sus-
picions on seeing my "work"(am now writing by matchlight,all
lights have gone out in "the Universe": my waiter has brought
me a candle. . . . I continue by remarking that the 85$ is still
at my elbow which proves how good a Prefect Nandin must be,
or else it goes to show how bum the crooks be hereabouts.
Remember me to [Louis] Kantor,please(who never an-

swered my last letter dated June or July)also to A. Wilson(who never saw his "portrait"(in prose)per a not too distant Broom) also thank you again for writing and for the dope bits and for The Krazies. I close,because the candle is damnéd wavery ——— ergo i-strain ———

yrz

<u>Best to Lachaise</u>

P. S. beware of Horse-y. He's harmless.

o Munson Munson * woe is me I lived too soon 2 sup with thee

* *The critic Gorham B. Munson.*

70 / *TO MR. AND MRS. JOHN PEALE BISHOP*

Paris, le ? mercredi
[December 13, 1922]

Gentle Inhabitants of the Crows nest

Know ye I(capital,in deference to Professor Vanity Edmund Eglinton Woodrow Fair Crowninshield [illegible] Wilson Esquire L.M.N.O.P.E.T.C.)have forsook things temporal and or liquid during a perfectly indeterminable period or interim bounded on the left by Will Power's Haunted House and on the right by an altogether singular or unplural desire to Work at quelque chose for some nights and days incroyable though This appear at "first blush":hence and for no different nor yet similar reason I shall have to beg implore and importune your pardoning pitying selves(or self as the case may not be)to accept my sincere apologias the feminine accusative after a verb of receiving anent Friday and Sunday evenings and including the indubitable Delanuxe Duet more inexcusable shame on yours umbly has never.

Owever;by Wednesday please **Cheezuz** I will be in a less unbodied and otherwise miraculous condition or hope so to be more and have my ising whence,should you both care to receive, or take,the before invited above bidden undersignedlybyoneof them guests to your rochefoucauldish bosom,will consider self or selves honoured unutterably and also imminently abashed and will cry as one voice¡Evviva El Salamandro¡¡

Do not forget,I beseech youses bot', that:the Boy(or Garçon)stood on the "burning" Deck;whence all but he had van-
ish-ed:and that Then(two)we did the nightly(?)chores(!):and
that Lars Posthumus of Cloaca by the Toititree Gawdz E swore
Dat De Gweat House of Weally should suffer wwong no mowe.
With which enervate origins permit me to clasp however respectfully your Omegas in farewell

(N-hot so G-hood or;The M-haiden's Pr-hayer.
O!Mrs.Delanuxe h-had a husbánd
and h-he was dou-b-ble j-h-ointed
she tr-h-ied to m-h-ake him eat out of her hand
but s-h-he was d-h-issap-h-ointed
                              from the s-handscript) *
           [EEC's note] *copywright 2987 A.D.
                          by Tears Eliot

71 / TO HIS SISTER

                                              [Paris]
                          Monday Dec. Something '22

Dear Lulu—
    Cabled you today my congratulations àpropos letter post-
marked November 24 and dated Indiana.   This letter I consider—whether or not you object—one of the most interesting I've yet received:—The Cambridge streak is almost defunct!
Incroyable . . .
    That you massacred it alone,sans aid of friends(who in my
case had been made for that purpose so to speak)is all the more
extraordinaire.   You have every reason to be pleased with your-
self(which is the only thing anyone can possibly be pleased with)
so cheer up!   A sense of humor is one of the things which C.
Columbo didn't discover,and is in fact priceless,and cannot be
acquired by any other means than you are employing at present
—three-hour-examinations of nth hand mentalities,etc. etc.
    I've not the least intention,upon my honor,of advising your-
self—which,if closely viewed,is a further cause of thanksgiving.
Don't forget that whatever I may be responsible for to date is
due to my having been on the defensive(e.g.,invasion of visiting
Penates;a letter a day keeps the doctor away thesis,ad inf.)

Having some time since(to be modest)discovered that to inhabit the amiable and succulent bosom of one's relations not to mention one's family is to—I use Mitchell's momentous words,borrowed from St Paul—"die daily",I have at least learned the synonymous lesson that to give advice is to croak momently. Or as the universally underestimated B. remarked,People Do What They Want To . . . you may have heard the phrase somewhere?

 ≡ You no doubt know that I like N.Y.
  " " "   "   " " had one helluva time prior to my attainment of said city.

 It isn't exactly my fault that
  (1) you are not me
  (2) " " " male
   (P.S. thank G.)
and,since you aren't(1)nor yet even(2),any "advice" from either would be highly ridiculous. A blind man could read as much and a legless man might jump to similar conclusions without difficulty.

 Don't,however,underestimate my interest in the latest earthquake—I assure you that it's entirely genuine:in doubting which you are missing the point of this unnecessary and otherwise enjoyable epistle.

 So far as the Taussig is concerned,I consider it a malheur: but one can treat malheurs like plastine as well as like bedbugs: by which,understand that I mean you can(if you've got a grain of sense)use them:whereas bedbugs are really unusable so far as I have had to do with the kleva lil reskels. Further, understand that I mean distinctly as follows:THE MAIN PROBLEM IS TO GET TO NEW YORK. Have a little brains and DON'T WORRY ABOUT ANYTHING SUBSEQUENT to getting to N.Y. If the Taussig is a good dodge,USE IT,solely because ONCE YOU ARE OUT you can look around FOR YOURSELF and—pardon my reiterating,GET THERE before you decide what's going to happen to you once you've got. I fully get that the F. would prefer you to go on to N.Y. with a girlhood friend—
   O.K.—Do it:
THEN—once you've done it—KICK OUT!¡

 Do you get me?
 If not,your dome must be a bat's nest.
 Which,guessing by recent évenements,it is not.
As for the business of being without a definite aim in existence:

remember(as Elaine,to whom I read your letter)remarked
àpropos that—every girl is in the same situation. (Given our
little régime plus its delightful W. P. Foundations,antibooze
amendment,and other longlegged trivialities of like nature
E.E.C.)—or,to put it blandly:OTHERS HAVE BEEN UP
AGAINST EXACTLY WHAT YOURSELF IS UP AGAINST
JUST NOW and HAVE FLITTED all the same,incredible as
this may sound—and don't take my word for it in the name of
X but keep your eyes peeled once you've arrived in N.Y.

Oh no—it's not one Wth as bad [as] it seems! COURAGE he
said and pointed to his GOGGLELESS GLIMS !!!—without
which there's no knowing what may happen

!

if(in the course of the above)I've advised,I hereby humbly
take back that or any advice.

For sweet Jesu's sake

Do what you want to

!

Love,

P.S. let me know by seismograph of any further shocks—that is,
if you'd like to—

72 / TO WILLIAM SLATER BROWN

Café de Madrid

Guéthary(B.P.)

[July, 1923]

Dear B—

thanks a million times for the K Kats! The batch which
G.Seldes brought over he wanted to put with his own collection,
so I let him—keeping the later arrivals myself,as you direct.

What news of yourself!

I got a postcard from Kantor saying he was passing through
England (Londres)en route to Germany and giving no address
in Germany so I waited:but I haven't heard anything more.
Now I'm sorry didn't write the hotel in London.

I left Paris day before yesterday,arriving in St. Jean de Luz
yesterday—tomorrow I'm moving to Guéthary(Hotel Suzan)
where I'll be until the 18th probably and where I write this.

If you care to write,address me at M.H.Cie [Morgan-Harjes Co.] as usual.

St. Jean is horrible;but here's much better(pensions everywhere about the district,at 38 fr. a day).

Dos is in Spain not far from me and Hendaye,at 10 pesetas per diem.

—Elaine & Mopsy left Paris avant hier on a pippy Tug for Biarritz (Hotel Carlton). I ought to have gone to the Baltic (Deutschland)where it's cheap but yew kno me Al and beside which,hate the German food.

It rains like Hel since I've left Paris but not as badly as when I left P. for Pornic last June. Beside,the Basques are far pleasanter.

I seem to have a rousing advertizer in one Bishop,who connects himself to S. Four En that"stinking dime novel";but who isn't ½ bad I assure you and(or so I imagine)greatly superior to one Bunny [Edmund] Wilson,his consequent in V.Fair.

I wrote you several letters recently and didn't post them. Proving that my spirits are in their usual decline,or what not.

What are your plans? How's Vesuvius? More lava?

Was glad to hear that J.Gould is still abstracting coin from feeble-willed benefactors. Remember me to the loose-lived lowbrow,if convenient.

Thayer says Nagle's drawings in latest Dial are good. Perhaps he even said very good. As I haven't seen the journal in ?, can't judge:but Dos,on arrival,intoned à propos N.'s rejuvenation at hands of a "blond flapper." He,N,deserves no greeting from myself,so don't tell him so.

J. D. Passos also remarked that yourself was working its head off for this damn finanseer,whazisname. "Why Foolish?" As for me, I struggle to occasional achievement if it suns(instead of pouring)will be content. The air smells of clover. I am waiting for the ½ past 3 train backwards or to St.Jean where my diggings for tonight lie hideously threatening me. All this because made the mistake of going to a city instead of to a village. Will know better next time.

The Basques are,as you may realise,a thick(if not sturdy) race with black hair,boinas,or whatever [*sketch of cap*] are called,and a Kat-like Kuriosity to put it mildly. They speak a tongue or patois approximating Esquimaux and don't seem to care whether it hails snows or merely piddles. Nothing can persuade me that these folks are inhibited.

(above)
SKETCH *accompanying*
letter to William Slater Brown,
August 12, 1923

(right)
SKETCH *accompanying*
letter to Hildegarde Watson,
December 11, 1933

(below)
from EEC's sketchbook,
France, 1917

(actual likeness
   of a
 Hammamet dude
 "playing
    a
    drum"
 at our cook's
 wife's sister's 3day
 noces
     —sandglasses
 optional;
         garters
 de rigeur)

[Guéthary, France]
dimanche 28 juillet 23

Dear Elos—

just received(in my seaside retreat)your two,together-arriv-
ing,letters—one fat and one lean;the latter enclosing a letter to
Elaine.

I took the liberty of forwarding both letters plus the enclosure to Elaine;because I think both are tremendously—to
use no harsher word—interesting. I dare say there was nought
to be done by yourself in the face of circumstances(or,better,
avaykn as the Greeks have nicnamed what is commonly translated by the little bon mot Necessity)and I'm at any rate highly
pleased that you took the trouble to meet,see,and receive the
subconscious wisdom of,the entirely worth-encountering janitress.

Dos is "a lovely gentleman"—Mrs. McC. [the "janitress"]
was dead right in that. Dos's aunt is,however,an aunt—that is
to say:the studio is Elaine's,rented(by courtesy)to Dos at a loss
of some,as it happens,three hundred $(this in your ear,strictly
and exclusively). If anything were needed to convince me for
one that Dos is a.l.g. the fact that he is wholly responsible for the
bringing out of my poems by a Mr. Selzer next fall(I speak of
sheer prospects)—that,in other words,he of his perfectly own
volition,dragged said Selzer over the coals,rubbed his nose in
merde,and otherwise frighteningly buldozed him to the extent
of signing a contract to print myself—would go to influence any
not neurotic jury that Mr. Dos Passos is one of earth's Loveliest
with a capital L gentlemen;I reiterate,aunts are aunts:so don't
make the mistake of blaming your bad luck on J.Dos P. !

As for the weakly and doubtless holy Benet accent aigu or
aigue we know not whether nor which this being after luncheon
(with a mezzabottiglia),all of my curses on that bastard's dull
bean. Here again,it's not Dos's fault. As for Elaine's responsibility—

One reason that I forwarded your fat letter(to me)to Elaine,
is:only partial accounts of the devastations in her front apartment had reached her(via a censor-subdued,and writing instead
of speaking,Mc C.) Them ginks was gotten by Constance—by
the way,should you get a chance,meet C.,who is one of the nicest
of human or otherwise beings—and being members,fullfledged

(he is a banker,broker,or whatnot)of the cocksucking leisure class to which I at present accursedly belong and from which yourself(here I thoroughly and irrevocably salute you)have mysteriously and God nose how escaped)they behaved as such.

Assez pour eux.

(Thanks,incidentally,for the Mexican red slogan!)

Words fail me to express our pleasure at your change-of-style(excuse a phrase of the x minus nth water),not only since illustrating the popular conundrum Why do young girls leave home? but even—or I err—since your previous letters. That the pursuit of hap. should have transformed P.Gay to the extent mentioned by you is perhaps unbelievable:but that you should have transformed yourself to the extent which your latter two letters indicate is more than merely incredible—I beg you to believe that it is delightful. (Being a confirmed Hedonist,I can render no more intense homage.)

Please don't get the idea,out of viscid silences on my part, that what happens to my "small" "sister"(end of quotes)is not among the interests of my own completely erratic and let us trust otherwise otherwise-than-negative existence. But I honestly don't believe for a moment that you—given the present,id est:N.Y.—are as dull. Once again I reiterate—take no advice from another(e.g. myself). As for the "female" of the How species . . . . should think 'twould remedy any and all susceptibility for counsel: if not,you are from my point of view woytless.

Courage he said and pointed to his pyjamas.

Think—no more than think—you would be beginning an excitement and subtracting forty six years of a life which only the stupidest of virgins can boast of by quitting the Library. A vacation among your FAMILY in CAPITALS ought to "brace" you for next to anything:even I used to feel exhilirated,in a more humble way,by re-mingling with the Penates Incorporated. ✳ ✳ ✳

[Guéthary, France]
12 Août 1923

dear B.

received few days since—forwarded from Paris—a letter signed 45 Grove St Hart Crane recounting that you were en route to a vacation chez Nail [Nagle] & enclosing somebody's idea of a wise crack at the Dial:for which much thanks!

Should it interest yourself & H. C. to know the basis of aforementioned apocalyptica i beg to mention

ⓐ that Dos,Seldes & self had a party

ⓑ   ″   E. E. Cummings was lugged to the rue des Grands Augustins police station for having pissed opposite the Calvados Joint of rue Gît le Coeur(time 3 A M)

ⓒ that Dos accompanied me;& even entered the station—only to be thrown out protesting.

ⓓ that Seldes,despite great tipsiness,followed Dos

ⓔ that next day i presented self at station(alone)& was given a kind of 3rd degree for not having reported change of address on carte d'identité—also threatened with expulsion from France,etc. etc. etc.

ⓕ that Seldes immediately visited m. Paul Morand,Quai d'Orsay

ⓖ that P. M.(so far as we now know)squelched both charges against me;& wrote Seldes a very pleasant promise that "C. will have no ennui."—

Perhaps wrote you the above(?)

Incidentally,none of us were in Paris on the 14th July.

N.B.—[Malcolm] Cowley was not in Paris during our little party. (Dos & I subsequently threw a shindig chez Cowley at Giverny—the 2 affairs may have been mingled by Captain Nemo of the News World) The only thing which made me sore(in the clipping)was the coupling of my humble self with Greenwich Village,alias the "Dome"—"Rotunde"—heapshit. If you know who did that, be so nice as to knock his block off for me;will you?

Turning to less theatrical matters,I am in Guéthary,between St. Jean de Luz and Biarritz(where Mopsy & Elaine are). Was just enjoying a model coat of tan when fell off a precipice & "sprained" my foot(9 days ago). Hope soon to walk. The trouble was I had to walk from where I fell to my hotel,½ hour; as hereabouts is a countrified locality.

Got 2 letters from Kantor—1st saying he was in Paris—to which I responded by wire giving my address—2nd wondering if I was coming to Paris. I wrote suggesting that he visit the midi;& haven't heard since. I'd like very much to see K.,eyes and all.

—If you should see Cowley in America,remember me to him and add that I'm glad to have heard—by a letter he wrote me before sailing—that the Giverny fracas left him uninjured. Incidentally,so to say—there was a number of the Dial which had new-and-improved Nagles(I speak from hearsay)—which number I never got but would like to have. & How—speaking of the Bertolett Boyz—is yourself? Elaine says that your nemesis is en viajo and that you are thereby profiting by a small vacation:congratulations. What—to Kontinue Kuriosity to its illogical Klimax—of one Thechair [Lachaise]? Miss Nagle is flourishing.

I saw a different kind of Thayer from what left America. (It was less agreeable,by far,than what had been my host last winter in Wien.) It was to be watched through a microscope while taking 2 of my drawings for Dial purposes. Unhappily, having no such instrument,myself smoked looking out the fenetre as I have misnamed room 29's sole aperture [St. André].

Received, in addition to other missives from G's Country, an epistle from M. Josephson(cf. coat-of-many-colors myth; Holy Bible)who is now flying the flag of Balai—but won't speak no bétisses,realising that yourself may be shinning up the pole untangling halyards. Sent Broom,via you(if agreeable)some sonnets which I beg on [sketch of bended knees] genoux will be either

(1)printed as typed,in order,etc.

(2)rejected entirely.

!¡Be good to the oesophagus!¡

75 / TO HIS SISTER

[Paris
September 15, 1923]
¿A cuantos estamos hoy?

Dear Simply
heartlessbloodthirstyun(im?)moralselfishstubborninaword-modernrelative. Thanks for yours of the 1 on bicoloured papyrus.

Am pleased to note an amazing changement de proprié-
taire in the cerebral hemisphere:the ancestral He abdicating
in favor of the ditto She. Buttons,a small flask of ripe water.

As you may guess I am glad to be in Parigi(as we call it
since the GAWLZ took to beating up antifacists in the extreme
or red suburbs. Poleasemans are anothers name,for these He-
rows.) A gent named Louis Kantor thinks we should visit
Deutchland Under Alles soon:he having already come from
thither via leaving New York. Possibly you did or did not gno
that one of the only three reviews of the ER "pleasant" to an
author's "eye" was L.K.'s,a friend of a friend of mine called
"Slater" "Brown",looks not too much like J.Christ and has at-
tacks of total inepticality and is a very pleasant person.

I am glad you are reading smutty books,living in New York,
drinking gasolene coctails,etc. A sister to be proud of.

As for the raising of the lowered clahses,I predict that you
will discover that we all never should cross those bridges until
we etc. or that is to say Worry Not Gentle Maid Lest Wrinkles
Thee Invade(Bunyan,Poem to a Corn and Bluejay Plaster).
(Elaine is looking to seeing you and I shouldn't be surprised if
Mopsy might drop in too,just to make sure the social side is
taken care. of. In which case,give your guests my love. . . .)

Were I a golfloving child of Westmorley:who wears their
knees halfway between their ankles and their genoux(in emu-
lation of Dearie,The Poifikli Dressed Man(?))should now be
romping to NY covered with dollars but aint so aren't. So to
speak. However,etcetcetc. Nor will anyone bet with me upon
Slacker Dempsy against Panther Firpo. My financial future being as usual behind me,I don't bother to look around at it
thereby avoiding the usual(in similar circumstances)imitation of
a Gatto with Its tale. Yes we have no bananas no I am learning
Spanish.

The droll histoire of drowning smiths tickles my nether
cranial noiv—as for Bigchief Abenaki on the warpath,what
sports you americans go in for to be sure! (Thanks for a sneak-
ing sympathy with the gangatbay.)

Tomorrow at niyuntoiti am due at Noodleville(Opytahl Amer.)for a W or violt rae on my longsincealmostbut notquite-curedfoot. Shall report to headquarters anent. The weather here is hot,or makes great heat if you prefer. I prefer fine to calvados,detest "mar",distrust Anis del oso,and drink beer also. ✳ ✳ ✳

[*sketch of sporty Basque*]

when you see me looking like this
please kick me in the conundrum
until when, if life isn't bliss
at least it isn't hundrum

anon

76 / TO HIS FATHER

[Paris
September 18, 1923]

Dear Father—

✳ ✳ ✳ I almost finished ORPHEUS,Histoire Générale des Réligions,by one Salomon Reinach—left by Dos in one of his flights from yon to thither—which you,as one who occasionally has been known to pulpit,doubtless know. If not,recommend (respectfully). I dare say I am reading a translation,or you may have.

"Le XIXe siecle a vu se développer,en Angleterre et aux Etats Unis,la sect chrétienne et rationaliste des Unitaires. . . . C'est surtout à Boston,l'Athènes américaine,que le christianisme ainsi épuré trouva un terrain favorable. . . . Apres Channing, le poète et moraliste Ralph Emerson(de Boston)propagea cette "religion des intellectuals",christianisme sans dogme et sans autre temples que les cœurs."(page 534)

After reaching two thirds of the book,I am unable to see how any even partially sensitive person could have anything to do with any form of Christianisme—but perhaps you haven't read,or have forgotten,my kindly friend Reinach's description of the Midi inquisition?(not the Spanish one). vide Chapter 10. Sans blague!!!

I see that De Wop Napoleon is making Someone's League of Small Nation's(whose I don't pretend to know)look like the inside of an institution for feebleminded folks. Fiume looms, Poincaré wrangles. As usual,I admire Russia.

77 / *TO HIS MOTHER*

[Paris]
October 24, 1923

Dear Mother,

* * * Louis Kantor is a man six years younger than I am who has worked for his "living" all his life(and is still on the NY Tribune),sensitive,generous. A friend of Brown's. He(Kantor) is now on a vacation somewhere:I hope to see him when he gets back. (We had several very spirited parties!) It was Kantor(as I may have written you)who insisted that Pound(whom he had met)take some poems of mine for an English magazine [the *Transatlantic Review*] gotten-out by Mr. P.'s friend one Ford Maddox (Hueffer)Ford,the change from Hueffer(if that's it) being due to Mr. F's wedding recently a female millionaire (hence the magazine aussi)or so they say. —In fact Kantor took me around the Pound's studio(I had been once introduced by Thayer,in Paris)where we had much and excellent tea.

(Note:Pound liked the poems,and is taking 4 out of 5(the 5th being too rough for the Hinglish Sensor). As you may know,I have for some years been an admirer of Pound's poetry: personally,he sometimes gives me a FatherComplex) * * *

78 / *TO HIS SISTER*

4 Patchin Place [New York]
Wednesday 27/2/24

Dear Lulu—still trembling,panting,spasmodically laughing, fitfully or hysterically weeping,I sit upon my unmade couch to answer or rather to not answer yrs. of long since;the occasion being the meat of my epistle which was as follows:

At 11:30 I uprose,raised my pinions,lit a stove and a radiator,observed 'twas sunny without(what?),and almost fell or sat down on the former which was fortunately still unhot apropos the frenzied ringing of my doorbell. I push ye clicker,an even if possible more fierce crash upon the cloche—I lean,palsied with terror,against the wall,thumb buried in clicker,whereupon a bespectacled figger abruptly enters the court—"lost" I exclaimed,and the word went like a dagger to my heart,when ye f. begins holla-ing "CUMinz cumINS"at which many voices answer,respond,suggest,ripostent,but not mine because GAS-BILL flashed thru our hero's foreconscious. Steps accompanied by let us say briefly feet reach my porte. A chauffeur, gigantic in furlined undies covered by walrushide-chiffon with a capute of the ditto material and spectacles suggestive of Daddy Doom inserts his pose upon the halfopened door—"Mr CUMINZ" yes I said "Are YOU mr cumminze?" yes I said "Mrs. Hutchins is outside and would like to see you"—whereupon I broke into a torrent of illiterate phrases,interrupted with "Why you're just after getting up" yes I said "Couldn't you slap on something quick?"—yes I said so he came back again just as I noted that my shirt came through my pocket on the left side of the King of Sweeden trousers nor could I tuck it in which remarking "She wants you to come to dinner with her" he remarked "So you'd better dress up" he observed so I undressed put on my·best suit and said weakly,still sobbing But i will Have to shave "Couldn't you shave quick?" he said kindly and teasingly yes I said entered kitchenette emerged reentered "For Christ's sake" he said "Don't tell me you're shaved" yes I said so handing him the clothesbrush he caressed my back-protesting "there's more on here than this brush will take off yes I said but I don't care about anything except what's bigger than a $ bill" laughter then we hastened out. The car,as I had learned when suggesting to the emissary that his mistress might like to come in,to which he countered that the car as already mentioned was not near,being held up by a stuck truck,the car we repeat was reached a pieds and I invited Mrs. Hutchins,wife of Robert Grosvenor Pronounced Grovenor Rabbit Hutchins Esquire The Banker in but she declined merrily and off we went to Wanamakers to lunch but I suggested the Lafayette whereupon she fell on both knees in the midst of the luxurious limousine embarassing me slightly and hammered daintily on windows etc. shut an opened door and persuaded him to stop. I tried to take her in the front door of which there R 2 but no she wood enter by the cafe whence escorted her to the dining room where she paid my check 4$somesense and gave the garçon Won dole-are at which he it I and the whole world skipped.

As for psychoanalysing why Youse chose to blowup on a examination,youse may infer have consulted Dr.Joy of Wien, who remarks:a complete report will be necessary or in other words when I watch your prancing bouche and gather the spot-less items which redolently tumble from ditto in a papernapkin while with my other paw I stroke your spindelmaginnis in ¾ time reciting sub voce the Sotto Rosa of Histrionides,then O Hera,will Sanyclaws come down the chimbley. Suggest mean-while that worries anent THE PHYSICAL aspect of l l & the p of h(vide AM.Const.)times Resistance to the PSYCHICAL gueri-son of same might normally influence yr. infraviolet immodesty to commit Harry Carry as per letter to me. Should not be over-inclined to arson for that reason. By this time the dream follow-ing the one you so accurately described in nonexistent terms of enormous ·resistance will have undoubtedly revealed all. A portrait of the (dis-)section man might help matters,since before him you were apt to fly the coop of knowledge. Speaking of which,don't take those frozen cats too seriously. There are all sorts of opportunities for sublimation equal if not superior to that involved in extracting viscera of faintlysmelling puss.

If the wind blows the right way,my middle-ear understands a hint that Mother and You are to appear in NY for vacation-days,stopping at the former's hostel off lower 5th? A kwhyet place. Should you intend to put up sola with elaine,she would be glad to give you a very comfortableIamtold sofa,till bearings could be got and safety devices installed in the unrapable room which has doubtless already been selected by Raymond Whit-comb for OWer YounG adVENTuress. We are both expecting you,so don't fail to show up even if you forget the vodka and Morocco Horatious at The Bridge which I personally don't cross until you impersonally come to them.

Yours for the exploitation of cortical divarications ✳ ✳ ✳

[4 Patchin Place
May 13, 1924]

Dear "D.D."

* * * the Independants found me not incapable of a
40″x50″ "ABSTRACT" canvas which they or it or both or
neither hung very well(by itself)—this lidel effut cost me 9 days
work and was dry on time,selah-sounds. It's pseudonym being
"Noise Number 12",Philip Davis will rejoice—I judge by a heart-
felt and muchappreciated addendum to his recently-arrived-
and-welcome-Xmas gift—that I have seen the light of reason
and am concerned with the everyday reality etc. instead of
floundering upon the guags of incomprehensibility. Before I
forget:have composed a wootchka or thkymblug(*ancient runic
form of versification)to fulfill his abovementioned plea—it
gallops similar to this:

> the bolsheveeks have bearded cheeks
> their leader he is Trotski
> we're glad we're not in Petrograd
> where youski would be shotski

Iski * * *

4 Patchin Place
[September 27, 1924]

Dear Mother,

* * * I have been very busy doing absolutely nothing at
Astoria,across the river,where the Famous Players—Lasky
Corporation hang out. Mr Frank Crowninshield,editor of
Vanity Fair,got me the chance to visit the studio during 4 weeks
on salary compatible with the environment(Richard Dix,Jaque-
line Logan,Beebee Daniels,Gloria Swanson,etc.) The latter
makes 7000$ a week,work or loaf.
Today my connection with the movies ends,at least officially.
Possibly I shall have an opportunity to write a story from
material furnished by one of the directors,Mr Paul Sloane,who

has been putting on "Jungle Law" during my stay. He has a "sure hit"up his sleeve but doesn't seem inclined to produce it. ✳ ✳ ✳

Almost forgot to mention that wrote a humorous bit for Crowninshield✳which he likes greatly. Therefore he has asked me to do much more ✳ ✳ ✳

✳ "The Soul Story of Gladys Vanderdecker," Vanity Fair, xxll (December, 1924), 52, 92, 94, 114.

81 / TELEGRAM TO MURIEL DRAPER

New York, N.Y.
May 13, 1925

MAN SILENT STOP BLACK MARIA SPRIG LILAC BUT-TONHOLE NEGRO EMERGING STOP AQUARIUM FIVE ALIVE IGUANAS IN PYJAMAS OF CHINESE GOLD LOOK

82 / TO HIS MOTHER

[4 Patchin Place
September 3, 1925]

Dear Mother —

it is delightful to hear from you — I just found your letter at the door,having myself painted since 1:30 circa(or 5 hours) without rest. Find that painting is what best takes the horns of unhappiness by the bull.✳

I made myself sick by the simple means of worrying,telephoning a lawyer,etc.;so have resolved to forget the messy machinery of incohate injustice for the nonce. Apparently,was not made to match wits with twofisted gogetters . . .

Probably have made clear the situation ✳ ✳ ✳ and were I a millionaire I should be cogitating the employment of detectives(imagine me using that merde! ✳ ✳ ✳ a likely canvass of my mentality if I say so moimême). Or in other words,am sitting on a large piece of almost nothing taking my own photograph with a shutterless camera. It seems to me that

father's brains(which I have ever admired,unlike my own)plus
the life which he has given to society in the economic sense of
that word ought to rise up,here,and somehow(my own apologies for b.s are static)magnificently Save The Day before it's
too late —

>mind you,he may know a Boston lawyer who's a gen-
>ius;and anyway,he is a famous man whereas I am a
>small eye poet. * * *

° This letter concerns problems arising from his divorce from his first wife.

83 / TO HIS AUNT JANE

[4 Patchin Place
November 17, 1925]

Dear Aunt Jane—
I first employed dynamite. It is dangerous,of course;but
also effective. When the walls [at 4 Patchin Place] had been
eliminated and the only thing left of the ceiling was a piece of
plaster slightly smaller than a postage-stamp and the floor was re-
muneratively reposing upon the insurance-agent-lady who
formerly lived underneath me and once wanted to know if I
spilled those ashes on the stairs etc.,I sent in one hundred
Pinkerton detectives,all dressed differently—some imperson-
ating ferrets,others mail-boxes,still others Intelligentiae—who
thoroughly searched the framework of what had been 4 Patchin
Place Top Back for two weeks(which I very much enjoyed at
the Ritz)employing microphones,dictaphones,audiphones,ec-
toplasmiphones and similar devices for the location of missing
data,not excluding Professor Von Bungh's new invention,the
epistolophonoradiogramopho-rheostat(guaranteed to discover
the whereàbouts of all written and unwritten objects)comma
but without success period. Nothing dashed,I paid Freud's
passage to the West Indies,where he psychoanalysed a native
who,having once worked in a jewelry establishment on 5th Avenue,might legitimately have been suspected of having wrested
my treasure from me,under cover of darkness if not equally
with false whiskers. Results being negative to say the least,I
next consulted Madame Zybysco Pysistratus(the well known
epileptictrance-medium)who told me to look in the wastebasket
of the first lovely woman I met,who happened to be above sus-

picion,thereby nullifying all preternatural testimony. Hereupon a bright idea struck me—I painted several of my friends(of both genders)with phosphorescent paint,waited for night to come,filled them with gin,and lowered them in wicker baskets from a deusexmachina or derrick into the ruins of my apartment,where they waited until morning without seeing anything peculiar. After this,I swallowed aspirin in huge quantities,read Epictetus,jumped out of the window and back several times,declaimed The Face On The Bar-Room Floor in Lithuanian, played hookey dumbbells and leapfrog with my shadow,and otherwise exerted every sinew to place myself in a mentally receptive state. Almost a week having elapsed,my efforts are at length crowned with quite unmitigated success;in fact,I found your letter only today,and(even more extraordinary) found in it your cheque a propos the repetition-compulsion of my naissance. I cannot express to you my enthusiasm upon this achievement but I can promise to visit the loosely called "corn-exchange"institution-for-the-decimation-of-savings-righteously-and-invidiously-acquired-by-fair-means-or-foul   tomorrow morning,granted the absence of vasculomotor inhibitions, plus a limpid appreciation of direction,which is not impossible (if uncommon)with me as a rule.

                    Unto which I affix my first,second,and third
                    initials:
                         E.E.C.(eec)

84 / TO MARIANNE MOORE

                                        4 Patchin Place
                                        January 19 [1926]

Dear Miss Moore:

thank you for your letter,enclosing the cheque for my poems in the January issue [of *The Dial*]. Watson told me,while I was visiting him,that you had suggested I write "theatre" for the next number;and I answered that I felt too unwise(suggesting [Edmund] Wilson as "your correspondent"). Since then I've been attending the Nemirovitch-Dantchenko shows and feel considerably less unwise. Would you perhaps care to have me write,under "THEATRE",some pages or even paragraphs or

possibly sentences "re" the russians? If so,I should be delighted. Assuming that a worthier has not been located,

[4 Patchin Place]
Monday [September 13, 1926]

Dear Mother—

thank you for the hat,neckties and handkerchief;and most of
all for your letter! I'm tremendously pleased to hear that Father is thrivingly inclined—not that I attribute said effect to
my own temporary presence(as you seem to do);rather,Herr
Sigmund is a mighty person for a' that & everything else.
Please let me know how the family enjoyed its latter chapters
[Freud's *A General Introduction to Psychoanalysis*] which your
correspondent absorbed en route to New York,(thinking to
himself that the day were at least one third unwon if the reading ceased with his departure). I should imagine that very
soon "Totem and Taboo" would be readable. This little book,
as SW [Watson] would say,contains more meat for individuals with religious cravings than the entire highly civilised universe of Six Mile Pond wots of! I trust that,once the General
Introduction is thoroughly digested, T & T will occur on Aunt
Jane's daily menu. Nothing like variety in this world. * * *
    Myself seems to be quite on the rampage,as usual. The play
[*Him*] will shortly find a typist,one is inclined to believe. Meanwhile I remediate it,attempt to comprehend its multifarious
meaning and indulge in vigorous parties(incidentally,the President of The Club's scotch is in need of improvement,or else my
watercure spoiled me for domestic products). If keeping busy
were synonymous with keeping happy,your humble servant
would claim a palm or three. Completed in two days and yesterday mailed an article on the tabloid newspaper the pilgrim
father and big business—all via psychoanalysis—something like
which wasn't?
       was? expected by my wellintentioned nitwit em-
       was not?
ployers, V.F.[*Vanity Fair*] Incorporated. My able vagabond
friend,Signor Joseph Ferdinand Gould,desires me to "do
as well by" him as I "can",apropos fact that is attempting to

have his History Of The World "typed and marketed". Mr.
Gould tells me, moreover,that he has fought no duels of late,
but has succeeded in making somebody tell "everybody" that he
is "of negro origin. Hoping you are the same,Sincerely yours,
Joe Gould". The [Harvard] coop's missive sounds almost pre-
posterously wallstreetish—why not,given the circumstances,try
another bookstore as Sherlock Holmes might put it? (Never
mind,for you shall have a ride in my pinkpoiple WollsYoyce,if
only as a token of my appreciation for the Conway Haircut
Sweepstakes a la Franklin)! My friends here in New York are
flourishing and glad to see me and greatly interested in the
Aerial Raccoonery and even threatening to hire one of the
Cummingsbuilt mansions [at Silver Lake, N.H.] as a wayside inn
for thirsty aesthetes—but I impress upon them the inherent
calcoolidge upwrongness of N.E.'s panaqual landscape and
vaguely rant of the colours of precise October. I also wish that
someone of the C. phylon would investigate M.R.Werner's
Barnum or Brigham Young(or both)emitted by Harcourt Brace
and Minus Howe. —But enough of recommendations!

1930–1939

[4 Patchin Place]
one three thirty

when through who-the-unotherish twilight updrops but his
niblicks Sir Oral Né Ferdinand Joegesq(disarmed to the non-
teeth by loseable scripture befisto -zr- P—nd subjesting etse-
mina our lightwrittens)and him as mightily distant from a fit
of the incheerfuls as am our hero but naturally encore when the
ittorian extroverts Well why not send your portrait of you and
your portrait of me? J,says sprouts,itch'll be pigged,if only in
the name of Adver the Tisement;but will they immaculate it
on t'other conception(meaning Brussels)which being respond-
fully preanswered we thusforth are proseeding.—Play in
Regress [Him] meanwhile(sub rosa s.v.p.)am trying to untangle
from Carpy D.M.(alias Kid)Liveright;with a view to otherwhere
(post quite the usual literally decades of shushment)pub- among
whispers of Too bad & Say foo & Every Lawrence Has A stalling
& What We Need Is More welfare to legs or the importance of
being arnnest & A William Bleats Is A Johnnycake But Achilles
Is Only A heel -lish a picturebook called CIOPWamong whose
Os occur likenesses of the unlikenesses beforementioned:but Ye
Kid is hitting in the clinches and ruffurree Brandt&Brandt's one
glasseye had an attack of sic unleashing pandemonium until the
audience was on my feet to a manhole(what Comma Indeed
comma Is civleyesehshun)?—Tears Lyut

I hope Variétés won't feel united,under the waistland or vice-
versa...
For the rest,I am proud to be "translated" as you select

A recent cable from interrogation point reads:Masser Zorach
maybe own one piece nicotine redman stop have dispatched
angel with suitable prayers for closeup stop no doubt Western
Electric will have them talking soon but however(signed)the
enormous room stop tulips & chimneys stop xli poems stop &
stop is 5 stop him stop

It is a pleasure to hear from you, sir!

[4 Patchin Place
April 12, 1930]

pleasant weather,Columbus!

'twas even more than a pleasure to read The NR#p 239 sixth 1 from top quotes THE MECHANISM OF THE THEATER . . . THE MECHANISM OF THE CIRCUS IS MASKED close quotes   welwell-welll perhaps Not lasciate ogni speranza Afterallll!

Ye Wear-ne'er [M. R. Werner] hath paxvobiscumbed else-wherishly*viz parry an burlin [Paris and Berlin] en root to the amen soviet yeastcake;he wanted i to go but $,if not sens fore-bad.   Am almost thru eheuing & reddy to sing "Whan that Ap Reely"
we hope to see yousesboths verysoon,Mudumunmushoo!

lay khyeu mangz
[The Cummings]
nbps) Q;Whence the phrase "virgin forest"?   A;Only G-d
can make a tree

Anon.(20thC American)

#issue graphically recommended by Sir Silbert Geldes this day of grace 4/12/30

*loaning us a Lachaise
HugeHead and Drawing plus
several Kuhns(and a Cummings

(From   HATS OFF to thea orthodox flea,
the   who attempted to bugger a bee
Sanscrit)   But eamerged from thea fray
in a familea way . . .
which is why wea do things so fee-blea

JOYBARN,nh
eyedz of kaylenz, '30

Gentle Denizens of Thalassaville:
                    hail!
                    We,the undersigned,

do hereby proffer our benignities and do very much trust that
you survived the Dreadful & Terrible Scene Over The Cut Of
Pig;whereof consequences still echo in our surfsmit hearts. Nor
shall years(neither time with his scythechariot)ever so much as
begin to obliterate—let alone erase—your generosities;to whom
ourselves are most fain if all too willing debtors:nevertheless it
is our purblind aspiration that you'll give us a whack at evening
things up without benefit of underto[w] and allowing for the
difference in density between aqua fresh & saline. As for True
Row,'tis a mere paddle by comparison with Dune City—but for
god's sake watch those O.Jene U.Kneelites and keep 1 weather-
eye peeled for the bishopy cook John Silver alias Heartofgold.
In the name of Harry the Hamlet,Harry the Kemp,and Harry
the Rogers Bruce
                    dingaling

À BAS LES BARRELPIPPILS
VIVE LA VIE
Shantyshantyshantyshantyshantyshantyshanty
hovelhutcabinhouseaboderesidencedemesnemanorcastlepalace-
                    farmshack

                                        ah,
                                          (wo)
                    Men.

---

* *EEC and his second wife, Anne, had been visiting the Edmund Wilsons at Provincetown*
("Thalassaville"), Massachusetts, where the Provincetown Playhouse had been estab-
lished by Eugene O'Neill and others.

Berlin
26 Dezember [1930]

ACHTUNG

Lux is nutn—to uss.

Why for instance:as a boy in a boiled shirt & swallow tails was showing the Nuptial Sweet at Hotel Britannia,Budapest,Hung., he fell flat on the back of his neck at our astonished fruite and —as I faintly endeavored to insert a helpful hand in one prostrate armpit—mercurially arose with the oracular remark(in French)"Par Don".   But before that occurence—to be exact, when we boarded the Schnellzug from Munich,Germ.,a wild-eyed official tore into the compartment,placed radio-receivers on our ears,wired the ceiling in a trice,and(presto)we were listening-in-on "Hal Lo Hal Lo Eats Raddy Oh" from the Hung. Broadcasting Co. Headquarters myles & myles away.   And don't let nobody tell you there aint magic in Mitl Uropa:why,I asked a ober in Wien for two vermouths please & instead received a cigar!   Yes,Berlin is indeed a big place,big and imposturous;but we have sat in the "Wild West" room at Haus Vaterland and looked upon the dunkeles when it was zweimal.   Prague,too, contributes her thrills—not to mention trying to explain to a head-czech on a hill that I'd lost the cocher and finally resorting to Ich kam mit ein(?)Mann(?)mit ein(?)Pferd(?)Wo ist er bitte? "The church"he responded laughingly"will be open at 2".   And, so it proved.   But . . . Keep all this dark from the Doser;as they doubtless are reading about S.Revol.etc.and starvation ad infinatio and besides we're planning to reenter Paris—do I babble on—for New Year's Eve.   The trouble with you,Comings, is that you don't no anything—

32 bis, rue du Cotentin, Paris
January 7, Wednesday [1931]

Dear Mother—

I've just returned from the place de la Concorde;whither went at an unearthly hour this morning & where waited on a traffic-island for 2½ hours. All with a view to viewing the obsequies of M. Joffre. Shouldn't have gone at all except that last night,after dinner, Anne*and I and a Paris-inhabiting American arrived from Rouen(mighty fine town!)dined near the étoile,left our bags(temporarily)at the restaurant and hurried to le star—precisely as a cannon exploded,searchlights hozed the environs,any number of youths almost fell from the trees into which they'd climbed and "cinq minutes de silence" oc- curred. Much the noisiest silence,incidentally,which your cor- respondant ever heard. Then happened salutes,another can- non,passing of limousines under the arc—whereupon everyone went home. "Well" I said to myself "tomorrow must be better than that!" and so today found me freezing my feet at the Concorde.

Said funeral itself was distinctly no great shakes—only ex- citing element being the warrior's horse,much-panoplied and dancingly wondering what everything was about—but the tril- lions of nomillions who crammed the vicinity of the Crillon, standing on anything from "pliants" to chimneys and each other, provided a spectacle which nobody could easily or uneasily have imagined. Not one ounce of sentiment—save when two spec- tators failed to uncover at the proper moment:then dirty cracks re "bosh" and "pas français",(I was hatless,fortunately,at the moment). Everyone taking the show as a free-for-all picnic crossed with a universal vaudeville. Or as one woman remarked when her friend asked her if she'd seen the horse?—"There isn't a dragon?"

However,that being over,shall now settle down to Paris. The short Rouen trip(you would scarcely think that Lausanne- Munich-Vienna-Budapest-Prague-Berlin voyagers would need a change again,yet the latter proved highly beneficial)made me wonder again at France;which certainly has more in it than the rest of creation multiplied by itself. Do you,perhaps,know and

recall the crazy houses and lacey gothics of Jeanne d'arc's martyr-village? I thought I'd seen them once,during la guerre;but no
. . . Never were stones so punctiliously petticoated. Never was weight so presdidigitatorily negated. And to add to our ex-citement,a London fog struck the ville at the very moment of departure,eliminating gently such tiny objects as railroad sta-tions! Nevertheless a train somehow arrived and we somehow as well * * *

The studio here,by the way,has only one disadvantage:toward 2 A M ten thousand neighing pigs,mooing sheep,bleat-ing cows,etc:wend unwillingly to a kind of yard outside our unique window. But,noise excepted,all's well—a bath,contin-uous hot water,a comfortable couch,three kitchen chairs(and such homelike symbols as a coffee grinder;bought by Madame, in French!) To be sure,there's but one sitting room,a bath-room(WITH toilet),kitchen,& a hall;yet after Raspail hotel life,what a relief!!! * * *

° *The former Anne Barton, EEC's second wife.*

c/o American Express
11 rue Scribe, Paris
9 avril [1931]

Dear Mother!

* * * While Anne was in Switzerland,who should find me out(having tried vainly at Le Lute Hôtel,Boulevard Raspail)but Master John Peale Bishop,erstwhile intimate ami de Bunny Wilson & present holder of Yeeeeee Oldeeeee Harpereeee Prizeee(=$5,000). He led me to Hotel Something,where Char-lot is rumored to be reposing after repulsed threats of knight-hood & gracious acceptance of legiondoneur,Crillon is the name—where Bea Shop,his wife(née Hutchins)& I & he had a drink! Another day he invited me to dinner. Upon which lat-ter occasion,while waiting for my hosts at Cafe Select,Boulevard Montparnasse(Open All Night)I began to draw a faggot(=fairy); appears yon Eveque [John Bishop] & announces "Elaine's in the car—do you want to say hello to her?" Having done this,I

next "enjoyed" a drink with Mr. & Mrs. B & Mrs. MacD[Mac Dermott](who seemed very well & said she'd recently produced a boy). This lady inquired for Scofield,Nagle,Mitchell,Yourself & Elizabeth. My informant asked if I'd received certain letters from "Charles Francis"? I said yes,but that couldn't take them seriously. In short,a cordial but unsatisfactory(as usual)time was had,for five minutes;then she remounted the Bishop's auto & evaporated with 2 vague addresses of mine. * * *

Numero deux—have applied for a Russian visa which,if am the lil lawd fongleroi they wish—should arrive in 2 weeks:intend to reach Moscow onor before May day(international celebrations):receive Russian lessons daily(except Sunday)at Berlitz(if open;if shut,chez remarkable woman of 45–65 who lives in one room with samovar,a stove,3 dogs(whippets)& one cat. The remarkable w. and the Berlitz teacher are,incidentally,one. I find the language just a shy wink harder than Greek. * * * Expect to remain a few minutes,days,or weeks;depending on how long five hundred $ carries me:to depart(via Odessa)past Athens to Marseille—where Anne may join me,if she decides to stay in France a bit longer.

Paris,nowanights,reeks with Etrangers;ah,but the trees are budding,& we've seen certain hours-without-rain! On dit that the Gingerbread Fair is in fling at the Nation Gate;as for I,it's Steam Swings we need! (Do you recall refusing to partake of an innocent merry go round under the Lion's Noze?:) But when it comes to flying!!! * * *

as I may already have written—Thought Morrie's "Liberty" magazine article somewhat pas cher(don't tell him so). Sub rosa—Brown asked Master W [Werner] to expose Wussia for the New Republic(a magazine "on" which Brown works),to which request M. Morrie replied,said B,that if he(W)wrote what he(W)really thought he(W)feared he(W)wouldn't be invited again;or words to that effect. P.S.,"Liberty" pays "in three figures"! The Hound & Horn article was certainly an elaborate model of a W.C.,did you think? (I may have a touch of recognition here,by the way;but that's one secret for the present;choostah maggyzeena wud). * * *

Guaranty Trust   (but i don't
4placedelaConcorde)
Paris
[1933]

Dear Foster—

re your letter(which just arrived)allow me to congratulate eimi!*a lucky book!

can report only vaguely on reception-in-general:
apparently one "Nathan" spectatorously called her
"the worst book of the month" before e was ever published;other nongentleunmen of ny's pressless sought
gants [*sic*] ("the funniest book of the month")—fearing
another him?—while curt cowflaps rolled in from ye
sticks inc as per etc . . . Silk Hat Harry(they tell)be-
holding a Hound & a Horn,sprach "of course I don't
mind for myself:but he really shouldn't have made
fun of poor Gene Tunney" so the wellknown thorn
was on trotsky's wing again but

you sound fine not to say hearty—so am I!

Paris amazing.   Almost a vacuum where the Americans aren't;
those who are weep concerning $(soon we'll be rid of them
even)hence nothing could suit better

Your humble and obedient servant
who trusts to receive his copy of New Hampshire
alias
   Jock duh Frog
   Count Sandy d'Essence
   Putana Madonna
   A.R.Bitz
   Herr von der Urinoir
   a gentleman with a hat or so
  long

---

* Eimi (*New York: Covici, Friede, 1933*), *EEC's account of his trip to Russia.*

> c/o Guaranty Trust
> 4 Place de la Concorde
> Paris
> May 26 [1933]

Dearest Mother!

your welcome letter of May 11th is received—not to mention its predecessor,enclosing a wealth of French currency past espérance—and we're delighted to find you well! * * *

* * * Marion's my pride and joy:as you've probably guessed. Coming to a new language or world she immediately took it by storm without losing any proverbial tête;this I consider an achievement. The "Vogue" people are doting on her slightest whim,creeping the boulevards on hands and knees to buy her orangejuice(with just the necessary goût of champagne)etc—as for Baron Huene,photographer de luxe,he wants us to visit him in Africa whenever he can stop snapping "the most beautiful woman and the most poised in Paris". A nice fellow,by the way.

We've already eaten in a tree at Sceaux Robinson(which is as dead as a doornail,owing to lack of tourists)and I've saluted your griffin for you—the entire country sends respectful admiration and the principal city bows to you with a smile of recognition and the engines haven't changed a semitone. One of these days,when am not too busy shopping for dinner(la cuisine Morehouse)shall eat a meal at La Reine Blanche. I fear that naught will compare with domesticity,howsomeever. A certain Mrs. & Mr. Pound(Ezra,son of Pound,Homer)graced our board,also M. et Mme. Malkine(née Ledoux,daughter of "Mr. Zero")also the folks which found us our gilded canarygage,to wit Walter(de pote)Lowenfels mit Frau(e?en?). Eimi is read at last by one Johnnie Bishop,whose dame give it to him on his birthday and in our presence viz. at le chateau de Tressancourt Orgival Seine et Oise whither we repaired last weekend;he raveth now. And much gratitude for enclosed clippings—apparently the rubes are ahead of the cityslickers!Foster outdid Damon meseems

it grew so cold here a week or less ago that la cuisinière attrappait le or la loom-bah-goe;she's over it today,and was yesterday;daybefore too. We've had excellent weather otherwise and anticipate perfection demain   *   *   *

94 / TO HIS MOTHER

c/o Huene,Hammamet,Tunisie,Afrique du Nord
fullmoon
September
[September 13, 1933]

Dear Mother!

here we are. The sea lives a few hundred feet away;this palace is built around a court;we wear handkerchiefs-on-head and bathingsuits-to-beach;the beach — uninhabited save for occasionally goats—outdoes any I've seen;the Mediterrané's warmer than to be imagined;about 20 minutes walk away lies Hammamet (meaning "City of Doves," they say) and patter donkeys and lurch camels(the worstputtogether of all creatures?)and howls a trumpetting phonograph and loll ay-rabz galore(with occasionally a wedding);behind us,a range of mountains borrowed from the Sandwich line,and not excluding a similacrum of Chocorua; the land here is full of cactus and low shrubbery and Bedoins whose mansions consist of shelters slightly larger than a bananaskin;heat equals somethingtobegotusedto,almost everyone(alias I)sleeps from noon till afternoon(3PM);the first evening Huene and Marion and I all sampled some cactusfruit,becoming full-of-thorns inside our faces and outside — without dire results;when people wish to punish people people throw people into people's cactuses,it seems;camels placidly nibble the whole shebang,not merely the smallish but the spike thorns;have already made many sketches and 1 watercolour;our host is Kindness Personified,offers me sanguine and easel and space and time;chameleons are splendid models;Marion's sunburn is becoming tan (you burn while you watch yourself burn and tan almost as quickly)of the premier order — as for me,shall shortly ressemble The Spirit Of Bronze;   *   *   *   today is the baron's birthday and a German lad who's visiting has constructed an imposing centrepiece from seashell and sand and snails . . . there are lots of snails;we lunch every day about noon very lightly and enjoy citronade at 5 and dine — also outdoors — facing la mer — about 8 and retire circa 10:30 and rise at 9 sharp(the master gets up at 6 to assist his Arab workmen in the completion of this palace,as I insist it is);Djeedee(?) and Muhammed(?)are the principal plus only servants;everyone does exactly as everyone likes,including the sun and a full moon! ❊ ❊ ❊

95 / TO HIS MOTHER

[Tunisia]
October 28 [1933]

Dear Mother!

❊ ❊ ❊ "time" [magazine] arrives con punctilio & Do those pipple spik Owt . . . why you'd never Guess that karl marx's Whiskers were on the point of taking over uncle sam's Chin Wood you now. Or am I wrong?

Tritesky traitsky treetsky troetsky trootsky
tritsky throughout
tretsky trahtsky troytsky
trowtsky trowtsky trowtsky

will make sum ambassador,que pense-tu? And le toothpaste Litvinof pour le vrai proletaire & les cigarettes Stahlean & le rasoir de sûreté Lenin. —I'll bet Morrie's Bonnie Scot against the hole gang though! (always a staunch American,albeit guggenheimized for ye noncee)

well,must now prepare for an Arab wedding,whither the cook is escorting us with the aid of our neighbour Marsr Henson's Renault. ❊ ❊ ❊

96 / TO WILLIAM AND MILDRED O'BRIEN

[Tunisia
Fall 1933]

Share Beel A Meeldred

I am writing from a little palace by the c,in the Shitty of Doves; and simultaneously waiting for Mohammed to announce D.Nay of fried partridges with wine sauce.

It all happened through Marion's charm. She had no sooner posed(not as you naughty folks are thinking,but gorgeously attired per Lanvin Vionnet Patou, etc.)for Europe's leading fashion-photographer,M. le Baron Hoyningen-Huené,up to French Vogue,than the good nobleman suggested that she occupy his Arabian villa in Hammamet,Tunisie,Afrique du Nord,during his brief presence therein and his subsequent absence thereout—i.e.as long as she wished. Now Marion is One GOOD Girl;hence small i am here(for the aforesaid baron is to put it mildly an excellent sport). Merely to complete a tableau of luxe de la luxe,maybe 'twould interest you to learn that there's a perfect beach within the proverbial stone'sthrow, whereon doth disport itself le ménage Keemansh-Mohrhooz; and that,my friends,in the altogether(sic). R oui tanned?!

Alles ist hier misteeriohsum. Take "Hammamet",for instance. There be those which would basely derive its derivation from the word "hammam",to wit "bath";making our townlet into Bathville. Now "hammans" are no places for Parsifals;hence I myself prefer "hamma"("dove"):being,as you both doubtless are aware,a Parsifal in excelsis. So much so,ye childrens,that when it occurred to me that it was an obvious fact that everyone hereabouts—both native-per-se and gone-native—was an ambisinister disciple of hermaphroditos . . . you will kindly except the K M duo beforementioned . . . when,let me repeat,this constatation temporarily beclouded an otherwise limpid horizon, verily verily our hero was not unlike a voice crying in the well-known shrubbery. Possibly this point may appear less impacted were I to add that,should J-m-s Sh-ll-y H-m-lt-n appear here on let us say a Thursday,on Friday(or next)morning the wandering fisherboy—plying his exhibitionistic trade by the dimpling wavelets of the Mediterranean Ocean—would accidentally corral an effigy of extravasated epidermis,which some wit had stuffed with a motley collection of horseshoes bananas and hotcrossbuns. Or,to descend to the sublime:our nexdoor neighbour,a Jahjah queen,is at present engaged in rifling the hilltops within a radius of 50 kilometres and therefrom removing pre-Roman temples;which he is enabled to do,not by an unlimited income, but thanks to the aboriginal craving for rectal relief which characterizes Northern Africa. (You should hear him tell about it all,in his inimitable Southern accent,to appreciate what life really isn't;to put it softly.)

Well,mayzamee,how are use? Drifting from West to East on the restless Atlantic tide,rumours have arrived re notable fowl of a bluish persuasion which(it is hinted)are e'en now aperching on this and that door-post of little old ny. Hath Metro his? What does it all . mean,anyhow? Would an involuntary expatriate recognize the Grand Canyon? Will such birds survive rough weather? How about fertilizer? —When time hangs ponderous,lean upon your stylos to enlighten our ignorant bliss.

Am having 1 hell of a time trying to inveigle Uncle Tom's Cabin to become a ballet for Lincoln Kirstein. Hoping you are not the same,

Veuillez agréer,monsieur et madame,nos sentiments distingués Et Comment

97 / TO HILDEGARDE WATSON

[Paris
Dec. 11, 1933]

A Christmas Truestory
(copyright)

It was vairy veree cold in Paris. All French lay under a brumewave. Brume looks like smoke,but(alas)within that smoke is wrapped a whole platitude of cold. Estlin and Marion were cold. The reevs were cold,too;both rievez. Sometimes the sun shone like a Turner,sometimes nut;often neither:seldom boath.
   Our tiny pair had come up from a little place called Africa where never,nevvair,is et kald. There in Africa were flamingoes and fairies and burros with long warm strong thonglike ears and even an occasional scorpion. Born under Libra,Estlin did not see the scorpion;which disappeared into a double you sea. Marion saw it,but she was not afraid and so their existence passed like a day in the night. Effrica . . .
   Well,we got pretty hungry. The Kruger Millions from home hadn't arrived. Possibly they were delayed by Xmas weather? All Frunce lay under a brumewave. Dicky Ames ran low,too;his thoroughbred dog "A-r-r-e-e-e" had to go and get his ear almost chewed off and hospitals cost money. Then,too,

there was Lah Shoot Dew Dough Lar & I don't mean maybe as Americans are always quoted as always saying. But this story is intended to cheer you up;so we decided to do something. And something we did.

We went to the "Guarantee Troost",a company of whimsical folks without much meaning. They keep a "male department" however. Estlin was taking the part of "a Guggenheim addict" in the current amateur theatrical called Lay Bah Fonds, so that was his bank; the Triste. Marion and Estlin walked up to the Mele Dep't with beating hearts,wondering why they'd spent 1 franc 15^c each in Lay Maytroe . . . Marion was upbraiding herself for not looking up a new photographer to pose for

when I found your letter,I did a kind of bow to friendship; I am still bowing,after Eggs Something at the Café Weber(with a more than mortal Cinzano Sec);I shall probably continue this salutation for centuries to come!

please tell Miss Moore that I deeply enjoyed her Eimi article—can't imagine why she should reproach herself:she never did like doytee woydz & Am's probably full of them. —Besides, penguins are among my favorites,were,will be

(also please remember the Cummings-Morehouse to the Ann(e?)H and to the latter's singe-savant-Et-Comment)

we peer through Varieties, hoping for a whisper re SW(in Hollywood column or otherwise)

love to M

& J

######## HEUREUX NOEL!!!!!!!!!!!!!!!!!!BONNE ANNEE $$$$$$$$$

p ps) i'm constructing a new bookofpoems

ppps) hope to see you soon.

[4 Patchin Place]
August 1934

Dear Mr. Rowan—

thanks for your letter

I happen to feel that there exists one way of "helping" crea-
tors;which is,not hindering them:and that there exists one way
of not hindering them;which is,abolishing "censorship"

after proudly issuing which Emancipation Proclamation,the
President of the United States may humbly request Ezra
Pound to take charge of America's "arts"

* *Rowan, then Assistant Technical Director of the Public Works of Art Project, Washington, D.C., had written EEC asking if he had "any ideas to advance us as to how the
federal and state government and local organizations can best materially help individual
creative writers in need and the general cause of their field of expression."*

99 / TO EZRA POUND

4 Patchin Place
1/2/35

Dear Pound—

may I insult my intelligence by reminding me that you are
intrinsically what ye knights & ladies of ye slippery pasteboards
have nicknamed A Trump,while extrinsically you resemble
what those self-appointed stewards of a heavenly realm or
"spiritual roofgarden"(as my leaning from his unitarian pulpit
with his economicosociologico background where backgrounds
belong i.e. in front of you mightily father entitled it) call The
Last ditto?

there is a miracle in NYCity. This miracle is worth your travel-
ling to NYCity. This miracle is a "natural" history museum.
As one(if not two)would expect,nothing in this museum is natural. All the animals are not alive(this would be natural)or

dead(this would not be unnatural)but stuffed. Natural history museums are made by fools unlike me. But only God can stuff a tree;hence the trees are not stuffed,they are merely sectioned. I ardently recommend the tree room,in which is a sectioned tree,cross may I add,conclusively proving that it began growing 500 A.D. That is a very big thing for a tree to prove,Mr P; but that tree is a very big tree. The "rings",which are how a tree grows,have been counted and grouped and marked in groups and the groups have been labelled with flags bearing dates,Mr P,from the centre or birth of that tree to its circumference or murder. Of course if that tree hadn't been murdered,& murdered crosswise,that tree would have remained a mute inglorious milton. Naturally this milton would have been alive,but science doesn't care for this. Science never did care for what is alive,you know;hence mitrailleuses. What is alive has no sections,either transverse longitudinal or sagittal. Besides,what is alive has a strictly unscientific habit of growing. Corpses(if properly prepared)do not grow,hence anatomy. Close the window,Mr. Manship,I feel a draghtsmanship. Science,as we both know,cares for what my father(towering like a doge through unpunctual air cluttered with wishless refractions from fragments of prettily coloured infratransparency) thunderingly described as A Spiritual Roofgarden. # ¶ # Donnez-moi un arbre,SVP.

But to return to the unnatural itstory ponderum:having heard the old tree's story,we thank the old tree and proceed (for we are proceeders). We are now in the evolution room. A tree is just a tree but now we have left trees on our right and we have attained to a hollow rectangle pardon me cube full of evolution; evolution meaning all about animals. So now,I take it,we are at last among all about animals. And what do we find in this all about animals room? Why,a tree! Yessir. And not a sectioned tree either. Not an alive tree,of course. Naturally not a dead tree. Know. This tree is even more unnatural than you or I could believe—for it is a manufactured tree. I mean even that somebody made it in his spare time out of the ingredients of a discarded musicbox and a pair of old bicycletires. But mark you:every inch,née centimeter,of this multifariously manufactured & ceremoniously synthetic phenomenon or tree is labelled;just like the real tree but not the phenomenon we just came from. That is confusing at first,Mr P,until I read you a few of the labels. Scientists are of course pederasts,as we neither know nor care;& unnaturally enough this natural history museum is a temple or cathedral of the scientific spirit,so let us get a little scientific spirit for ourselves. Standing beside this strictly scientific and not alive and not dead and not even stuffed tree,Mr P,let us pretend(P is for pretend)that we are pederasts(no offence)comma too. I reiterate:to put the whole thing in a nutshell—let us start at the bottom. What is the bottom of this tree? The bottom is PROTISTA. What is the beginning of the trunk, just above the bottom? PROTOZOA. Welwel. What happens then? A branch,bedad. The name of which branch is which? Wel it seems to be two branches. I mean that there seems to be a fork,with two whichs,one which being ENTEROCOELE and the other which being MESO-BLAST. Pardon me,I have skipped a jellyfish. Not Forgetting COELOMATA but of course they don't really count. Let us return to the fork,please. It is something to hang to,if you don't mind;and I do. On the first branch are hanging starfish,sea-cucumbers,fishes,frogs,birds,an opossum(how did he escape the NRA?)apes,and merely what men call men. On the second branch are hanging spiders,crabs(not what you think)bees, earthworms,clams,snails,and a squid. I am sure I have forgotten something. Never mind. And you don't. Whatatree whatatree.

"Owe loog" a scientifically spirited descendant of the sea-squirt, aetas 9 in its last shortpants,gulped(entirely jumping before my at the moment merely cephalopodic self & totally—for an unnatural nonce—Owening not only the dendronous mechanism in question but All Evolution Personified. "Disis" our eventuel concatenation of rotiferous animalcules triumphantly continued "howe LOIF biggun!"

"Ugh-huh" its oledur bruddur almost fatally hazarded

—that sir,is Miracle Spirit for you:and well worth the uprooting of a foliate & doubtless immemorial phobia re H_2O plus x(And How)alias seawater.

But if anything else were required,My Consort will be on the dock to greet you in case the Official Committee of Welcome am asleep

gertrude steinie
let down her heinie
all on a summer's day
as it fell out
they all fell in
the rest they ran away

100 / TO EZRA POUND

[4 Patchin Place]
January 7 [1935?]

superruthianX transoceanic swat fabulously incinerates pilule
pink As Cowards Sheer and blushful beholder's bereft bor-
salino bounds proudly from soi-disant brains(item who in serene
glee suddenly stood on my head)paragraph

& so let's all begin next year all over again & let's all wake up on
the wrong side of the right & turn on the raddyoh & so let's all
get down on all fours & let's all become one big mitotic family &
all grow together like two little cells or something & so let's all
of us shut both our eyes wide and tight counting 1935 until I
say BOOdle when you drop another five billion conundrums
into Big Jim Farley's chaise percée because didn't Pollyanna the
Glad cry "doles are degrading" or something or what?

Item now the Murrikin pippils are a Patient pippels so long as
there's a Doctor in the house particularly when one of his feet
happens to be all the way down their Alimentary Canal while his
other hand is affectionately groping their Rectum Hesperorum.
We-wee, I didn't raise my P.W.A. to be a C.C.C. is ein chic
diastole if you've mastered the Longfellow or can step six rounds
with a Thanatopsis,poisonally ah pif furs dat unmitigated mo-
notony which is aptly occasioned by belatedly breathing on red
combs through green toiletpaper(& they shot McKinley). Item
the now one of two Broadway hits—"Thumbs Up" by John
Murray Anderson—harbours an excellent frankly- antikikeanti-
communist skit which frightens your welldressed audience almost to laughter(Did We Not Recognise Russia? Then Why
Allow Such Travesties On The Stage?); you'd like even more
however the even however less hoipolloi tapdancing of a very

certain Paul Draper whose mere accent grave(not Ruth, Muriel) recently I am informed informed(via picturepostcard from Moscow)some succulent aspi&perspi-irrational crony It Won't Be Long Now before Wussia Wuns The Wurld

owe, the petty of it paragraph. Jimmy(James)Light directed the then unknown O'Neill at MacdougalStreet's Provincetown Theatre which smelt like its formerly horses. Eleanor F. (Fitzie) Fitzgerald,a hothearted Irish nolongeryounggirl (who had nurtured her god Emma Goldman's A. Berkman & cordially outkicked the equally h.h. & l. police who arrived at her diggings to snatch him for anarchy during Ye War)insisted that Him be produced. Jimmy,I think he had vetoed the same,said oke & directed. Sibley the Watson put up le cash. It turned in that Him ran 45 minutes too long,horrifying all O'Neillists — whose idol had meantime moved uptown & was pouring thousands of $ into Ye Theatre Guild per Seerious Drahma beginning the afternoon before and ending the evening after;one ate,it is said,in the middle thereof. Jimmie took the book of Him to me;said:you cut what you think you can cut & I'll tell these pricks that's final. All NY "theatrecritics" puked except John Anderson(Hearst's Journal);Gilbert Seldes stood up on his toes & took a poke for art;crowds gathered;Him began "making money" — so Fitzie began paying the longdue backrent of the theatre so Watson put up de l'argent again. (Erin O'Brien Moore as Me). Paragraph. Years past. Light sweated(sic)over moneyworries by Night;his wife wrung sheets & painted a few but good pictures which almostnobody almostbought. Finally Hollywood. Two yirs passed. He returns, poor & a ghost;but a good ghost & Madame looks better than formerly even. "Gene" (O'N)now divorced,then married "Carlotta" hay hactress;inhabited France,hay shatoh;ordered on dit Moxie By The Case & on sait rit cosmic crab (Lizzierus Luffed). Time,present — James struggles with punks called "The Theatre Union" which produce Proletarian Melodramas at Eva(l'Aiglon) Legalliene's 14th Street Pippil's Tearter. (She moved back uptown). Fitzie is Unioning & a lot of exmacdougals & Jimmie is trying to sell them the idea of doing Coriolanus by making the crowd a Red Mob. Yes & do they like it? "Nothing" he said to me wistfully "is so conservative as a radical".

My own father being perhaps America's earliest exponent of a (then preexisting) "science" called Economicosociologico,very am naturally ignorant;wherefore cordially second your timeless suggestion that condoms become currency. A night-watchman in a floristshop encouraged my hope of snow;adding—just as your correspondent was sailing forth to destroy all comfort-stations & join the nearest Red Corner under mistaken Und Wie impression that Taste is not the Root of Aristocracy & vv— "IDDUD GIFFUH LODDUH GOYS WOIK"(meaning "iddud costtuh siddy $15,000"). Croyez-le ou non,cette neige n'est tombé qu'une fois et ça c'est pendant la nuit de '34–'35 while self was exploring Big Bad Bushwaws At Play meanwhile noting good friend Max Eastman ("art is communication")'s also Trotsky son * * * (whom Marion & I'd brought because his father highly approved and the kid seemed sort of kind of lonesome etc.)steer straight for the only woman in the room who inherited thirteen millions...dada. Ich glaube nel instinct

    Air For Muted Dumbbells
      by Kumrad Nyez Neyeoo
    (author of Lenin's Lullaby or
      day soitnly uhvengt Kirov)

        here lies a national hero
        (who goverened by fits and by starts)
        framed(it was well below zero)
        in a garland of petrified farts

          "but my good man—how can I knock you down
          if you don't stand up?"

101 / TO EZRA POUND

4 Patchin Place
January 29 [1935]

Dear Pound—

delighted to learn that you're casting your anchor and blowing newworldward!!!!!*

as to hostelries:you'll probably have to pay more than you mentioned if you stop at,say,the Lafayette(or else be bathless):there

are a few cheaper dumps in this vicinity but all somewhat dismal. Uptown,on the contrary,am told they're pleading for cus-
tomers—whereof I know nothing.

It's been colder than socialism here. Maybe you'll bring us a
real blizzard;so far we've enjoyed mere tempests. Dos Passos
tells me that "Bob"Minor is (a)in New York and (b)irritable.
The kumrads sound as if they'd folded. I recommend the Irving Place Burlesk(stripteasers in excelsis)& to hell with I.D.
Ology

—as usual

EEC

la signor(in)a sends congratulations to the seafarer. Let's know
when

> Lily Langtry & O.Henry
> used to live at the Chelsea
> Hotel—that's supposed to be
> circa your price ✳ ✳ ✳

° *Pound decided against this trip to the U.S.A.*

102 / TO JOHN PEALE BISHOP

4 Patchin Place
January 31, [1935]

Dear John—

> by way of glimpsing that esteem wherein the un-
> dersigned holds you,learn that he feels no need to
> apologize for my hitherto silence;yourself being
> one of the rare,and proud,souls who appreciate
> human what are called failings ✳ ✳ ✳
> have been epistling with Pound,whom yessed in
> Paris for a full ½ hour under lurid misapprehen-
> sion that his "Douglas" rave intended "South Wind";
> and he ups and hands Am [*Eimi*] such a boost as
> would knock Karl Marx's whiskers out of Benja-
> min G. Woozeythought's cabinet d'aisance;utterly
> destroying Kingrolls Punk Shovehard;so,meaning
> to show appreciation,I downs and forwards a dol-
> laredition

E R [*The Enormous Room*] with arrow pointing
to introduction . . . "the rest" so far "is silence"

Speaking of brainstormers and barntrusters and buggery
boobs—how's Mason Dixoning? does Hooey long? sommeil
aux porcs. `A bas Stalin. Mort aux vaches

Vive
the "basilique
d'esprit"

103 / TO EZRA POUND

[4 Patchin Place]
Saint Valentine [1935?]

Dear Pound—

I appreciate and approve of your reaction to the ER preface*
and am profoundly glad this little pickaninny feels unworthy
to convert any maneating missionaries

as 1 castration complex to another:"fuck" has been changed
to "trick" in n e w [*New English Weekly*] today arriving with editor's compliments.   This(said our hero with illdisguised re-
straint)settles the ? of Angleterre

I hear that No Thanks will occur in three editions(simultaneously)
> (a)"holographic",modestly priced at $99.00 per copy;and
> consisting of 1 poem—"the boys i mean are not refined"
> but keep it under your hat—by me written with pen and
> ink
> (b)&(c)successively less violently valued,and in which said
> poem is represented by its number and by a note refer-
> ring the reader to said (a) and by much blank space
> —also sub rosa—sub watch—sub ward

should a responsible(i.e.honest)European publisher wish to
make shine while the hay suns,let him or her(i.e.not it)so state
in writing to S.A.Jacobs,48 Charles Street,New York City,
U.S.A. who's prepared to furnish what are aptly called sheets;
thereby

Rebecca Haswell Clarke Cummings,
EEC's mother

Dr. Edward Cummings,
EEC's father

EEC and his father

EEC aged two

Family group at Silver Lake. EEC on the horse

EEC and "Elos," his sister

Family group. *Left to right, back row:* Father, Mother, Aunt Jane;
front row: Elizabeth, EEC

S. Foster Damon and EEC
at Harvard
(Moses Photo Studio, Boston)

M. R. Werner

John Dos Passos
(*Brown Brothers, New York*)

EEC, 1917

William Slater Brown, 1917

EEC, 1918

J. Sibley Watson
(Ned Hungerford)

EEC and Hildegarde Watson

Gaston Lachaise
(Paul Strand)

Scofield Thayer
Plaster cast by Gaston Lachaise
(John D. Schiff)

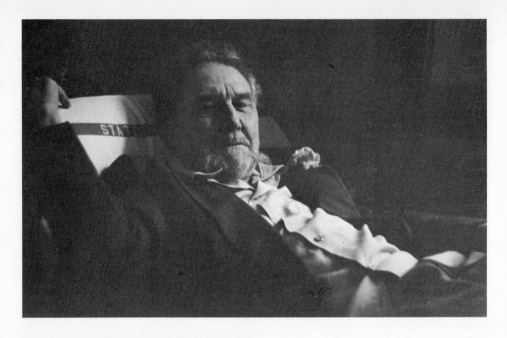

Ezra Pound, 1949
(Marion Morehouse Cummings)

Marianne Moore
(Marion Morehouse Cummings)

EEC in the 1920's
(J. Sibley Watson)

Anne Barton

EEC, circa 1939–1940
(Manuel Komroff)

Marion Morehouse Cummings
(Edward Mueller)

EEC, summer 1939
(*Marion Morehouse Cummings*)

A. J. Ayer. Portrait by EEC
(Marion Morehouse Cummings)

Allen Tate
(Marion Morehouse Cummings)

William James
(Marion Morehouse Cummings)

Sir Solly Zuckerman
(Marion Morehouse Cummings)

EEC and his daughter, Nancy,
early 1950's
(Marion Morehouse Cummings)

Joy Farm, Silver Lake, N. H.
(Marion Morehouse Cummings)

(1)saving the itless considerable time & money

(2)insuring that both versions(native and foreign)are identical as to content

(3)eliminating 1,356,249 socalled typographical errors — since J. sets up every poem himself on his own machine & a cloud of witnesses not excluding your humble proofread all

but speaking of tickets & theatres I'd rather plant potatoes in a blind man's pocket than suffer a single trick,or even an asterisk,at the prehensile hands of those lousy limies who are just so good no milkfed moron would trust their fifth cousins with a red hot stove he tactfully concluded,proving his opponent's point avec ees

° *EEC's preface written for the Modern Library edition of* The Enormous Room (*New York, 1934*).

104 / TO EZRA POUND

[4 Patchin Place]
February [1935?]

there,Mr P" Mr C said,tightening his vagina femoris by a not to say skillful adumbration of the trochanter major dexter(& with almost unequal pomposity flicking a horsebun off his left eyebrow)"we perceive the crux or gene of the matter." I too was at Bennington College,The Higher Education,meaning que les · demoiselles — of all dimensions and costumes — sit around eachother's rooms quaffing applejack neat;to read for 45 minutes,for 25 $. 1 girlinmate observed dreamily "we had a behavior problem here..." "what" I suggested "is a behavior problem?" "Williams" she answered "college is only 47 miles away. One night some of the boys—they had been drinking—climbed into several 2ndstorey windows and were found kneeling beside the girls' beds..." "anything happen?" I inquire. "Well" she remembered dimly "the faculty" (whose function is to unexist except when a BP arises)"decided it had better install a nightwatchman..." "anything happen?" I almost whisper. Vaguely "well" she said, and almost hopelessly "he arrested the first man he found on the campus that night..." "Who was?" I

venture. "The professor" she prettily murmured "of physics
..." & as your correspondent entered ye lecture halle 200
maidens were chanting for the 3rd time a poem concerning
Buffalo Bill—but what was the crux?something to do with one's
deciding to appear in public before one's(nonpubic)hair had
disappeared...—ah yes:vanity,sah!—there,Mr P" Mr C said, extracting a Woosevelt nickel from his armpit & carefully if not
decorously laying same on the astonished herrober's tray plate
or goingawaybasket "is the chromosome of the crisis." And with
that he farted so suddenly as to extinguish a Swedish match
held at some distance by a Lett named Doomer Fees who was
momentaneously sitting in his Chinese laundryman's garret-
window at the redolent crossing of Eggshit and Cowpiss Ave-
nues,Leningrad,duh brongz...

Bravo JoeGould—Esquire!!   where isn't Das Gingrich?wrote
twice but sans riposte °

we,I received Active Flowerword † & it's the only "anthology"
have liked (Profile excepted,if you wish);at Marion's suggestion
I even intoned pp179–181(at aforedit Kneeling Academy;
only to find,muchmuchmuch later,that meine hostess vas a
kumrad—however;"sombreros")and   especially   enjoy   pages
45 185–6 189–209
even made a visitor read&understand 185–6,not long ago.
Paragraph. Your own poems which I most aime are absent.
—Say isn't that a whale of a pp207–9 not that anything could
top her
      the lucid movements of the royal yacht upon the learned
                                 scenery of Egypt
     :......the shadows of the Alps
imprisoning in their folds,like flies in amber,the
                    rhythms of the skating rink

Thank you very much for both letters including the appreciated couplet & muchissimo re Notty [?] work at the cross-
roads. He & Jacobs seem already intercommunicado. My
greetings to George R et I

° *Arnold Gingrich of* Esquire *was interested in publishing a portion of Gould's* Oral
History.
† Active Anthology, *ed. Ezra Pound (London, 1933).*

snow,

March [1935?]

NY

Nuncle

this is a brave night to cool a courtezan unquote

if it would give you any sort of a kick to see Eimipublished in Albion,go ahead—provided there are no(sic)alterations. Otherwise,good nuncle,absent thee from felicity unquote. Ditto re poems. Leer. Omelet.

I like very much your extremely flattering "thoroughbred"-"steamroller" metaphor(one of the fool's favorite toys,when he too was young,happened to be a "rollerengine" & at least two of his friends were Horses)

Marion having quote turned on her charm,G— departed with an article which he didn't seem much to care for & about 40 poems. Don't know whether;but he said that if I'd holdup publication of No Thanks for 15 days he'd kill unquote a page of Aiken,substituting for the corpse a selection from C plus a drawing(by C);I arranged my quote end of it.

O yesOyesOyesOyes

"I'm always interested in the mental coefficient" I said (speaking of maladies)"and suspect that every disease has a large one;if we could only understand it". That's the way we were goingon. "Well" G said "I had a malady for 7 years which didn't have any mental coefficient". We were goingon like that;quite illiterately. "Really" I said:and then he told me...for 7 years his face swelledunrecognizablyup at the most unexpected moments—the first seizure(italic mine)occurred shortly after his wife's baby had been born—G asked the doctor who'd delivered her what to do and the doc said put cold water on it and forget it—things got worse;prodigious pain,partial paralysis,etc.—final seizure on a train,with his wife playing nurse& G practically non compos:she insisted he see another doctor—he did—2nd doc told G that the first doc's advice was "like telling a woman 'you're just a little

pregnant; but don't pay any attention to it;nothing will happen'"
(verbatim)so G had his tonsils out and is now "knocking on
wood" & hoping for no more seizures. (His own words for what
he said to doc one were these "I'm getting inflation—will I
burst?")PS the pain had something to do with "sinus"

how would YOU like to edit a magazine unquote for 25
people with 4 ciphers always after them:see Freud;persecution,
comma

more arrows to toi Sebastian mboi

v

s

SCIENCE

(just forwarded to me by a friend who is now in Hollywood)

> "The encounter(of the earth with a comet)would prob-
> ably not be harmless. A continent broken up,a kingdom
> crushed,Paris,London,New York or Pekin annihilated,
> would be one of the least effects of the celestial catastrophy.
> Such an event would evidently be of the highest interest to
> astronomers placed sufficiently far from the place of en-
> counter... Such an encounter would then be eminently
> desirable from a purely scientific point of view;but we can
> scarcely hope for it,for we must admit,with Arago,that
> there are 280 millions to one against such an occurrence.
> However,although the probability against it is so great we
> need not entirely despair.
> Popular Astronomy,by Camille Flammarion"

106 / TO HIS AUNT JANE

4 Patchin Place
some time in space
[March 11, 1935]

Dear Aunt Jane

* * * am fighting—forwarded & backed by a corps of loyal
assistants—to retranslate 71 poems out of typewriter language
into linotype-ese. This is not so easy as one might think;con-

sider,if you dare,that whenever a typewriter "key" is "struck" the "carriage" moves a given amount and the "line" advances recklessly or individualistically. Then consider that the linotype (being a gadget)inflicts a preestablished whole—the type "line"—on every smallest part;so that words,letters,punctuation marks &(most important of all)spaces-between-these various elements,awake to find themselves rearranged automatically"for the benefit of the community" as politicians say. Oddly,this malforming or standardizing process is technically called "justify"ing:thanks to it,the righthand margin of any printed page which has been "set" on a linotype has a neat artifical evenness—which the socalled world-at-socalled-large considers indispensable forsooth. Ah well; you should see the army of the Organic marching against Mechanism with 10,000th-of-an-inch (or whatever)"hair-spaces";you should watch me arguing for two and a half hours(or some such)over the distance between the last letter of a certain word and the comma apparently following that letter but actually preceeding the entire next word;you should hear my printer's blasts against his "operator"(as is called the Slave of the Linotype)when said unfortunate playfully smashes the machine while "he's thinking of giving Rocky-feller a bomb or something"(like all "operators",or all I've met, this bird is a communist). But something tells me we'll succeed—!

you may be amused to know that the other day there came a letter from Hollywood,a letter written by an excellent fellow and stating that a Mr. Von Sternberg(who directed,among other films,The Blue Angel)wished to purchase one of my paintings ("cheap"). Don't try to persuade me that those nitwits are going Intelligent:I know much better! Much . . . ❊ ❊ ❊

107 / TO EZRA POUND

[4 Patchin Place]
April 4,1935

Dear E.P.

yes,shall send you merci [*No Thanks*] hot off the Quoidonc. Respectfully prospectus hereby submitted(gratissimo)

Messer Gingrich bought,shortly after poems,a by moi versus-cranks article;at $150. (I only had to rewrite which & ain hoid uh woid sins). Re thy financial queery:Oinis is paid $450,on dit, for his monthly crap . . . pretty damn shitty — seeing as how another pugilist has just(on dit)been offered by your favorite perfidious Albion $250,000 plus 40% of any excess profit for one(1)go;which meer buggertail the latter(a hebe)is even rumored to be considering!!!NOW will you believe in the DE-PRESSION?(ecco enclosure).*

Paragraph

I met Stravinsky today — it is not a stone,thank God;he is a rock

* *Enclosure missing.*

108 / TO HIS AUNT JANE

[Mexico, D.F,
June 13, 1935]

Dear Aunt Jane —
"antes de ayer" as the Spanish are said to entitle "day before yesterday",was redolent of excitement-Plus. After a series of misadventures which I'll presently sketch for your esteemed delectation,Marion and I awoke halffrozen and almost penniless in a 16th rate hotel 8000 feet up in the air in a place called Mexico by the Mexicans and Mexico City by other people. Gulping one of the oddest breakfasts in human history we rushed to Wells-Fargo Express Company,expecting to find a letter from Mother,whatever mail had accumulated at Patchin Place during our absence,and a telegraph-order for $50. Absolutely nada(nothing). Very fortunately I'd changed my trousers,with a view to impressing the aborigines. And in the watchpocket of said trousers occurred — believe it or don't — one $5 bill! With which our hero dashed to a cambio(money exchange office),emerged with 18 pesos(Mexican dollars),wired urgently to Mother,and received — that very afternoon — at the Wells-Fargo mail department,a notice directing him(or me)to visit the nearest Western Union and collect "a sum of money" (in Spanish). Mother,being Mother,had wired $100:she had also written a characteristically cheerful and hearty letter;which promptly followed the telegram,giving us good news of Eliza-

beth and Carlton and containing this sentence:"A letter from Jane says she has $500 for you 'when he comes home—Perhaps he may need it by that time.' " —Well,my dear Aunt,you could have knocked me down with a proverbial plume!

Why?

Here's the story.

About 3 weeks ago,in New York,I ran into a boy whom I'd met years before in Paris. His father was running a magazine: he'd lent me a quiet room to work in and asked if he might publish some of my poems and nigh dropped dead when I told him he could have them for nothing. The boy's mother ✳ ✳ ✳ (whom I'd also met in Paris)—one of the world's wealthiest professional beautifiers(or cosmeticians,or whatever you call them). See any Cold Cream Bureau. Well:this lad had recently married & was leaving New York,with his wife(who appeared pleasant enough),for California,via Mexico(where he wanted to do some painting of Indians mountains etc.). The conveyance was a Packard "straight 8"(ask Philip),purchased secondhand with cash furnished by beautificationary devices;in other words,a present from Mama. Lad and lassy enthusiastically invited Marion and me to share their racer to Mexico City,to be the houseguests while in Mexico,and to drive up in style to California. Now it so happened that nothing more pat could have arrived— I'd had my hardest(to date)year in New York,No Thanks had been published despite 14 publishers,and our only chance of $ seemed to be Hollywood,where 2 of Marion's old friends were highlights in the socalled motionpictureindustry(one a director,one an actress). Therefore(having frankly explained our pecuniary difficulties,which were graciously poohpoohed)we accepted the abovementioned generous invitation & thundered away;bound eventually for Los Angeles and its suburb Hollywood,via New Orleans,Mexico City,and San Francisco.

So far so good.

The lassy turned out to be a complete moron of the omnivorously show-off variety. This didn't exactly surprise me;but it hurt Marion. After all,one woman doesn't enjoy seeing another make a fool of herself of her native land and of her husband. The lad(completely under moron's influence)disintegrated with a velocity which both hurt and surprised Marion and myself. To shorten an incredibly painful,if somewhat brief,story(you may yet read it somewhere;my pockets are full of pencils!)we found ourselves faced by the following problem: how to get to Hollywood,minus everything which our formerly wouldbe hosts had so cordially and even insistently promised. We decided to Lay Low until Mexico City,to there collect $50 which Mother had spoken of sending,to then move to a cheap pension with edible food(the native variety is appalling:or ask your doctor about Mexico,Typhoid,malaria,etc.),to temporarily relax(both of us were shakey with fatigue both physical and spiritual),and to trust to Luck. * * *

109 / TO EZRA POUND

Silver Lake, N.H.
October 3 '35

Dear Pound—

haven't heard from yer honor in a number of epochs & am naturally suspicious:what with Roosevelt growing whichfully Boulder at Hoover dam & Robinson Crusoe translated into Basic for the benefit of marinated moujiks & social discredit goosing Father Coughlin in the Alberta & the Quintuplets still taking nourishment & Lawrence puking posthumously all over his Doubleday Doran & Mussolini busily barking up the woebegone arsehole of Solomon! Sure an' 'tis a fine hoblate horange yer cronie Joymes Jace has uprightly decided to walk blindly upon. All the more cause,I'm thinkin',for a couple o'dizzily undelapidated & otherwise prematurely noncrepuscular correspondents like our blessed selves to hark forwardly backward into the pettifoggering salaami o' the ringstrakers & to cry oop fer a Mann named fer instance Thomas

"For distance in a straight line has no mystery. The mystery is in the sphere. But the sphere consists in correspondence"—what was I atellin' you—"and redintegration"—a translator's word, to be unsure—";it is a doubled half that becomes one, that is made by joining an upper and a lower half,a heavenly and an earthly hemisphere, which complement each other in a whole,in such a manner that what is above is also below;and what happens in the earthly repeats itself in the heavenly sphere and contrariwise. This complementary exchange of two halves which together form a closed sphere is equivalent to actual change—that is,revolution. The sphere rolls—that lies in the nature of spheres. Bottom is soon top and top bottom,in so far as one can speak of top and bottom in such a connection.   Not only do the heavenly and the earthly recognise themselves in each other,but,thanks to the revolution of the sphere,the heavenly can turn into the earthly,the earthly into the heavenly,from which it is clear that gods can become men and on the other hand men can become gods again."   (Joseph And His Brothers, page 205–6,Knopf publisher)

compare Gaudier [–Brzeska].

Come come,me fine boyo,quoth the flyder to the spi:haul up yer catgut out o' the pretty pond o' putrid politics & bait a strong rope with all o' yourself & jump you out right inwardly at the Isful ubiquitous wasless&shallbeless quote scrotumtightening unquote omnivorously eternal thalassa pelagas or Ocean

And just to prove there is nothing provable or I'm not joking, shall be sending you(in the was of an aeon or twain unless it's tomorrow-come-yesterday)one book of a ballet [*Tom*] which nobody here will produce by the oozing artichoke of impassioned ishtar

110 / TO DAVID HERTZ*

[4 Patchin Place]
9 mai [1936?]

Dear Dave—

your letter is as generous as you are.   Thanks
.#.
＊ ＊ ＊· improbably shall revisit California in 6 shakes of a lightyear,even perplexing Dinah.   Should like to see the rather long,but beautiful.   And the we are all well.   Not to mention a surely particular not to say firmly unique lookingglass(the homemade;with the pink moon in it).   I also want to learn how to lie on thunder precisely and slide up to all the most glorious girls at 70 mph.   Anybody behind us?   Look:4 are now stepping from stirrups of chevrolet into what sunlight immensest;1 quakingly wagers another it's colder than maybe tomorrow; comecome(a 3rd earthily cries)cowards die many deaths;& sand there shall be with our franks I mean sand et comment I mean sand by the jollyhut
..?..

take that white horse out of the blue bedroom before wrangel's
folly begins throwing telephonepoles at heaven knows who it
might make some of or are they waiters stop besides your don't
breathe ouch this Marion Dick Armitage Elise(what)the-hellppp
                    ...anyhow...
9 cheers for la vie

                    —salut!!!!!!!!!

111 | TO EZRA POUND

                                        [4 Patchin Place
                                        1938?]

        only come in Spring°
          e.g. when you feel
        i.e. don't auden your spender for any agent procurateur

item ⌠ "the more you shall ask,the more they will want"(Karl
      ⎰   [Marx?])
idem ⌡ "stick to your guns,doughboy!" (General Marx)

        re my error ("art is communication")
     remember that all "political minded" people, including women
                                        are simple people
      ″   ″   ″ simple people think
      ″   ″   ″   ″   ″   ″   that they are
      ″   ″   ″   ″   ″   ″   ″   ″   ″ honest
        which means nothing,which doesn't mean that they
                                                        would
        trust you(or even me)with a red hot stove

          ⎡ When Count Keyserling toured America,a statement
          ⎮   was
          ⎮ forwarded to all concerned,telling exactly what &
          ⎮   whom he liked to
          ⎮ eat drink & leigh,advising of the minutest details—
          ⎮ including   laundry—&   otherwise informing   this
          ⎮   country
          ⎮ that somebody had arrived. That's how you should be
          ⎣ handled kid & don't forget it

Marion is trying to get you better terms via some
livelier publishing bureau. I'll write or wire
if anything turns   ↑

° *Pound was planning a visit to the U.S.A. He arrived in New York on April 30, 1939.*

112 / *TO J. SIBLEY WATSON*

[4 Patchin Place]
2 14 apocalypse [1939]

Dear Sibley—

as Plato forgot to say to Aristotle I'm trying to borrow money.
This would be just simply lousy news in the best of milleniums;
and merely much worse if the borrower could offer security
collateral or whathaven'tI,instead of a vague possibility of in-
heriting 2 or 3 thousand dollars at some semicolon of the soi-
disant world's hertory when half a hen's arse might well be
worth its hollowness in hippopotami:however,honesty is the
best poverty as Aristotle immediately answered

recently a somewhat olden acquaintance who rather tends to dis-
believe that what he calls folks can even enjoy the finer things
of what she calls life on what I call a strictly munificent income
of $55 a month(not including rent)at least forever,it being the
proverbial member in good standing of a society more or less
dedicated to shall we say equating the invisibles with the visi-
bles by which I accidentally ask you to believe insurance,of-
fered me a ten dollar bill;meaning that if anybodies you know
haven't given their final shirt to the kumrads in hopes that
kahm de susshul revelooshin will ole it strubbriz("But I don't
like strawberries!—Kumrad,kahm de susshul revelooshin yewl
It strubbriz and yewl Lahk strubbriz")your correspondent'll
be the bestdressed kepitullizd under 14th st:which really makes
the faintest difference;if actually none.   Otherwise,as afore-
time! ✳ ✳ ✳

[4 Patchin Place]
jeudi [February 17, 1939]

Dear Sibley —

à propos de bloodless r,perhaps enclosed*might interest(if you didn't notice it).   Merely adding
   1) "columnists" stink
   2) Learned Hand is a wonderful name
   3) happen to have seen Brandeis coming into a New Hampshire clearing:he has fine eyes
   4) a once(also now,this is a great year)professor of economics who became the noman for impurely fabulous Case call up Uruguay and buy it Pomeroy said to me in the quote depth of the depression unquote "when anything" meaning anything "gets too big it falls to pieces" meaning pieces;and prophesied a separate N,E,S,& W
   5) heard some time ago that the top US army aviation officer,being asked why so many accidents to passengerplanes especially around the Rockies,answered you see the instrumentboard has become superhuman;and recently read that same's somewhat halved:but when M & I were at just 14,000 in complete mist between El Paso and Los Angeles a copilot of the brandnew('35)Douglas politely invited us in to behold all the pretty dials,which looked so like NY-by-night that I might have wept — if mercifully a much unjust too lofty mountaintop hadn't appeared quite all of three solid subjective inches away
   6) somebody who admitted he died in an earthquake observed between spoonfulls of Battle Creek seaweed that '42 would completely mark either the total disintegration or rejuvenation of the humanrace,and am pretty sure he hadn't read the first edition of Yeats' A Vision
   7) this,however,might mean something:compare Stravinsky's orchestra for Le Sacre with his orchestra for Les Noces

which is more than plenty for "immediate requirements" thank you most kindly for the 300 and am literally American enough to hope I'll be able to "make my own way" "some day" "soon". Seem to remember mon père telling me the best thing which could happen to you would be that what you want to do most should give you a living;anyhow,feel this is so * * *

* *Undated and unsigned newspaper article on Justice Brandeis, Judge Hand, and American economic policy.*

114 / TO WILLIAM CARLOS WILLIAMS

4 Patchin Place
April 15, '39

W si W—

this is a free country in a pig's arsehole number 305; and you would be a fine fellow anywhere,as votre was not the first to c'est and if friendship equals any personally conducted cruise Cap'n Fud guaranteeing Signor Pud [Pound] will meet all the right people I climb trees to avoid on earth may heaven give us each something all better

if etc the comet in question himself-not-a-can'to pound one afternoon,circa fünf,crying Marion pause This Is Doc Williams a beautiful admirer might usher you gratis into petchin's mubbul pelles. Until quite recently we were charging 25 cents to see me impritchoor:and publishing with the wellearned proceeds a leaflet whimsy comehither treatise lipshits or innuendo entitled Give Ireland Air

—à bas A Bas
¡vive Vive!

115 / TO JAMES ANGLETON

4 Patchin Place
May 31 '39

Dear Angleton—

in certainly printing a certain poem, *you and your confrère have paid me one deep compliment,and I heartily thank you both am not a "critic" — I hope — am a learner or impossibly someone who loves(which cannot be measured)what couldn't and will not be measured. Mostpeople are amorous of misunderstanding:tell them "I can't tell you" and they bark "so I'm lousy,eh?" But I can tell you "your magazine cover's the best I've seen" and improbably you won't mew "he thinks the contents stink"

enclosed — everything your correspondent has to say about my pictures;should be very glad indeed to have you quote it
* * *

° *In* Furioso, *the periodical of which Angleton was an editor when a Yale undergraduate.*

116 / TO EZRA POUND

4 Patchin Place
Thursday [1939]

Dear Yank

we returned last Sunday;since when(your warship being at sea)the enclosed envelope*has roosted on our door,waiting to crow. Much as I mostly loathe all joiners gettogetherers civilizationsavers and friendsofwaterclosets,more am glad that Ezra Pound has met the only living American young composer [David Diamond] * * *

we still wake up circa noon and still fall asleep toward dawn and still want to hear about a certain district known but not loved as of Columbia so why not 'phone GR 7-3919 beginning Saturday if you're still possessed of the twentieth part of a fin.

° *Enclosure missing.*

117 / TO HILDEGARDE WATSON

Silver Lake, N.H.
September 18 1939

Dear Hildegarde —

about 3 weeks ago,an individual or individuals of unstable habits or propensities decided I'd write you a letter;and try to tell you what a good time Estlin and Marion had this summer,thanks to SW. Then I said to myself "maybe Hildegarde would wonder why you wrote her instead of Sibley". Then myself said to me "nonsense:Hildegarde will understand perfectly. Beside,she might enjoy getting a letter from you". Then I rushed out into pitchdarkness,with a twelvefoot pole of no earthly value,to poke at two porcupines who were sitting in the best appletree; and did it,over and over,without any effect whatever. Then I fell into a mighty depression entitled Why am I fond of porcupines? which(before entirely disappearing)involved not merely Hitler and Stalin but actual fleshandblood humanbeings like let us say Abraham Lincoln. Whereat Mrs Samuel Ward [a neighbor] leaped nimbly from her odd little house(which was screaming with radio)and shouted "the German planes is over New York it's terrible aint it":I answered(evasive as always)I don't give a g G damn. The bottom thereafter nearly fell down off most of the wells in New Hampshire;while a queer wind blew,and Florence(who is not a city,as we thought,or a coon,but an English female born in Nova Scotia)became slightly aloof and wanted like anything to see her ancient mother—so what? the point being,Estlin and Marion haven't washed any dishes for 4 solid months("my dear" he often says to her,and means it "this is a dream")

some paintings and poems may(here's hoping)have made themselves

did Sibley ever see Ezra Pound?he zoomed into Patchin,all of a gloat and gasping against ✳ ✳ ✳ the heat and juggling all his mythical realities like "Possum" and "Brancoosh" and "Uncle Jarg";but I'm very fond of Ezra,and S is the only person I know who could have done any good,unless it's yourself! This correspondent will probably never forget the morning he woke on a hill with a brook beside him

1940–1949

[4 Patchin Place]
treize mai [1940?]

Dear Ezra—

have done what less I could to more your most generosity
around little joe [Gould].   Eg wrote Can(unquote)by;pas d'answer.   Then a pleasant ba from Stephen Rose Benét,at whom
had officially been referred my naked suggestion,claiming
ignorance of & curiosity re j g:replied phenomenon vide CPs
twosixtyone [261 Central Park South] must however be viewed
to be perceived,gave its address.   Coached Joe,which expressed
willingness sans astonishment con skepticism but(to undersigned's delight)announced Steve was "up my alley" apparently
via John Brown's body a certainly bookofthemonthclub selection
probably for years ago.   Ye candidate once depuis materialized;
there'd come no word from fame

Marion and I've glimpsed intermittently that steady admirer of
your warship named Fox.*   A sort of tortoise,I like them.   Full
of kangaroo.   Beaucoup freundlich

also rabbits.   John Reed.   Popped en route to Canada.   You
saved his mangled life.   You did a good job

high see can't casts no shadow itler & itler

* *Douglas Fox, who with Leo Frobenius explored African and Australian cave paintings.*

[4 Patchin Place]
dimanche [1940?]

Dear Gilbert—

concerning Lysistrata-the-second,*may I give you a brief written
reaction in place of the long oral one which circumstances pre-
cluded?merci.

Unless wiser men than myself are very vastly deceived,the Greeks(whatever they weren't)were — &,I should like to observe, still are for those lucky mortals who haven't yet tumbled into some barbarism—a luminous mature complex & rarely developed people

to interpret this rarely developed as primitive,this complex as simple,this mature as infantile,& this luminous as black,may constitute(for our mutual friend Jimmie Light)a pleasing tour de force

for me,it's an obscenity typical of the Ultra-epoch Of Superconfusion;id est a gruesomely perverse(=cruel)obscenity—the negro race being,per se & in its own right,A 1.

Such is my reaction,honestly expressed to an individual whose honesty I esteem;and now may the ignorant undersigned add that 'twas good seeing you again?

* *Production of* Lysistrata *by an all-Negro cast, directed by James Light.*

120 / TO HIS MOTHER

4 Patchin Place
[May 6, 1940]

Dear Mother—

Well,you could have boosted me over Memorial Hall with a waft of the proverbial feather when I got Jane's excellent(to put it very mildly)letter with your delightfully indomitable postcript! * So 'tis standing upon your eye you've been,madame— we've all heard of folk standing on their hands and heads and even walking thereon;but this rings the Ringling bell. Now(at last:and better late than never)your obstinate aesthetic offspring realises where his prodigious fondness for circuses comes from;and especially my adoration of acrobats. Wouldst learn a secret? Strictly between you and the moon and me— for the moon goes down but the moon comes up—acrobats have always been,& will always remain,the only truly and honestly miraculous things * * *

* *Relating his mother's recovery from a serious illness.*

Silver Lake, N.H.
August 8 1940

Dear Angleton —

* * * mailed you,at its own suggestion,a chocolate éclair fresh from the kitchens of Rapallo;trust Furioso fowarded same

I like Charlie Chaplin as is and my lightning raw;know nothing & care the proverbial less re Master Archibald(or Mistress Disney)'s "policies concerning anti-" or pro- "Hitler" or Big Lord Fauntleroy "ejaculations":but that last's a good word;and maybe,mah frenz,some dismal little dumbbell with a borrowed mustache might wake America out of the dryest wetdream on record

glad the poet Wallace Stevens sent you poems. I never wrote him * * *

122 / TO HOWARD NELSON*

[4 Patchin Place]
November 10 1940

Dear Mr Nelson —

thanks for your letter

the poet Hart Crane would thunder there'd always been and would always remain three sorts of people:warriors,priests, merchants. I imagine an artist(whatever his art)is a kind of priest,or perhaps vice versa;no artist surely is a moneymaker and no artist surely is a mankiller. Also perhaps:if enough skindeep socalledpeople are so confused about what they are that they'd itch rather than not be what they aren't,this so-calledworld will change hisher skin

also surely:if nobody ever escapes something(e.g. I avoided the American army,by visiting France with a Norton Harjes ambu-

lanceunit,merely to have myself drafted later and serve six
months at Camp Devens)only whatever is artificial perishes

* Who, while in the Marine Corps, began a correspondence with EEC which continued
intermittently for some years.

123 / TO EZRA POUND

4 Patchin Place
F. 1941

Dear Ezra —

your 14 Nov. (adorned with six Pegasus & 1 settingupexercise) *
greeting crashed Patchin on Monday December nine. To Hell
with subrosa & entrement sororities or fraternities,very particularly the pythian orders of moose. When callow thou hast
attained my humble servant's Experience,all thesey thosey get-
togetherys merely mean goosing one's self into a plentifully
perforated brownpaperbag,the worser to swim winedark
Hellesponts inc.

now something different's a fellow gets word to pay 250$ or hear
a jailsentence or fulfill his jury—"duty" (which he's already succeeded in dodging once)—the poor guy "serves". At least I
did. And that's a distant wail from muttering thankyouplease
to the Karl Wheeler Markam chair of contaminated desuetude
in Archibald Benèt's parlor de burys

swam at "Times Square" last "election eve" to watch me lose 15
berries re W. W.[Wendell Willkie], having(also to please my
family)once voted for the gent with artificial teeth that fell
asleep president & awaked Hughes. Mob = 42nd–48th. 3(three)
its looked as if they were trying not to be blown by horns:other-
wise nothing did everyone whatever at all.

Jim Angleton has been seemingly got hold of by an intelligent
prof & apparently begins to begin to realise that comp mil ser
[compulsory military service] might give the former a respite
from poisonal responsibility . . . maybe he's developing? Per
contra:last summer Ted Spencer dropped up with two dubs,one
the farflung Bessin Ganzesse yclept Laughlin;which mistakenly
afterward wrote addressing me as "immoral and rustic bard"—

who promptly announced "what I need is a thousand dollars and when I need it is now";celui-là muy languidly replies that so would everybody including him like a thousand dollars. Light house Robbie was correct.

The full is so world of a thing full of numbs,
& all we should think be as finger as thumbs.

Beside "Treasure Island" I put "Lorna Doone" Spring is coming. Two penguins salute you from our mantlepiece. The lady sends love & the elephant wishes bonne chance

P S and right soon

° Refers to the Italian stamps on Pound's envelope: six with representations of Pegasus, one with a Winged Victory (the "settingupexercise").

124 / TO HIS MOTHER

4 Patchin Place
[March 29, 1941]

Dear Mother —

* * * when you told me over the 'phone that you felt "ashamed"(I notice the same word in your good letter,received yesterday)I almost laughed out loud. There — says I to myself — is the genuine 101% New Englander! "You New Englanders" remarked Charlie Malamuth in Moscow,sagely wagging his handsome head "are strange folk." We are. I began to realise it years ago,when my friend Gilbert Seldes accused me of what he called "the egocentric predicament". If Gilbert had been a Catholic he'd have used another phrase — "the sin of pride". For what he meant was that really,underneath everything,I considered myself pretty dam omniscient. — Well,our hero (being a New Englander)vigorously denied all. But very gradually I began to notice that if something happened which prevented me from doing as I pleased,then(by Jove)I tended to feel downright frustrated:nay,even personally insulted! Talk about "childish"! Maybe,some day,I'll be blessed with a touch of true humility * * *

[4 Patchin Place
July 2, 1941]

Dear Warmonger —

delighted to hear from you!

wellwell:now that Hocus & Pocus Inc. har aving hit hout hin the hunblushing purlieus hof mudder rahsyah,mere oy polloy like I may(if you will permit me to mix a metaphor)sharpen our spoons and carve one deep breath

war comma at best comma's a gaseous thing semicolon but by gorry not until Hingland's W.C. got really hactive did us hill-williams start sleeping in our masks. I wonder what 151 th rate politicians like his jakes would ever do without bovine billions on billions just adoring to let go with both eyes in order to be led by one ear? Particularly,my erudite friend,don't read that liddl mesterpiss about yee poore prayinge Russianpeasants —unless, which Heaven forfend,your doctor has ordered you to the stomachpumps. Why,Morrie,the supercolossal twerps of ultra gigantic moviedumb(and thanks for flexing a femur in the Trib!)can slop better slip:nay,even(as one M.R.Werner hath it) a Waldo on a Frank's vacation ought to do emerson . . . although,of course,"the English make the best servants" (anonymous)

'twill be a stirring sight — King Herbert The First riding all the way from Times Square to the White House with Anne Corio on his saddlebow to inaugurate the Return To Reason,or,Why Bundle For Britain When You Can Fuck A Duck? Then will the Werner-Cumains Rubber Woman Company,seizing time by the foreskin,shower humanity with incredibly elastic and strictly indestructible canards. Then men will drink to Sir Francis Drake in beakers of scintillant cowjuice. Hoover will hand unto Howard Dietz a few Swiss francs to keep him from shearing his sheep before they're hatched;Maria Rogers will give short talks in Iroquois to the Sioux nation explaining what democracy means to every good American:Smut Alley will nominate Jack Frost for secretary of the exterior and Joseph Ferdinand Gould

will inherit the Mills.   Ducky's no name for it,pal;if you ask
Bing Crosby

but enough of crystalgazing.   The pen is mightier than the plane

126 / TO EZRA POUND

[4 Patchin Place]
October 8, 1941

Dear Ezra—

whole,round,and heartiest greetings from the princess & me
to our favorite Ikey-Kikey,Wandering Jew,Quo Vadis,Op-
pressed Minority Of one,Misunderstood Master,Mister Lone-
lyheart,and Man Without A Country

re whose latest queeries
 East Maxman has gone off on a c-nd-m in a pamphlet arguing everybody should support Wussia,for the nonce. "Time"
(a loose)mag says Don Josh Bathos of London England told
P.E.N. innulluxuls that for the nonce writers shouldn't be
writing.   Each collective choisi(pastparticiple,you recall,of
choisir)without exception and—may I add—very naturally desires for the nonce nothing but Adolph's Absolute Annihila-
tion,Coûte Que Coûte(SIC).   A man who once became wor-
shipped of one thousand million pibbul by not falling into the
ocean while simultaneously peeping through a periscope and
sucking drugstore sandwiches is excoriated for,for the nonce,
freedom of speech.   Perfectly versus the macarchibald maclap-
dog macleash—one(1)poet,John Peale Bishop,holds a nonce of
a USGov't job;vide ye newe Rockyfeller-sponsored ultrarum-
pus to boost SA infrarelations.   Paragraph and your excoed
Billy The Medico made a far from noncelike W.C.of himself
(per a puddle of a periodical called "Decision")relating how his
poor pal E.P. = talented etc but ignorant ass who etc can't play
the etc piano etc...over which tour d'argent the wily Scotch duck-
fuggur Peter Munro Jack 5 Charles Street NYCity waxed so
wroth he hurled at me into New Hampshire a nutn if not in-
candescing wire beginning "stab a man in the back but do it
three years too late":'twould hence appear you've still some
friends,uncle Ezra,whether vi piace or non

now to descend to the surface;or,concerning oldfashioned i:
every whatsoever bully(e.g. all honourless&lazy punks twerps
thugs slobs politicos parlourpimps murderers and other re-
formers)continues impressing me as a trifle more isn't than
least can less and the later it's Itler the sooner hit's Ess. Tune:
The Gutters Of Chicago

> ("make haste" spake the Lord Of New Dealings
> "neutrality's hard on my feelings"
> —they returned from the bank
> with the furter in frank:
> & the walls;& the floors,& the ceilings)

As my father wrote me when I disgraced Orne* —forsan et
haec. And the censor let those six words through

hardy is as hardy does

* *District of France, in which is located the prison where Cummings had been confined in
1917.*

127 / *TO MARIANNE MOORE*

4 Patchin Place
December 15 1941

Dear Miss Moore —

> Thanks for your essay in the May
> "Echo"(and who,by the way,wrote
> "an" excellent "editorial"?)
> which Mr Peter Munro Jack,more
> than oddly enough,has just shown me.
> You have(unlike many learned
> "critics" of this obloquyflattery
> unworld)a gift:appreciation.
> You feel and you express your
> feeling. That's miraculous

[4 Patchin Place]
March 21 [1942?]

Dear Ezra—

today is March 21,the First Day Of Spring;we honour you and
it,as(of November 6)you honour it and us. Beauty also sends
love

I have no and never had any and never shall have until having's
obligatory(which God forbid!)radio. This is not out of dis-
respect for you;it's into respect for me.* So happens the latter
individual doesn't begin if abovementioned endlessness occurs.
Maybe he's odd. Or maybe to corrupt—i.e. spiritually betray—
more people most quick equals the instrument of delusion beforementioned. As for de gustibus,all you young sprigs are
plumb unlucky:I,per contra,had as a kid a real musicbox

oldage entails,of course,socalled disadvantages. E.g. have spent
some months wrestling with(1)a game leg—"sciatica"(2)a bum
back—"sacro-iliac";both were eventually diagnosed(via Xrays)as
"arthritis". Am now up,& somewhat about,in a most imposing
corset;which I hope to be rid of before the time when birds
migrate. Maybe all said nonsense might be blamed on the war?
Anyhow,something's taught me what I never suspected:that
health is a thing of wonder;yes,all healthy people are per se and
incontrovertibly miraculous

"health and a senseofhumor"—that's my 82year mother's favorite slogan. And speaking of humor,Fox wrote me a high letter;
his first museum job's(guess)arranging a May Day ikon show;
Litvinov will appear in person. Why not? According to "Time"
mag,that very museum is very very advanced:every gallery being
wired for sound,pictures are interpreted while you gaze at
them;I gather nobody so much as drops a nickel in a slot,the
wisdom just gushes . . . and harken—by way of hoisting the
maninthestreet out of lamentable ignorance & through Art's
Portals,what do you suppose? Perfumes. Yes,the public's
nostrils are approached:did I say approached?tittilated. Now
match that,Mencius Praecox

shall presently hazard a prepliocene quatrain;mightily begging
you to vastly believe(a)that all characters and incidents thereof,
being purely fictitious,are not intended to refer to,and do not
refer to,any existing or extant person or persons(b)for the
simple reason or effective cause that—as thou likely wottest not
—such unfolks never were ever alive at all at all. I've translated
out of the original pakrit,running asterisks wherever plausible

> life might be worse
> no mouth can cr*p
> but somebody's ears
> are licking it up

which happily is seldom

° *Pound's "American Hour" broadcasts on Rome Radio included a talk on EEC's work
(May, 1942).*

129 / TO ALLEN TATE

Silver Lake, N.H.
August 18 1942

Dear Allen—

am delighted(being myself a student,however humble,of the
white arts)that you and Caroline [Gordon Tate] have completed
a novel by Bill [William Slater Brown, *The Burning Wheel*].
Quite useless to append:let but this triumph of telepathy honour
me with its arrival,I'll peruse the dit opus avec that disinterested
hindsight which asocially adorns one who hath never signed yet
(nor will ever,con Heaven's Good Help,sign)a blurb;who getteth
not lifts out of camels,neither diddleth his fellowyak par wireless—cries of "à bas ubris";sounds of knocking on wood—or,at
long least,who right vastly abhors all reversely snobful tossings
of pine before swirls. It helps nobody ps

Marion and I'd like mucho to visit les Tates chez eux. Shall
give you a wink when am off my at present peculiar diet. Also
at present,may nothing but scotch drink and little of which

greet jean l'évèque [John Peale Bishop] for The Queen and her
proud pawn

Silver Lake, N.H.
August 20 1942

Dear Miss Gooding —

here's hoping you'll accept a sincere apology for considerable
silence

am not 40 but almost 48.   Glad you appreciate the Rilke letters.
It's better that mostpeople should laugh,even at,than cry;isn't
it?   You'll find whatever I have to say about me on the jacket of
Him;and in the prefaces to CIOPW,the book without a title,
Is 5,the Modern Library edition of The Enormous Room,Col-
lected(wrongly:rightly Selected)Poems.   Nobody,believe it or
not,knows "why" anything.   Since you "go in stages",you're
perhaps beyond the Cummings "stage" already.   However that
may be,it's impossible to have "enough emotion";as for "experiences",the most profound I know are breathing:and
"enough words" would be a fine title for every novel.   No woman
is illdressed.   Live first,"want to" afterwards.   I suggest that you
read Shakespeare's Hamlet aloud,slowly,3 times;and The
Agamemnon of Aeschylus(see Loeb Classics)silently and more
slowly,4:then,if you like,let me know how you feel

* The singer, now Cynthia Gooding Ozbekian.

131 / TO M. R. WERNER

4 Patchin Place
June 15 1944

Dear Morrie —

* * *   "every coin",an obscure Yankee scribe once remarked
in Moscow,"has two sides".   E.g.:humanly speaking,this otherwise fair city scarcely exists.   For what is war?   "Nous vivons
dans un apocalypse" said Marcoussis "il faut être très intelligent".
War is an apocalypse,a "revelation":literally(in Greek)an uncov-
ering;a taking off of something(your hat)and a showing of
something else(your head) — not,as mostpeople ignorantly sup-

pose,a taking off of your head.   War means that true individuals show their true individuality:it also means that all unreally human beings become really unhuman.   Alors?   "The kick in the teeth"(and I had one yesterday;'twas number X^n)is bad,very bad;but always finitely bad.   Another thing,however,is infinitely worse.   Let us pray to Le Bon Dieu,my friend,that we may never turn into teethkickers   *   *   *

132 / TO ALLEN TATE

[4 Patchin Place]
October 30 1944

Dear Allen —

thank you for an always welcome letter,long(to my shameless shame)unacknowledged.   Olim [unexplained] approaches. Marion's walking in the hospital pool   *   *   *

lady reginald humphries(belie
-ve it or don't) had a vulva so wee
she disposed of the sexual
needs of lord rex through a l-
audably disciplined flea

133 / TO HILDEGARDE WATSON

4 Patchin Place
[Spring, 1945]
vendredi

Dear Hildegarde —

entirely agree with you about le philtre.   Never until Bedier had I realized how a story can be greatly told.   If "Tristan Et Iseut" were merely onedimensional(human),Marc would be the true hero;as Arthur is the true hero of the Launcelot and Guenivere romance.   Magic adds another dimension:whereupon Tristan and Marc both become heroes.   Finally,fulfilling every com-plexity,comes a third dimension — "la courtoisie de Dieu".   Did any mere treatise on the meaning of that Courtesy which is Christianity ever begin to touch our poet's ten words "les hommes voient le fait,mais Dieu voit les coeurs"

today a long awaited letter from Mrs. Moore arrived. Shall try to write something for the catalogue [for a showing of his paintings at Rochester]. And if you'd very much like me to make a speech,I'll more than gladly do my best;although,toutfranchement,should infinitely rather not. Singing birds shouldn't talk

yesterday a wop came out of a store,got into a parked car,backed up,knocked down Marion(who was standing in the rain,waiting to cross 6th Avenue)and would have run over her if passersby hadn't yelled. She got up,made him drive her to Patchin Place, took his number,changed her clothes,lay down for a few minutes,then arose,made tea for me and a couple of guests,and rang the big elephant-bell. I thereupon descended from my pied-à-ciel to find her radiantly entertaining the company

134 / TO HOWARD NELSON

4 Patchin Place
May 26, 1945

Dear Mr Nelson—

allow me to congratulate you on many things,e. g. being "the only second lieutenant in the batallion",losing nothing more than your "clothing"(most of the socalled civilians hereabouts are playing admiralissimo like mad;having long ago parted with even their sense of humor)and enjoying a fine ocean-view. Speaking of <u>La Mer</u>,how about <u>La Cathedral Engloutie</u>? It might perhaps cheer you to hear that America's leading critic of music,my friend Paul Rosenfeld,dearly loves Debussy

your extelephonic bard reminds me of a mighty scientist of my acquaintance,who may or may not be mad:anyhow he insists that my little poem "ygUDuh" exemplifies the very latest(post-Einsteinian) mathematics. As nearly as I can make out,science is halfwaking up to what Santayana(in his "Realms of Being") calls "eternity"—nothing everlasting,something nontemporal. Let me add that I am not a Santayanian. But as William Blake

has far from infrequently observed,only the imaginary is indestructible.   If Mr S,being a disappointed poet,delights in calling this only indestructible actuality "nonexistent",that's his funeral
* * *

never met Gertrude Stein;but,as a "speaker" at [Harvard] "commencement",recited a few of her Tender Buttons which laid "them" in the aisles.   "They" also fell noisily for Amy Lowell; whereas President L [Lowell] (solidly seated a few feet from tremblingly standing myself)didn't.   (The year was '15).   As much of G's latest book as your humble could subtract from the whir of again&againingness seemed goodcommonsensical,nay better uncommonnonsensical,prose

my own tiny theory re the latest unpleasantness may amuse you. Le voici.   Once upon a time,there was a country inhabited by very ignorant and disunited red communists.   Certain very united and ignorant foreigners arrived(the usual "dirty"—so ignorant that they called the aborigines "Indians")& did-in said aborigines by force and by fraud.   Today the proverbial wheel has come full circle.   A new species of red communists,even more ignorant than their predecessors but excessively united, are doing-in the ditto-ignorant but disunited descendants of the former doers-in-by fraud and by force.   Et voila * * *

135 / TO LLOYD FRANKENBERG

[4 Patchin Place
1946?]

Dear Lloyd—

6,000,003 thanks for your both good letter!

if I'd seen a Human Fly,pausing just halfway up the outside of the Chrysler Building,produce from his left hippocket a five-poster bed in which he immediately lay down and fell peacefully asleep,maybe the aforesaid achievements would seem less extraordinary ¶
several millenia ago,when I was on safari in Bozoland,my dusky native bearer(especially chosen for his fleetness-of-foot)spon-

taneously pursued a desultory shot inexplicably departing from the carefully unloaded mechanism of my supercrocodilegun in the exact direction of the local Crown Prince's Uncle(a charming old multiwidower)and,neatly plucking that egregious faux pas from our almost-victim's nightblack vicinity,returned it to me with the courteous explanation "white-man drop some-thing"; which,at the time,struck me as a remarkable bit of tact:but no longer

again,when not unrecently called upon in Paris by Eduard Sept ("a broth of a bye" as Dan Parker would say)to dedicate the infamous House Of All Nations,then enjoying its opening night,I felt considerable amazement à propos of the costumes of my audience(all,naturally,members of the fairsex)which consisted of a onecentstamp;nor was "the shock of recognition"(as Edmund Wilson would say)precisely diminished by the observation(made by glancing in a fiftyfootsquare mirror which perfectly reflected a queue of unmistakable males stretching far beyond the Opéra)that via His Majesty's explicit command each prospective patron of the royal if nefarious establishment had been provided with one of those convenient gadgets employed by French postal clerks for the purposes of cancellation:however,I somehow pulled myself together and delivered the requisite oration in what a goodly gathering of peculiarly unsympethetic newsfolk were so generous as to entitle impeccable esperanto — but that sans exaggeration herculean effort seems as naught,Lloyd,compared with your double own

finally,let me state frankly that until receiving this brace of epistles I'd been impressed with the sangfroid of a gorilla who, during the late unpleasantness,casually reached through the bars of his bower in Hambourg's worldrenowned zoo and,extracting from the merest spectator a very complicated timebomb which the latter had foolishly concealed in his navel,instantly swallowed same;without the slightest damage to anyone present including the Kaiser,for whom(oddly enough)it was never intended:we therefore "live to learn"

allow me,as a gesture of affection and esteem,to enclose a poem sent this afternoon(by request)to a doubtless unspotted editor named [Theodore] Weiss * of a N. C. lilmag of announcedly nonpolitical tendencies;or at least they call stoutly for contributions which shall attain "the guts of tradition" . . .& kindly comprehend,my friend,that I'm in no manner shape or way attempting to compete with anybody,including that maneatingcoterie of mailed lyretwangers,for irrevocable specimens of whose impenetrable affluvia the undersigned remains your(speaking mildly)debtor

° *The poet, editor of* The Quarterly Review of Literature.

136 / TO PAUL NORDOFF

[Tucson, Arizona
Jan 31, 1946]

Dear Paul—

delighted,and more than,to hear you've been(however briefly interruptedly or otherwise painfully)composing:that's infinitely the best news you could have given me!

perhaps the undersigned dimly appreciates your major difficulties through a hereabouts minor version thereof;anyhow,am only beginning to(perhaps)begin to work,or(in other words)to be. Arizona's inhabitants are doubtless agreeable by contrast with Michigan's;but(believe it or don't)I've never before seen so many ghosts at once. Ghosts of what? Haven't the feeblest idea—can merely affirm they wouldn't inexist an hour East of Chicago. Particularly confusing isn't the unfact that almost nobody ever seems quite real,& is the fact that almost everybody appears bent—sic—on gooddoing. Mais assez de ca;or(may I quote Confucius?)"gentleman blames himself,ungentleman blames others". & I'll quietly add that,if Tucson produced a Shakespeare the Battle of Agincourt would become a submondayschoolpicnic for ungrownnonups

heartily wish Marion & I could have seen that wonderful Xmastree;the next best thing's your description. (Does the Tao sign, then,equal the Venus' mirror— ♀ —which means "female" in scientific plantlanguage as Mars' spear means "male"— ♂ —& the "perfect" or male&female sign ☿ means what laymen call a flower?) On Cristmas Eve I sat opposite a Papago Indian(married to a New England archeoethnologist;both,let me reassure you,très sympathique)simultaneously discussing the fall of Catholicism with a kind & impoverished granddaughter of Majeska & the rise of aesthetics with Waldo-Pierce-the-painter's lively & enormous sister. Marion was meanwhile just a little(but don't forget the wideopenspaces)way off,seated at a tablefortwelve-orso;she survived charades,whereas moi je me suis sauvé after glimpsing our host disguised as a-bull-at-a-bullfight & he wore real steer's horns . . . tintinaBULLation,mon ami * * *

137 / TO ALLEN TATE

4 Patchin Place
June 6, 1946

Dear Allen—

here's your(7 x 9¾)frontispiece *

it's a simple linedrawing in leadpencil—nothing complicated & gaudy—because "Santa Claus" is neither gaudy nor complicated. It illustrates the play's almost final moment—Santa Claus revealing himself to Woman—because that's the play's climax. And it symbolizes the whole aim of "Santa Claus"—which is to make man remove his deathmask,thereby becoming what he truly is:a human being

I hope that you and an extremely sensitive fellow Morrie will like my drawing. If anyone should ask why only half the face appears,tell it him or her that the face's other half is still in the shadow of the mask(death)

* Allen Tate was then an editor of Henry Holt and Company, publisher of Santa Claus.

138 / TO HIS MOTHER

4 Patchin Place
Sunday January 5 1947

Dear Mother—

* * * Cyril Connolly,the editor of "Horizon" magazine (much the best periodical concerning socalled literature;& pub-

lished in London)has been wining-and-dining Marion and me in celebration of a(let's trust)soon-forthcoming English edition of 1 X 1. * * *

he told us one story which might amuse you. The "literary editor" of one of America's biggest(CBS?)radiorackets,a woman,was questioning Mr C before he "went on the air" — "and what is your religion?"she asked him. "Cummingism" he replied. "What?" He repeated the word;then,since she obviously understood nothing,added "I'm a devotee of your American poet,E.E.Cummings" — "you mean you <u>were</u>" she corrected him. Mr C was surprised. "No" he maintained "I <u>am</u>." The "literary editor" gave him a pitying look. "How can you say that" she asked "after the terrible things he did!" "What things?" asked Connolly. "Living in Italy and broadcasting for fascism:don't you know he's a traitor?" Connolly blinked. Then he understood — "you're confusing him with Ezra Pound,aren't you?" he asked politely. She shrugged. "O well" she said "it was one of those three — Eliot or Pound or Cummings" * * *

139 / TO HILDEGARDE WATSON

4 Patchin Place
January 22 1947

Dear Hildegarde —

an extraordinary human being [EEC's mother], someone gifted with strictly indomitable courage,died some days ago

she was eightyseven,very deaf and partially paralyzed;young of heart and whole of spirit. In her will,she asked that her eyes(which had never failed her)be given to any blind person who through them might see. And her last letter to me and Marion (obviously written with supreme difficulty)ends "Please excuse this writing"

such things I find wonderful:and,feeling that you love what is wonderful,I want to share my admiration with you

4 Patchin Place
February 17, 1947

Dear Mr Cornell—

thanks for your good letter of February 10

Marion & I are naturally delighted to hear of your success
with Ezra. Please accept our heartiest congratulations

thank you also for enclosing a copy of Mrs Pound's letter;&
let me add that I'm glad she's aware of her indebtedness to
yourself

finally:thanks for the two statements,one in behalf of & the
other by Céline;which I've taken the liberty of forwarding to D
Jon Grossman(219 Washington Street,Winchester,Mass.)who
expresses great admiration for Céline's prose & is,moreover,
personally interested in the Céline case. I presume you're already in touch with Milton Hindus,whose A1 article on Céline
& censorhip appeared in The Sewanee Review about a year
ago?if not,his address is 5459 Blackstone Avenue,Chicago 15

as for me,it so happens that(atop all my various other failings)I
never under any circumstances sign manifestos or join groups—
& almost never participate in "symposia". Despite(& possibly
on account of)this fact,my sympathy with Céline's cause is far
from negligible. To say that I wish him & his supporters the
best of luck is not to exaggerate. I don't,however,regard Céline as a poet. And he is not my friend. Pound was(perhaps
is)my friend;& I consider that any human being alive today
owes him an immeasurable debt. Why? Not because,as a re-
former,he has tried to pry an unworld out of its nonexistence;
but because,as a poet,he has created particular beauty in an
epoch of universal ugliness

please remember me cordially to Varèse & Patchen if you see
them. And here's hoping for an early spring

° *Ezra Pound's lawyer.*

4 Patchin Place
samedi [1947?]

Dear Ezra—

the question Is Joe Gould Crazy strikes me as,putting it very
mildly,irrelevant.   For "crazy" implies either(crazy)or(not).
And badold goodyoung either-or is okay for movie—i.e.
2dimensional—"minded" mobsters;be they "intellectuals" or
be they "proletarians" or be they neither or be they both or
etc.   But Joe happens to be 3dimensional:i.e. human

4 Patchin Place
March 21 1947

Dear Mr Friedman—

your good letter is welcome.   Thank you

as it happens,taste is what matters to me;& I feel I don't exaggerate in saying that my taste isn't everybody's nor should I
wish it were

take,for example,the above address:"4" signifies a delapidated
house perhaps 100 years young,perhaps younger.   If asked
"why" I live here,I'd answer "because" here's friendly,unsci-
entific,private,human.   Actually I live here in 2 places:away up
& away down.   The larger(groundfloor)"apartment" is really
Marion's;but she shares it with me & we both share it with the
socalled world—& sometimes entertain(more often are entertained by)our few friends.   The smaller(topfloor)"studio" is
where I go to be alone & do my work

now between upstairs & downstairs,on the middlefloor,resides
a man(I use the word generically)buried in a perpetual night-
&-day bath of radio.   I have been at some pains(& pleasures)to
understand this man,& feel justified in stating that the under-

signed is not incapable of describing said man accurately. Radio is to him perhaps a shade more indispensable than eating;much more important than breathing,in any case. He is a "young" man,little,very lonely. Whereas Marion & I are so complexly constituted that we cannot live without privacy,he is so simply misconstructed that he cannot live with it. Needless to add,the socalled world—being based on what "psychiatrists" call "the strength of weakness"(sic)—is 1000percent his: not ours. If this little man simply halfturns a little knob,"life" becomes literally unendurable for the individuals under & over him . . . & they have no redress whatsoever. None

but(by God's Grace)this little man is friendly,not in his way unintelligent,& wellmannered. Being friendly,he doesn't want us to hate him. Being not in his way unintelligent,he somehow realizes that individuals may be innately different;& although he's very sorry for us because we can't "enjoy life",that's that. Being wellmannered,he feels that the fact that I've been peacefully living here for 20some years(whereas he moved in recently) gives me a social status superior to his. Were he illbred,he would feel himself an intruder & hate me for not being an intruder. Were he stupid,be'd be unable to imagine how anyone could exist minus a collective delusion. If he had no love in him,he wouldn't give a damn. But,being himself,he respects others. He lowers his gadget until(a)he enjoys it while(z) others are not destroyed by his enjoyment

all this—the 2 perfectly different tastes,the 3 floors,the old house—is a metaphor,a parable;& I'll thank you most kindly to keep it to yourself,unless you care to share it with my trusted friend Professor [Theodore] Spencer:for(believe me or don't) the last thing I'd like to do is to hurt the little man,the beneficiary of "science",the middling-weakling. I felt that perhaps this parable,this metaphor,might help you to understand me. If it doesn't,I'm sorry. If it does,I'm glad. That's all:except that I'd be very happy if you'd do me a deep favor. Never,come Hell or High Water,read a word of mine or look at a picture of mine or(if possible)even think about me & mine while any mechanical unsubstitute for experience is anywhere even slightly audible

* Who was then a Harvard undergraduate planning to do his Honors thesis on EEC and who has since written two books on EEC. See also Letter 149.

4 Patchin Place
April 25 1947

Dear Ezra—

Hearty <u>congratulations</u> from Marion&myself on your <u>grand</u>-fatherhood!!

As for Uncle S's Archeological Academia:I cheerfully grant that conceivably same might be rendered at any rate infracontemporaneous via perfervid activities of some 6fisted Sir Galahad(Launcelot,si tu veux)more than hypothetically ensconced, against sure suffocation,by—kindly allow me to mildly suggest—a seamless suit of stainless steel superarmor which(encore conceivably)12 "good" nonmen and women,all machine picked diplomatists of The New School For Soft Knocks,might semisuccessfully(later)subtract with cautiously&how-orchestrated caressings of(putting it softly)an hyperblowtorch. Soit. Mais moi(espérons)je me suis pas—&,God willing,shan't be—so humanitaristically de- or im-personalized as to glimpse in any search(even the abovementioned)irrevocable triumph of m over m as something remotely approaching major significance. Not that 'tisn't quite pleasant to know whence one's après-demain(or demain,let us modestly say)meal arriveth. But more & more,as I grow,is the antediluvian undersigned delighted by Doctor Jung's terrafirma riposte when a desperate wouldbe dogooder demanded what can be done to make better the world?quote Jung,make thyself better. Truly a Greek might have said this(and did)yet imagine a Swiss! We're,Madame GStein announced just before her departure,in for a strange epoch—well,only a few days ago(when our nonunhero was worth 25 bux)the very most vulgarest mag in even America offered him 500 for "right" to reprint,come next Xmas,a little moralityplay called Santa Claus—naturally I couldn't accept the(if such it were)compliment but that's neither ici nor là

4 Patchin Place
May 27 '47

Dear Ezra—

re latest letter:having mircrotelescopically explored the hypere-
insuperstein expanding-&or-contracting universe of finite-
butunbounded chinoiserie which only our illimitable contempt
for soi-disant fact impells us playfully to misnickname your
handwriting,Marion & I have concluded(not before frequently
crashing through the skylight of script & discovering each other
in the cellar of ignorance)that you pay me a multidimensional
compliment. Merci

concerning subsequent postcard:its absolutely decipherable
queery regarding the recent juxtaposition of two Harvard graduates somehow suggests a pronunciamento of JFGould viz
"the only reason a woman should go to college is so she can
never say O if I'd only gone to college" &a)DHThoreau's
description of the shantih Irishman. I found your friend
[T. S. Eliot] wearied(as was natural)& kindly(as is surprising)

You might be enlightened to learn that the other day,at what
amounts to a booksellers' banquet-to-publishers somewhere
uptown,Mrs. WWilkie & Mr CCanfield & other ultraintellec-
tuals exhorted fortissimo any & all Caxtonians present to(1)
delete intolerance from,&(2)insert tolerance in,all & any manuscripts submitted by aspiring & other authors. The ample
audience(quoth my trusty informant)swallowed its lambchops
sans blush

I still feel that the proper study of mankind is woman & how
did you like Mr Watts elucidation of your current idiom in the
Yale Poetry Review?

4 Patchin Place
June 1 1947

Thou rogue—

if anyone living could induce me to abandon my native land in her hour of greed,'twould surely be use;but the(as it happens) undersigned prefers beauty

so much for who runs may read. Per contra(alias entr' our-selves)a not unrecent peep at Tears Eliot,or maybe 2 1-s,has mightily confirmed my negligible suspicion that be it never so humble there's no:Solly,after entertaining that hombre for 15 minutes you feel like taking out a patent for manipulating the dead

quite another preternaturally distinguished cosmopolite once-uponatime told Marion & myself that he soberly spent a non-nonsensical afternoon meandering all over some suburb of Stalingrad formerly entitled London while crying loudly(& very voluntarily)"caviar for the upper classes,peanuts for the lower classes". This beatitude,it seems,had been imagined by an enlightened butcher. Well,we were amazed. Finally I said "Freddy [A. J. Ayer],wouldn't 'peanuts for the prole-tariat' have been better?" but he couldn't seem to decide. And that,since you don't inquire,is what's wrong with Europa

all my heart is on a new hampshire hill gifted with blue moun-tains. Yes;&,but for the miraculous persistence of what(I very fondly assume)we mutually revere as the touchstone of human nature namely(in 5 syllables)a sense of humor,thou couldst take ye holee pinke unracee & stick same up Joe's cornucopia

* *British zoologist, Chief Scientific Adviser to Her Majesty's Government since 1966.*

4 Patchin Place
lundi [1947?]

Thou (Rogue)$^{n\,3}$ —

* * * or as Sing observed to Wing when the Hoo
dynasty quite expectedly collapsed
>   give our sadists carte blanche in atomics
>   let our massochists flaunt economics
>   — if I understand Freud
>   noone need be annoyed
>   while our narcissists stick to their comics
period * * *

147 / TO HILDEGARDE WATSON

[Silver Lake, N.H.]
September 21 1947

Dear Hildegarde —

well,you're a saint(not to mention anangel)sending me,for the
second time,just a book whom I'd never met and who would
cheer me most!

this am enjoying even more than Rilke's "Letters To A Young
Poet";& perhaps because here I recognize a variety of feelings to whom I want to cry "you are my own!" — rootfeelings
who perhaps have,over a span of some thirty years,become
poemblossoms . . . but of course these feelings are no more of
me than of Count Keyserling and DHLawrence(and a Chinese
professor who spoke,long ago,at Yale;saying that the East
does not want "progress",does not want lipstick & movies
& equality of the sexes & le jazz hot & "democracy")& of many
other human beings since the beginning of beginning but also
before. "Better to follow your own dharma"(writes Keyserling
in "The Travel Diary Of A Philosopher")no matter how base,
than the dharma of another,no matter how noble. Never will
mankind become human(cries Lawrence,in an essay which Ed-

mund Wilson miraculously includes in "The Shock Of Recognition")until it rises up and smashes its machines. And,in your latest gift,immediately find a vivid contempt for precisely what Santa Claus encounters as a WheelMine:the evil of all Western "knowledge",alias "science",based on a "conquest of nature"!

have you,by some chance,a copy of "Life" magazine for September 15? If so,glance at an article called "OUTSIZE GOVERNOR". Note the climactically arranged photographs — man dancing(p 59),"resting his oversize feet"(60),eating supper barefoot in the kitchen(62),& finally "IN BATHTUB Folsom has to double up."(64). Can someone imagine what any moujik coolie or hophead of any crevice of the Orient would sense, upon receiving such a gospel? Maybe you & I can at least suspect . . . "mad". Ah, but Lear was mad;but mighty creatures & colossal beings have been mad:but the magnificent earth màcy become mad — it's not Madness we hate or fear! Madness may be noble or base;but not mediocrevulgarobscenedull

148 / TO CICELY ANGLETON

4 Patchin Place
November 11 1947

Dear Cicely —

a fine book you sent us;so fine that Marion & I feel sure its author is(as one strangely perceptive NY reviewer suggested) Isak Dinesen. And there's an extraordinary person! Believe me or don't:although Out of Africa,Winter's Tales,&(my favorite)Seven Gothic Tales were all ballyhood by some "book of the month club",I've scarcely met anybody,literate or il-,who could appreciate her achievement. A "writer" to whom I lent the Seven returned them coldly,remarking 'twas a pity she didn't know the past tense of English irregular verbs — true enough! over & again,Dinesen will put "did say" for "said" or "did think" for "thought". Alors? She builds(like Shakespeare)a multidimensional world:like him & like El Greco & like Bach, she composes fugually. To watch a Dinesen motif state itself almost imperceptibly — & then occur upsidedown & reoccur wrongsideout;to finally emerge,triumphantly&magnificently

As Is—makes the undersigned marvel that what Ezra Pound aptly called "the mamie-slept-in-the-sewer-school" of "modern writers" can dare lift their mommapushedpoppaoutofthewindow "democratic" unheads. After spending a dollar to buy the Seven,I worked about ten days discovering the plot of The Roads Around Pisa;& should enjoy learning how long it took(or,if luckily you've never made friends with this masterpiece,will take)you to do the like. Could all the Flakners in Missouriissippi ever dream of Peter And Rosa? And what a miracle of momentous complexity is The Poet! * * *

149 / TO NORMAN FRIEDMAN

4 Patchin Place
January 27 1948

Dear Friedman—

the heartiest of congratulations from Marion and myself!

can well imagine how you felt while the gods pondered,& even earlier;since our(as he's doubtless already boasted to you)nonhero was once a candidate for honours [at Harvard]. He remembers a tiny room,an imperceptible me,& a quite immense Don Quixote smoking a huge & perfectly black cigar—Professor Gulick:a friend,luckily,of my father—all at the moment this myth of a man suggested this un of a me discourse upon freeverse(then a scandalous novelty)& Greek choruses. Somewhat to even my surprise,I promptly remarked that they closely resembled each other. A weird expression miscombining pity & terror climbed over his face:he abruptly rose;turned,stridingly reached a window:wideopened it—& Spring came in

4 Patchin Place
March 29 1948

Dear Ezra—

thanks for a very fine gift;conveyed by a most refreshingly
cheerful young man named Fjelde

although can't judge Ted's opus,*can(entre nous)whisper it's
excellent sailing till scholarship docks,in latter few pages.
His devout world-state-individual trinitarianism must more
than delight your current Confucianist demon

news(?)-that,having sold usa Hoi a hyperriproaring trip on the
Soviet superhearse,sellers are trying to get into reverse without
stripping gears. Joseph Ferdinand [Gould] says "a war with
Russia would mean a civil war in every country that fought her".
And "why not in Russia?" asks Marion

one hears Italia's hostels are ⅔ unreserved;grâce à tourismo's
misdoubts re forthcoming plebescite. Imagine having the
chance to see that show & staying hereabouts! But one mustn't
forget that by going abroad one would meet everyone one most
wished one had never beheld

* *Probably Theodore Spencer,* Shakespeare and The Nature of Man (*New York,*
1945).

Silver Lake, N.H.
June 15 1948

Dear Hildegarde—

your fine letter came(as I'd deeply hoped it might)on Saturday
morning,the 12th;just before Marion & I squeezed each other
& not numerable items of baggage into improbably that pin-
nacle of progress,a "SUPEREIGHT";belonging to an exBen-

nington girl—she wanted a Lincoln but had to take a Buick—
who(loving us dearly)suddenly offered to translate ourselves
from Patchin's doorstep to Joy Farm at grande vitesse & avec
de luxe,Et Comment,confort modern(e). Let me add that the
glittering windows of this padded palazzo swam down & up
with a flick of a fingertip—while the motor was running:while
it wasn't,dynamite wouldn't budge them

your unearthly experience with Signor P(the strangest part
of which,I feel,is that if he'd only spoken his own language
anyhow one member of the martyred audience—you—would
have understood him)somehow suggests a moment(near Massachusetts)when a Tydol-man or an Esso-youth,unless 'twas a
Shell-boy,pressed something which made the vast streamlined
nose of the Fisherbodied phenomenon abovementioned climb
skyward:revealing an absolutely oceanic emptiness;islanded
by one lonely little perfectly static lump of a nothing-if-not-
inoffensive engine,labelled(via hugest scarlet letters)"FIRE-
BALL DYNAFLASH". Even our hero was surprised;& as
for the hostess,she couldn't believe her proverbial eyes

Marion survived the cruise nobly * * * whereas I'm still
recuperating—a change from urbs to rus generally floors me;&
this time I was properly tumbled. But martins have come to
our birdhouse;& a family of purple finches reside just outside
the little room where you spent a night,two years ago:& in spite
of rain-rule yesterday proved a brilliant exception)we're wel-
comed by robins chickadees thrushes vireos chipping sparrows
& whitethroats & an indigo bird

Silver Lake, N.H.
August 20 '48

Dear Nancy—

* * * As for Him:thanks!!! You give the first deep glimpse
received by its distant author. Only one other human being
went to my play & wrote me about going—bu. she,also,is a distinguished individual;being Margaret DaSilva,widow of Carlo

Tresca,America's leading(murdered just a few years ago in NYCity by the USSR)anarchist

the present director—no Jimmy Light,*but plumpyoung & very respectful—did drop over to Patchin;& received my permission to cut the show to suit himself,for he seemed a nice chap(though quite unable to conceive of any dimension beyond EitherOr:thus,either the play's about a birth or it's about an abortion;but which?)yet never did I get so much as a program,so can't tell who Him now is. The first Him was a charming & handsome & tall & sweet youth named Billy;think he later became a radio-celebrity. Billy's father was tremendously proud of having been Keely-cured(I remember him ordering & solemnly drinking a beer to prove it)while his mother—a lovely creature—was mightily concerned with astrology:Either a day is favorable Or it isn't . . . "reason" again. It might amuse you to know that M DaS,herself a huge woman,objected ferociously to Me—& the one & only(also first)Me was,is,& ever shall be,Erin O'Brien Moore;bless her ⁂ ⁂ ⁂

* *James Light directed the first production of* Him *in 1928. The leading roles were played by William S. Johnstone ("Billy") and Erin O'Brien Moore.*

153 / TO LLOYD FRANKENBERG

Silver Lake, N.H.
août [1948]

Dear Lloyd—

⁂ ⁂ ⁂ it is more than most kind of thee,monsieur,to warn me of le public's reaction to 2 Wild Words(see how they run). And yet the(however painful)fact that America is not a free country doesn't,I feel,justify anyone's behaving like a slave or three

or(in the lines of the Bad Bald Poet)steady
    there once was a cuntry of owe
    such lofty ideals that know
    man ever could mension

(imagine the tention)
     what might have offended jane dough
selah

Silver Lake, N.H.
August 27 1948

Dear Hildegarde —

*   *   *   how infinitely more than wonderful for Jeanne* that she has you & Sibley!! I've never forgotten & shall,I hope,never forget my dying night alone in your forest,with healing of fragrance under & around me;& my waking into a mystery of rebirth

yes,most heartily agree with you — my little picture is luckiest. Of Chicago,seem to recall an artmuseum with the most beautiful Monets in this world,an astonishing semioceanic muchmore-thanlarge lake,a very refreshingly authentic polloi,& some good lively winds:plusorminus the most eerily false wouldbe-"social-ites" unimaginable. Re "flying" which equals isn't,I fancy we quite agree. Last Sunday's NYTribune "magazine" featured an "as told to" tale of how it really feels to travel faster than sound "by" the first man who ever did it & lived. The hyper-scientific climax of this hero(a prominent killer,holder of Silver Stars & Clusters & Purple Hearts galore)'s experience(?)struck me as an unparalleled reductio ad;it was(in caps)"just like stand-ing still" for him,as he sat all sealed up("like a bank vault")in his supergadget watching a pointer go from "0.9" to "1.0"   *   *   *

---

* *Daughter of Sibley and Hildegarde Watson. The "dying night" refers to the crisis EEC went through when his first wife, Elaine, left him.*

Silver Lake, N.H.
September 22 [1948]

Dear Paul—

it's good to hear you've outgrown your "great depressions".
I've the very great honour to inform you that you're way ahead
of me!   Am possibly emerging from an impossible & v.v. one at
the socalled present writing

which only makes myself happier for your friendship

concerning uncertainty(alias insecurity,or whatever mostpeople
fear)I rather imagine that insofaras an artist is worth his spiritual
salt he can never get enough.   Only when Columbus is in the
middle of nowhere do the members of his crew invariably(&,
from my viewpoint,rightly!)stage a mutiny & threaten himself
with at least seventeen kinds of superdeath

but who'd care to not discover America by mistake?

156 / TO A. J. AYER

Silver Lake, N.H.
September 24 1948

Dear Freddie—

*   *   *   one mild winter morning,45 years ago,some friends &
I made ourselves a fine snowfort(with plenty of iced snowballs)in
the frontyard of the house where I was born.   This house stood
(& stands)at the corner of Irving & Scott streets,Cambridge.   All
around lived nothing but Harvard professors—Taussig(economics)on my left;&,behind him,Lanman:WJames on my right
—yet(more than oddly enough)the very tough town of Somerville began only a little way up Scott street.   —Presently a smallish mob of muckers(as we always called the youth of Somerville)materialized,& their führer-commissar suggested a friendly
snowfight.   I & my friends enthusiastically accepted the sugges-

tion:war broke out. Suddenly the boy fighting beside me dropped as if hit by lightning. In less than a minute our army was annihilated. The muckers swarmed,horribly howling in total triumph. —Why? Very simple! Whereas our side had merely iced its snowballs,our enemies—& not(as we'd naively supposed)our opponents—had put stones in theirs. More briefly:Cambridge's idea of a fight was not Somerville's

however could you dream that Marion & I would love you less because some(any)mob of muckers(& once Cantabridgian USA is about 90 pc Somerville just now)gave you the stoney snowball?

—sois pas si bête

157 / TO AN EDITOR

4 Patchin Place
October 22 '48

Dear Mr———

if I could make you realize how an artist feels when his work is mutilated by the very person he trusted to cherish it,you would be a wiser and a sadder man. If I were a killer,you'd be in Hell now. Being only myself,am trying as hard as I can to forgive you. But don't commit the blunder of reviving your crime

158 / TO ARCHIBALD MACLEISH

4 Patchin Place
December 20 1948

Dear A M—

please pardon;or anyhow kindly believe that our nonhero never intended the slimmest of slights re yourself & E P: nay,I've heard me denouncing(& him a staunch hater of R [Franklin D. Roosevelt]) the hole of America's free press unquote on your honour's behalf:while,concerning l'auteur du retour,may not actions speak louder if(only & if)the undersigned feels he can better serve beauty en masse than alone,l'Académie'll enter my horoscope;shouldst thou meantime need a whitehorse between 4 & 6 of some l'aprèsmidi d'un,advise your admirer Marion * * * & now, sir(with liveliest Christmas goodwishes to thy & yourself)

—EIMI

159 / TO HILDEGARDE WATSON

4 Patchin Place
December 23 1948

Dear Hildegarde—

how wonderful! You-&-Sibley understand me;understand that I'm perfectly helpless unless I'm loved by people whom I can respect—understand that such people are very much rarer than rarest,& why?it's not that respectable people don't exist;it's that what I'm trying to do,or rather who I'd like to be(the only value which,for me,makes my living worth while)quite incidentally but inexorably unmakes most "values";rendering them less than valueless

almost any two but you-one would say:why doesn't he do this,do that?why,when he has such&such a talent & could surely score a success there or here,does he renege & refuse;balk,stall,backtrack;hide from,dodge,or even insult those who'd like to help him;put absurd obstacles in his own way,& otherwise play the neurotic to perfection?

you understand how a true poet came to create a certain being ("Out Of The Rose";in "Stories Of Red Hanrahan") [by W. B. Yeats] whose face

> "was the face of one of those who have come
> but seldom into the world,and always for its
> trouble,the dreamers who must do what they
> dream,the doers who must dream what they do."

Am I wrong about myself? Does my picture of me fail as a likeness? Well,then;I'm wrong—perhaps perfectly wrong. But if so,you understand the so;& always your understanding gives me a mighty joy!

4 Patchin Place
Wednesday [1949?]

Dear Archie—

(as am aware I have already been guilty of entitling you during several populusques [readings?] with that Cal tennessee Roamin mars Tate)it would give me great pleasure to find myself your however briefly guest

I hesitate,however;since "arthritis"—without or avec a soupçon of "fibrillation"—makes social planning something like a furbelow,& please do not think I'm complaining:if only because I am. At any moment,our far less than negligible unhero(supposing he chances to exist)may desire supersoundless hyperhorizontality. And this is a f-ing nuisance;Monsieur. If which doesn't depress you(as it does me)dandy & fine;otherwise I'll climb from NY's teno'clock Monday morning local into a Cambridge aunt's attic. Wire me which. But let us certainly dine;& thine be selection * * *

[February, 1949]

EZRA POUND
SAINT ELIZABETH'S HOSPITAL
WASHINGTON
D.C.

HEARTY CONGRATULATIONS* TO THE CAPITALIST SYSTEM IN PARTICULAR AND ANDREW MELLON IN GENERAL

ESTLIN AND MARION

* *On Pound's having been awarded the first Bollingen Prize in Poetry, for* The Pisan Cantos.

4 Patchin Place
February 9 1949

Chère Madame—

what a pity I'm not a "critic",who can "explain" the poems which
puzzle you!

poem 1 [*Poems, 1923–1954*, 435], you'd then understand,tells
how time will gradually take away everything from a human
being & leave nothing(i.e. zero,or the letter o). This poem says:
<u>two old once upon a(no more)time men sit(look)dream</u>. A cou-
ple of old zeroes—who are physically two(<u>o o</u>)but spiritually
one(<u>o</u>)—are <u>sitting</u> & parenthetically <u>looking</u> & <u>dreaming</u> of
<u>once upon a time</u>(a time which is <u>no more</u>)when they were really
men. Toward the poem's end,these two lonely zeroes (<u>o o</u>)have
moved closer to each other(<u>oo</u>). Notice how the words "men" &
"dream" are opened,revealing "<u>me</u>" & "<u>am</u>"—in this way the
poet says "it's not simply these men who are old;I <u>am</u> an old
man myself,the poem's actually about <u>me</u>"

"chas sing" [*Ibid*, 436] is the name of a Chinese laundryman on
Minetta Lane(maybe Street). This poem tells you that,in spite
of his name,he <u>doesn't</u> sing(instead,he <u>smiles always a trifle while
ironing nobody knows whose shirt</u>. I can't believe you've never
done any ironing;but,if you have,how on earth can you possibly
fail to enjoy the very distinct pictures of that remarkable process
given you by the poet's manipulating of those words which
occur in the poem's parenthesis?!

ah well;as Gilbert remarked to Sullivan,when anybody's somebody everyone will be nobody

Silver Lake, N.H.
July 8 1949

Dear Eliena—

how are you? I've enjoyed many a daydream depicting your
flight from NY to M's V [Martha's Vineyard]. Sometimes you
had a falcon on your left wrist & a royal bengal tiger between
your knees. At other moments the car was full of monkeys who
have bright blue behinds;& an ostrich sits beside you,now&again
dipping her head in the sandbowl which you'd kindly provided.
Then(for a change)there's nobody but you:gorgeously attired
in circusspangles,with a glittering crown & the most wonderful
irridescent harpshaped wings in the world. But however you
appeared,you were preceded & followed by an army of motor-
cops;lefthands at salute:caps over righteye;& a shamrock em-
broidered upon every heart

Silver Lake, N.H.
July 9 1949

Dear Allen—

thank you much more than kindly for a most(putting it very
mildly)luxurious gift, *which only yesterday came from The
Cummington Press "with the author's compliments". And what
a title! I tend(however)to queery the bun at the back of what
Ezra would probably call yr head

the latest biglilmag of-by-&-for uncle tom's [T.S. Eliot's] lapdogs
complacently avers(page blank-319)that their Master's Voice
occupies a complete "album" of "five 12-inch records"(as against
e.g. the notable vox humana of ATate:1 disk). Couldst thou—
coming,as you do,from a piece of the world where(am reliably
informed)male americans still speak of The Redcoats—possibly enlighten an ignorant Yankee as to just how this particular bit of British fair-play occurred?

° *A copy of Tate's* The Hovering Fly and Other Essays (*Cummington Press, Cummington, Mass., 1949*).

165 / TO GEORGES MALKINE

Silver Lake, N.H.
August 10 1949

Dear Georges—

✳ ✳ ✳ the avoidance of a certain Island by our gently Americanizing friend strikes me,at least,as wise:& why not? Coney, when last(many short years ago)glimpsed by your correspondent,equalled a strictly innumerable mass of remarkably unlovely nonfigures so closely adjoining oneanother that literally nobody could sit down. Certain progressive blades presently clambered out on a difficult promontory labelled No Swimming or Trespassing or the like,& began diving off into semifreedom of incompletely-humanized-water. I was 3rd or 4th in line;& about to plunge,when we noticed that our immediate predecessor hadn't as yet reappeared—the lifeguards soon found him & nobly but vainly worked for a whole hour to make him alive ✳ ✳ ✳

166 / TO JOE GOULD

Silver Lake, N.H.
August 10 1949

Hon. Joseph Gould
Minetta Tavern
Greenwich Village

Sir—

are you by any chance inferring that a lifelong devotee of jai-alai cannot count his own thumbs in the dark? How could any man who saw it ever forget that almost incredible triumph of the Colatura Nine? You were riding Snowball,6 ⅞ hands;& (slipping for a moment under his abdomen)cleverly sneaked the puck from "Burp" Smith of the Tigers:to gallop the entire width of the tank for a basket.   Then(as pandemonium rained & people died like flies for a glimpse of your interstices(Eleanor Roosevelt seized one dripping hand by its union label & escorted him,more dead than dead,through Columbia Heights to Saunders Theatre;while The Supreme Court declared every other day Sunday & a grateful nation's organized schoolchildren(brandishing real tommyguns furnished by courtesy of the Perfect Garment Ladies' Universal & Local Friendly & Protective Association Inc)sang "O Please Make Us Criminals Too!"

—respectfully

167 / TO EZRA POUND

Silver Lake, N.H.
August 23 1949

Dear Ezra—

I am becalmed

at present,prose(or anyhow mine)seems worthless:poetry alone matters—in painting & otherwhere.   I spent several months persuading(espérons)71 poems to make 1 book who called himself Xaîpe.   Now et comment The quote Oxford unquote Press registers alarm nudging horror;poems are nonsellable enough(paraît)without calling the poembook by some foreign word which no Good-American could either spell or pronounce

thanks to Dorothy & yourself,Marion & I've enjoyed a defense of poetry(in a periodical of that name)by HC:clearly a nice chap.*   Kel woild

the Master Of Absolute Zero lunged over il-y-a-quelques-jours riding his firebrandnew jeep.   "Everything in physics" he remarked daintily "now points to an act of creation—a couple of billion years ago.   And since all matter was then at one point, it"(matter)"must have existed in the form of light.   All you can say is:Light WAS."   "Sounds like the Bible" Marion(after a pause)suggested gently.   "Exactly" he pleasantly agreed if a soon-arriving photograph of my little picture of Omar's head should happen to remind his mother of him,the painting's hers.   But if not,I shan't feel sad;or even disgraced.   So may she please speak with the frankness of friendship

Marion sends love to you each

—here's to a breeze!

° H.C., *"The Anti-Poet All Told,"* Poetry *(August, 1949), supporting Pound and other modern poets in the Bollingen Prize controversy.*

168 / TO A. J. AYER

Silver Lake, N.H.
[1949?]

Dear Freddy—

* * * & speaking of Sigmund [Freud]:a petit oiseau tells me himself will shortly join Pasteur & Harry Tomdick as a movie-hero,if that makes syntax.   May I ask you something? How would you describe the unc [oncious] in your own words? How would you define it(having first conceived it)logically;or c(w)ouldn't you?   Very seriously:I should like to learn.   Have fought for F against many—including the selfstyled killerof-Americangenerals,who woodenlikeimifhewurgood.   But viewed (et pourquoi pas?)as the founder of a religion of the entocosm, Freud strikes me as pitifully sans—about as s as Marx(mesocosm) & Einstein(ectocosm).   Que penses-tu? * * *

169 / TO GABRIELLE DAVID°

Silver Lake, N.H.
September 5 1949

Dearest Gaby—

* * * a poet & painter easily understands how you feel about leaving any beloved place—he's always putting huge pieces of myself into whens & people & wheres & animals & trees & stones. For human creatures(& I hope we're human!) "things" equal illusion;actually,nothing's inanimate. And yet— never doubt—if only we can transcend the hate which makes us willy-nilly become what we most detest,& somehow can achieve the capacity to love(through thickest or thinnest or neither or both)then our Selves will survive:no harm can touch Them. So,because they are noone but we,we'll never perish. Incidentally;I never met anybody worth(as we say)his(or her)salt,who wouldn't rather suffer the tortures of the damned than resemble all those unpeople who turn up a radio(till it screams-bloody-murder)without ever really hearing anything

as for appearances—when you see me again,I'll be as bald as twenty crabapples(& not,alas!one twentieth as tasty)but worrying about old age has been done,once-&-for-all,by a very great poet named Quintus Horatius Flaccus. And I certainly consider it the depth of nontaste to do what somebody's already done best

° *Landlady and friend of EEC and his wife in Paris.*

---

170 / *TO HILDEGARDE WATSON*

Silver Lake, N.H.
September 18 1949

Dear Hildegarde—

* * * have stopped pretending I don't dread(it's the first time in all my life!)returning to nyc. I do. Et pourquoi pas? For a couple of decades the topfloorback room at 4 Patchin Place,which Sibley originally gave me,meant Safety & Peace & the truth of Dreaming & the bliss of Work. But—as I remember tell[ing] you very bitterly—in March of '48,John Cooper Powys' friendly successor(a NewZealand writer named Hunter)collapsed:whereupon "Mrs C———",mad K———'s "representative"(who,'tis rumored,keeps him lockeduptight in a Milligan attic)seized Hunter's room,adjoining mine;& refused to let me rent it. Instead,she rented it to a radioactive pair who presently sublet to radioactive Miss L——— & ditto friends

two miracles occurred last winter. A JohnsHopkins teacher named Elliott Coleman(whom I mercifully met through my friend Allen Tate)produced an Horatio Street hideout,whither I could float(after dying my limit of deaths)& lie flat on the silent floor & shut both eyes & open a 3rd & be elsewhere. Then,through Paul Nordoff(the only composer who has set poems of mine to music which I not merely like but love)Marion & I spent a weekend now&again in the Spring Valley bungalo of one Mrs Nancy Laughlin;who(parait)summers in Florida

mais quoi faire maintenant? Move? Mais ou? Vacant rooms either don't exist or cost a queendom . . . & tsf's partout. Leave nyc? But Marion finds work,as you know,in nyc making photographs;&(as you also know)she has arranged our 2ndfloorback room as a studio—here the sittings take place,& here she does all her developing & printing. If only that 3rdfloorfront apartment were my:then we'd have only 1(& a relatively mild) auslander in number 4;& am certain John Cooper's outraged aura would stand up & smile

171 / TO JAMES LAUGHLIN

Silver Lake, N.H.
September 23 1949

Dear Laughlin—

there's one poet you publish;and he's very young—the youngest (am certain,rereading Personae)alive

—congratulations

172 / TO EZRA POUND

4 Patchin Place
[1949?]

Dear Ezra

mayhap like the "chasseur" of Cocteau's Les Mariés,am now aiming(through "my" trusty agent)at a fifteen hundred dollar "advance" re one book of poems. Cautiously I now s-q-u-e-e-z-e the trigger . . . Miss B *(I say)"please understand that this book does <u>not</u> contain 1500 poems."   Have also explained to her that, since a dollar = 30 cents—in Greenwich Village,anyway—1500$ would really equal 500$ <u>i.e.</u> what Miss B thinks I might not impossibly receive.   Perhaps she's touched by my financial ignorance;anyhow she has promised she'll do her best

when the cash comes tumbling downtown Marion will line up our most "promising creditors" & give each something(no doubt a publisher reckons I should get all of 100$;"times" being what they aren't).   If both Marion & I survive this distribution,will promptly plot our Washington campaign:otherwise the one of us who does go to jail—assuming there is one—will comfort the other

* Bernice Baumgarten of Brandt and Brandt, his literary agents.

173 / TO R. STEWART MITCHELL

4 Patchin Place
mardi maigre [1949?]

Maecenas Mitchellissime—

thanks for the handbook!*   How coonily dost thou marry irony & scholarship;therewith not merely rendering digestible per most ignorant me some subtle occurrences of a long bygone day,but(a feat at least many million times worthier)walking in the prodigious toeprints of him [Gibbon] whose genius penned that not perishable hyperbole
   "By the repetition of a sentence and the loss of a foreskin, the subject or the slave,the captive or the criminal,arose in a moment the free and equal companion of the victorious Moslems."

"hysteron proteron,chaos is come again"(Roget)—the hoi are again polloiing;cette fois almost en face,their ostensible aim being the renovation of an ex-dog&cat-hospital so what we call people may live in it.   How,by contrast,mellifluous seemeth thy salomemignon tristan&thebarber plus WC existence this correspondent will not attempt to express.   But by Jesus i hope to outgrow these bastards,if it takes seven centuries   *   *   *

° R. Stewart Mitchell, Handbook of the Massachusetts Historical Society (*Boston*, *1931*), *of which Society Mitchell was the Director.*

174 / TO R. STEWART MITCHELL

[4 Patchin Place
1949?]

Dear Stewart—

to say that your thousand dollars are welcome is to be guilty of
an understatement;needless(however)to add,I value your letter
more than the cheque

incidentally,Stewart,I once enjoyed a small allowance;later,
when the wolf knocked twice,aunt Jane would come arescuing.
Now her "maid" H——— —a proud & neurotic Roman Catholic,with good taste in flowers;whose character I used greatly to
admire—plus H———'s recently acquired "fiancé"-gone-hus-
band,E———'s(page Sigmund)a semimoron,have apparently
takenover 104 [Irving Place]. We learn from a trusty exservi-
tress that they're drunk upstairs & down;with feet on the mantlepiece etc

so far,so dull. But here's a quaint quirk. Marion & I,as well
as Elizabeth & Carlton,have at various times heard Jane's bitter
complainings re H——— & E———;& have ignorantly offered
to help Oust the Wickedtwain—I say ignorantly,since(come the
crucial moment)my aunt invariably turns turtle;assuring us that
E——— & H——— are the mainstays of her career.

well,I rather hope you'll drop in on poor Jane & take a good
peek,if only for the historical furtherance of Massachusetts
society ✳ ✳ ✳

1950–1954

[4 Patchin Place
1950]

Dear Bernice—

some months ago a Frenchman(whose name's in the NY tele-
phonebook)calling himself Dr Saul Colin inveigled me into
meeting a fragile old man(also French)named Jean Wahl,who'd
been rescued from Nazis etc & who had,quite without my
knowledge,"translated" some poems of mine for his Editions
De La Revue Fontaine 1945:

when the Revue arrived,I found(to my astonishment & horror)
that JW had made a mess. And so—not wishing to bawlout un
vieux bonhomme—I wrote Colin,asking him to make his agéd
friend understand that he must not "under any circumstances
whatever" do any more "translating" for me

Colin kicked & fussed & denied & couldn't believe & eventually
regretted. Then he turned up with another Frenchman yclept
Alain Bosquet(vide enclosure) [enclosure missing] whose mission
was to "translate" some of my poems into both German &
French. I told Monsieur AB that somebody else(Eva Hesse)had
already translated certain poems of mine into German;but that
you would get in touch with him. Please do so;& be stern,for
I've suffered. Among all the other provisos you can conceive,
please state that no "translation" of any poem shall go to any
printer until I fully okay it. Incidentally,Eva has—am sure—
rendered(& very well)the first poem of the herewith AB's list
[missing]

undiscourageable Colin also wants me to let his(French)friend
Adolphe de Willy,11 West 57,issue a book comprising my poems
&(on facing pages)French translations;the whole being illus-
trated(decorated or whathaveyou)by Fernand Léger. Please
investigate this matter. Again:I insist on having the right to
absolutely okay everything. And under no circumstances whatever—to quote myself—shall anybody illustrate(or etc)such a
book . . . think of what Jacobs did with PuellaMea! PS I never
cared for Monsieur FL's candy-cartwheels. De W should,
meeseemeth,pay handsomely in any case * * *

4 Patchin Place
January 30 1950

Dear Sibley—

perhaps you can help me. I cannot see how to go on unless am
sure of 5000$ a year. While my mother lived I had a very small
but regular income;& after she died,my father's sister used to
give me as much as 2 or 3 hundred$ from time to time—but the
aunt's money is now tied up. I "earn" anyhow 1000$ a year in
"royalties" & "permissions"—that I can depend upon;with a
dollar worth 30 cents. Marion's photographing helps out,&
sometimes we sell a watercolour,rarely an oil. With herself
cooking-in,our bills here(including 125$ for rent,all our food,
laundry,occasionally even a cleaning-woman,electricity & telephone,& about 50$ for medicines:but not including the doctor
or the dentist)come to 350$ a month. The taxes on Joy Farm
were 306$ last year;& the upkeep of the place is something,
though very little. I owe only 800$,somebody owes me 75$,&
have 30$ on hand. Recently the socalled Bollingen Foundation
seemed eager to produce a "grant",but that fell through. Shall
try the Guggenheim people again,but they(after awarding me a
scholarship,years ago)refused a "renewal". I can't(& should
never pretend to)teach;but can,& do,"read":always "clearing ex-
penses" & generally "making" a few $
                         —vive la vie!

The only thing I have of any value is the farm;which I'd be glad
to offer as security(if that's the proper word)

177 / TO AN UNIDENTIFIED CORRESPONDENT

4 Patchin Place
April 12 1950

Dear Mr Parker—

unplays need doctoring. But if(as you assume)there exists an
"art of directing",it surely consists in allowing a play to "express"

itself i.e. to be (re)born. And if every word of <u>Santa</u> <u>Claus</u> is distinctly spoken,by human beings deeply familiar with the American language,my play's "meaning" won't even slightly matter

what,by the way,does life "mean"?

re staging:I suggest you have a negative i.e. perfectly plain set (almost invisible at first,brightening gradually,& at last wholly lit)& that you drop a curtain(depicting the final moment:Santa Claus removing his deathmask)between scenes;while a small orchestra makes serious music cleanly for a few minutes

178 / TO HILDEGARDE WATSON

Silver Lake, N.H.
June 18 1950

Dear Hildegarde —

Marion & I came here 4 days ago,& are not quite yet we. Noone could(what a change from NYC!incredible)have been lovelier, on the day of our arrival,than Nature;with all her glory & silence & sunlight & thrushsong & peacefulness. But half the house was full of 2 native plumbers uptotheireyelids in repairs —"only man is vile". I somehow manoeuvred one of my fellow-villains into the position of persuading me that I really didn't want a trench(of depth unguessable by beast or man)dug almost to the next world:& in another week,"the waterworks" may be properly functioning

by why does Little Estlin find it so hard to understand that everything almost(& almost everybody)'s perpetually disintegrating;as well as re-?

last night I spotted 2(one as big as a saint bernard)porcupines sitting together under the barnfloor;they'd been placidly eating-away its timbers. But my pistol was in quarantine for two weeks chez le caretaker(whose littlest daughter has been down with "scarlet fever";while his wife suffered the subtraction of "a dozen" gallstones,one "five-sided—she's keepin' it"—at Dr

Shedd's Conway hospital). Therefore I could do no more than call Marion & show her our guests. The bats,usually innumerable after twilight upstairs,have behaved remarkably well,so far;only 1 perished:perhaps a sudden change of temperature(making prewinter of summer)decided them to hug their homes in our luxurious ceilings

when cosmos has regained her temporary sway over chaos you must pay us a visit,& behold Chocorua Mountain in all His magnificent lights-&-shadows. * * *

179 / TO EZRA POUND

Silver Lake, N.H.
Independence Day 1950

Wwaall—

as the prophet Ez might virtufully observe:you can have your Mr Best(after all,hasn't Jimmie J [Joyce] his,in the Hamlet scene from U?)though could nearly forgive him the founding of the most unXian church some centuries before Paul the Pharisee or Doubting TAcquinas(not to be confused with Doting Tommie,hO.huM.)when I remember that upon a certain portal of the ny Mu of Na Hi occurs a supposed quote from old Di Color Che lui-même(re dolphins unless it's whales)very prettily concluding "and they snore in their sleep"
                                        —give me the Broad

180 / TO EZRA POUND

Silver Lake, N.H.
july 12 1950

Dear Ezra—

so my letter's obscure? Tiens. Can't compare with your last,I imagine

same(postmarked JUN 27)began "being as it iz, as sez Ari StoTL. etc." My letter,in reply,begins by giving you your

"Mr Best"—'Αριστοτέλης;no very far cry,meseems,from ἄριστος:"the father of logic" as he's frequently called—& ends by a salute("give me the Broad")to Plato("son of Ariston, orig. named Aristocles,and surnamed Πλάτων with ref. to his broad shoulders,πλάτυς,broad . . . He held that the object of philosophy is beauty":Century Dict). The middle of my letter is a distinguishing of Christianity(vide New Testament) & the SaulPaul-Acquinas hypersystem—au fond Aristotelian—so headily espoused by your ultra-marsupial friend. Incidentally, I hand "your Mr Best" a bouquet for certain observations;which have perused on a wall of the NYCity Museum of Natural History:they relate to either dolphins or whales(forget which)

& now perhaps you'll interpret the enclosed [a letter from Pound] which please return

181 / *TO EZRA POUND*

Silver Lake, N.H.
August 15 '50

Dear Ezra—

so you know more than the birdsters? Fine & dandy. I don't. And what I've learned from a very few birds(who have honoured me with their friendship)leads one ignorant* biped to guess that poor birdsters are doing their wingless utmost

thy fondness for Mr A [Louis Agassiz] reminds our unhero of something delightful:a dearest friend of his childhood was(& is)the Indian elephant of The Agassiz Museum,not far from whose wonders I was luckily born;& there's not a wrinkle in his skin,for in those days you gave your public its money's worth

—salut!

*[EEC's note] I even find it interesting that—large & by—birds beautiful-to-hear dress quietly,& birds beautiful-to-see can't sing;&(nota bene)the real killers are neither beautiful-to-see nor beautiful-to-hear [There follow lengthy quotations on the

blue jay from T. Gilbert Pearson, ed., *Birds of America;* F. Schuyler Mathew, *Fieldbook of Wild Birds and Their Music;* and Chester A. Reed, *Bird Guide*.]

reperusing Agassiz Scenario,observe with pleasure that its definitely prosaic part goes to Tippling Tom(Meaculpa Marsupialis;Donne)whereas,by what may be roughly entitled a fortunate contrast,someone who shall remain nameless receives the distinctly poetic role   *   *   *

182 / TO LEWIS GALANTIÈRE

Silver Lake, N.H.
September 8 1950

Dear Lewis—

your fine&dandy letter(duly forwarded)was plucked from a diminutive postoffice in the Madison station of the B&Mrr,near one end of that narrow mirror which old men entitle Three-MilePound;was jounced—via my model A(immediately succeeding Mr F's farflung T)Ford almost several miles to this marvellous hilltop;was escorted,through a clearing(with Mount Chocorua & six friends in the nearness)& behind a cool big silent barn,toward a grove of whitebirch & norwaypine;& finally found herself opened by this(no trifle better than he should be) body,lying in brilliant afternoon sunlight under only heaven

then it's night,Paris;& we're climbing Montmartre:to Zelli's;& a charming girl sits at our table,& we drink&dance&talk&live—I can even remember how very skilfully your 50francnote thanks her selves at our depart—&,awaking palatially next day,I wander into an adjoining stanza to rouse your slumbering effigy; which(opening each after other its wild both eyes)quietly observes "O,that's very unfortunate"   *   *   *

Silver Lake, N.H.
September 16 1950

Dear Hildegarde—

Marion was much more than delighted to have your letter;& no
wonder,since it contained the praises of both Sibley & yourself!
Did either of you(incidentally)ever glimpse a remarkably flimsy
"portrait" of Miss Moore by Carl Van Vechten,which she thinks
noncomparable? I was really startled:until that "cuspidore" incident jumped into my consciousness,& I saw wee me friend-
lessly cowering in The Dial while its editor lectured(some 45
minutes)against "spittoon". * Yet I love the lady still!

could you tell me whether or no SW has read "Our Enemy,The
State"(by Albert Jay Nock;whose "Memoirs Of A Superfluous
Man" you & Marion & I heartily enjoyed)? I ask because,if
not,I'd like to give him a copy which a NY bookstore found for
me recently. The poet Eve Triem—whose work you may have
seen in "Poetry" & whose name(am amazed to discover)is pro-
nounced "Treem"—first mentioned said opus to our unhero.
Sibley would share my admiration of the author's quite unbelievable courage,if not my enthusiasm for his thesis * * *

* *Marianne Moore had urged EEC to change "spittoon" to "cuspidor" in a contribu-
tion to* The Dial.

184 / *TO EVE TRIEM*

Silver Lake, N.H.
October 1 1950

Dear Eve Triem—

you are far(far)ahead of me in reading. I red(& better,was red-
to)many years since;then,at college,a little more reading with
much difficulty occurred:between these epochs are three or two
marvellous meetings with human beings & five or four vivid
adventurings among printed pages. Once le monde appeared,
my books disappeared;almost. Yet am cheered as I remember

a soothing dictum by Fritz Wittels "you don't need to read. You write"—here's devoutly hoping

thank you,Madame,for your Good Wishes;& please accept mine

concerning la guerre & her effect on a younger (unquote)generation:am perhaps growing aged;for cannot honestly sympathize with you. If those lads of "the helpless look" dropped it & became what was anciently termed COs,that would be something respectable. Respectable also would be a young man who truly loved war—not to mention a youngest who(stranger things have happened) let a war swallow him to fight against war as a soldier. But our heroless doesn't respect even myself whenever he drops a tear over the very appealingest shallwesay(speaking mildly)subsheep * * *

185 / TO HILDEGARDE WATSON

[4 Patchin Place]
Vendredi 8 Dec. [1950]

Dear Hildegarde—

I was delighted to receive your letter;& should have said so long ago,if hadn't been gifted with what might perhaps be called physiological prescience concerning a trip to Vassar:now that's happily over

abandoning an excellent train at 6:40 on Wednesday evening, our nonhero was met by a kindly & far from either warlike or southern teacherofpoetry named RobertELee,& driven to "Alumnae House";there,encountered my womentor(an excellent imitation of MarianneMoore)named Miss Loughlin;was driven to a large hall;read,to an ample & extremely enthusiastic female—I certainly shouldn't describe it as feminine—audience, from 7:30 to 8:30;was driven back to AH & well fed(con scotch); was led into a vast baronial chamber,where answered questions of possibly 100 students(most of them tongue-tied)for 45 minutes;was driven to REL&(pregnant)wife's house & enjoyed a few drinks with Miss L & her EnglishDepartment-subordinates— Miss L,by the way,forbade the students to ask me for autographs & saved me from a newspaperman—was driven back to AH by

REL at half-past-midnight;went to bed under a canopy & to sleep(avec nembutol)circa 2:30;was awakened by telephone at 7:30;was called for by REL & driven chez elle for breakfast (delicious);was driven by Lady Lee,with R on my right,to his "class" of maybe 30 shes,who asked me questions(under his compulsion)for 15 minutes;staggered out,crying—to my astonishment—at the assembly "well,write poetry for God's sake; it's the only thing that matters" & was driven by R's spouse to Poughkeepsie station,boarded an excellent train,&(to make a short story long)arrived about noon of yesterday at the Grand-CentralTerminal,NYCity,NY,USA or should we write UN?

'twas,& is,wonderful to be here again(not to mention alive)

186 | TO SIR SOLLY ZUCKERMAN

[4 Patchin Place]
December 11, 1950

Thou rogue—

heat ease wease vair deeb ray-gray high lairn huf zohz heggs-payr-yonz weash hease hall mah-ee fohld high wooed-say plis heggs-eb mah-ee heggs-kyooz eef pho-zeebluh han bill-if me high ahm mohz sawr zohz suck-awtach pairsohn har kohz-eeng hyoo hall zaht troobluh bud-ah zang-guh hyoo tayn-uh-towzun tah-ee-muh

as for the photographs(taken,if you recall,in semipenumbra) they strike me as kuh-nokOOt;wait till you see yourself kee-doh

c'est la saison de mistletoe et holly partout paraissent les paysans de solly

[4 Patchin Place]
sunday [1950]

Dear SK—

please don't be stupid!

I wasn't laughing for scorn,but from joy;because(if my telephone didn't deceive me)you said you liked best the poem about
"a nigger and a little star"—& it so happens that this poem(24)is
one of two poems(46 being the other)which a "friend" & "critic",
who saw XAIPE in ms,did his very worst to dissuade me from
including . . . on the ground that the word "nigger"(like the
word "kike")would hurt a lot of sensitive human beings & create
innumerable enemies for the book. Of course I said tohellwith
him;but the incident depressed me;just how much,I never quite
realized until your voice took the curse off those eight lines & put
glory upon them

or so I seemed to hear. But even if I misheard you entirely,the
point remains

4 Patchin Place
vendredi [1951]

Dear Marianne—

but if that little bouquet were so big
that all Brooklyn easily might throb &
wander beneath its petals,the admiration
with which Marion & I regard you would
not even partially have been expressed

—veuillez agréer
Mademoiselle

[4 Patchin Place]
January 8, 1951

Dear Jimmy—

Could A A perhaps do something quick for Joe Gould? He's
almost on it now. Seems to totter between Minetta Tavern &
Goody's Bar,with occasional stumblings in the direction of
Dorothy Day

—here's hoping

[4 Patchin Place]
January 11 1951

Dear Joe—

you and I've been friends for quite some time. But we're not
going to be friends much longer unless you sober up and stay
sober. Verbum sap

[4 Patchin Place]
Feb. 10, 1951
samedi

Dear Hildegarde—

* * *

again & again have tried to picture the glories of a quick trip
abroad(or a trip anywhere;except to Joy Farm next summer)
with Marion(who deserves a true vacation if anybody ever
did)but sans success. Later or sooner I always glimpse a
miserably exhausted me—tortured in his "iron maid"—waiting&
waiting&waiting for some plane or train or boat or maybe hotel-
room which doesn't dream of materializing. It's quite easy,of

course,to enliven this dismal image with imaginary duels(based on a real denunciation of Eimi's progenitor by the Moscow radio) between heroic EEC & ultrasatanic agents of KumradSteel. But the trouble here is that Marion becomes a hostage—something not precisely endurable. Tell me now,Hildegarde,what do you think:am I suffering from what "the liberals" entitle "failure of nerve",or from something else most beautifully described by Quintus H as "nec pietas moram";or may my unending timidities harbour a diminutive amount of truth?

192 / TO JOHN DOS PASSOS

[4 Patchin Place]
April 3[?] 1951

Dear Dos—

& a more compelling invitation 'twere unpossible to imagine; even sans Va's bluebirds! Hereabouts(I blushingly add)mere human events have transpired,including my aunt Jane's death & what EPound terms contemptuously "a Gug" [Guggenheim Fellowship]. Former—which released somewhat heterogeneous feelings because "your aunt outlived herself by ten years",as Master Awk oracularly observed—implies amongothertrifles the exploring of 104 Irving Street Cambridge from eaves to cellar;a chore which Marion has already semiachieved. Latter(& this entirely pleased me,since Mr Moe all-on-his-own resubmitted my lastyear's downturned application)should make plausible a glimpse,after perhaps 13 winters!de l'Europe;et aujourd'hui même the pilgrims applied passports. But please don't suppose our nonhero's otherwise loafing. Only avant-hier did he face a small & farthestfromselect audience of "New School" addicts;& will beard on April 20 that antique institution of female furtherance yclept "Mount Holyoke". Dos,if an honest weekend appears I'll most certainly warn you:but meanwhile please make— for Marion&myself—profoundly immediate bows in the lucky vicinity of your very charming lady & your très photogenique daughter &(if any appears)a mockingbird;I've never seenheard one

[4 Patchin Place
April 17, 1951]

New York,April 17—AP. A plot threatening the existence of the Episcopalian hierarchy of Great Britain was believed,on good authority,to have been uncovered here today. The alleged instigator of this nefarious scheme,whose motive cannot as yet be determined,is suspected of having urged a prominent photographer of this city to falsify,in some unrevealed manner,a certain document whose exact nature(in the interests of domestic security)remains a carefully guarded government secret,known only to the President & his advisors,the Cabinet,the Supreme Court,the Congress,the Senate,& all their more intimate associates. Rumor(however)persists in affirming that the forgery in question was to have been eventually signed by an obscure Greenwich Village literatus,who discovered his predicament just in time to prevent an Eliotic England from travailing to its very ankles. A story,even if possible stranger,was being widely circulated in the nation's capitol tonight with regard to the identity of the presumed plotter. He is said to be Dr. Enzo Pound,a well known ornithologist,& co-author with Kung Fu Tse of "The Unwobbling Pigeon".

194 / *TO FAITH WILSON*

[4 Patchin Place]
August 3 '51

Dear Faith—

* * * we've just returned from a not quite 12week jaunt in Paris Rome & Greece,made plausible by the double luck of a "Gug"(as EPound would call it)& a poetry prize* (which I owe to MaxEastman;who voted & voted for our undersigned,year after year,until something happened). Let me add that I left America halfdoubting Europe would last the month out;& arrived in NYC,not merely sans doubts,but marvelling "Europe will never perish!"

the Greeks,quite incidentally,are the only people I've ever seen
who really like Americans:& why not?   You should glimpse a
huge map(hanging in a building where an exposition was
progressing)to show the Soviet penetration of Greece—all but a
little strip in the middle.   Then,with America's help,out went
the Rooskeez.   And long long long live Ho Parthenōn!!!   Italy's
lively & brisk(& glad to be rid of fascism)whereas the French,
though surfacely gay,have the strongest communist party outside Stalin's demeane;& they can't forget their occupation-
liberation throes(if I know them) *   *   *

* *From the Academy of American Poets.*

195 / *TO HIS DAUGHTER*

[Silver Lake, N.H.]
September
14 1951

My Dear Nancy—

thank you a millionmillion times for the marvellous gift!   A red
wheelbarrow!   A genuine(wooden)one,not some pseudo tin-
bathtub with a rubbertired diskwheel;praise be.   Why,I was so
surprised it's hard to even begin to explain.   Quite incidentally,
the only poem of Doctor WCWilliams—someone whom the undersigned should respect,since he(WCW)(too)received the Dial
Award—which ever truly pleased me as a poem should(from
finish to start & vv)is one affectionately concerning a red wh-b.
And as for surprise:perhaps the only equally-surprised human-
being is,or was,my little newyorker pal MorrieWerner;when he
demanded pointblank why I called myself "a good Republican",
& I instantly answered "because the Republicans have an
elephant".   Morrie looked at our unhero as if Morrie's head
would come off;then he moaned that I was kidding him,"no" I
said "I mean it":then he almost fainted from shock(but what
better reason could anybody have?)   After some terrible moments,Morrie's weak faint trembling voice asked dazedly "but
don't you like donkeys?"   "Yes" I admitted frankly "but not so
well as elephants".   There was a frightening pause.   Then he
slowly whispered "je-sus-chr-ist".   Now I must rush out & take

a peep in the woodshed just to make certain nobody's stolen my treasure * * *

196 / TO JANET COHN*

Silver Lake, N.H.
October 8 1951

Dear Janet —

the YMHA announces a production of <u>Him</u>.   What about it?

am asking because I wish to make absolutely & irretrievably SURE that my play is played strictly as written.   And by "as written" I mean,among other things,no alterations(alias "interpretations")of any sort(due to would be originality on the part of a "producer",a "director",a "scenic artist", orwhatever) i.e. nothing even infinitesimally resembling the appalling (sic) 2nd "Provincetown Theatre" "production" [1946]—where whole passages were garbled or omitted;where Mussolini of Act Two Scene VIII appeared as GrouchoMarx;where the Three Weirds, minus their rockingchairs & knitting,stood & faced the audience; & also where instead of the drama's metaphysical tragic-ending (Imagination becoming Reality)the players poppedouttogether shouting "Yes, We Have No Bananas".   Such was my reward for accepting a merely verbal promise

this time I must have a written statement,signed by some actually responsible person,who agrees(1)that he will follow my script exactly in all particulars from start to finish,&(2)that whatever he does will be subject to my ok,sans question

* *Of Brandt and Brandt, literary agents.*

4 Patchin Place
April 2, 1952

Dear Billy—

greetings,Herr Mahler!& know that(during a welcome diminu-
endo or lull in our sundry & respective ailments,Marion & I
adventured the AThayer show:furthermore,that we can't thank
you enough for making this pilgrimage possible

not only his selfportrait,as extraordinary in its own way as a
Rembrandt,but certain marvellously sensitive not to say charming drawings(especially one of his little son)delighted our souls.
And as for the game—there are,you may recall,two pictures of
hung ducks—"Wild Fowl"(at or near the left end of the very wall
through which you enter)is as Just a piece-of-painting as I've
seen.   Marion was enchanted with the featheriness of the upper
bird's breast:but your friend has also painted this creature's
precise weight;& such simultaneity strikes me as miraculous.
(We've all seen a lady's gown so nicely rendered by Mr Sargent
that you could nearly hear it rustle;but, alas!the poor girl herself didn't quite weigh a quarterofapound)

enfin:please believe that Patchin's Master & Mistress most
deeply appreciate Your & Alice's greatly generous offer of assistance in the finding of a Nortonian de luxe hypercolossal
mansion.   I'll probably write in about a week,specifying musts
shoulds & mays;till then

—toujours!

* *The philosopher's son, a painter, and with his wife, Alice, a New Hampshire neighbor
of EEC.*

4 Patchin Place
April 14 1952

Dear Elise—

your hunch is correct:am 101pc contra "nonobjective" "art"
(NYCity,also,is bursting with untalent).   Incidentally,seems a
trifle odd that all these supersubmorons should worship Picasso;
who used to make pictures,& once declared there's no such thing
as "abstract" painting & cried out "respect the object"   *   *   *

* *The California painter.*

199 | TO EZRA POUND

Silver Lake, N.H.
June 25 '52

Dear EP—

'twas good to hearseehug you

now that am collecting my(scattered in ny-va-wash-ny-bost-NH
transit)selves,let me kindly thank the author of epistle to the
human fly for generous greetings,excellent counsel,& instruc-
tive MaxB(enclosed)enclosure *

shall keep an eye peeled for Thetis' boychild,dodge Yandel-
lic "confluence" †,& probably pluckupcourage to cherchez la
Beatrix [Beatrice Abbott]

you may be pleased to learn that in his traduction of thy friend's
Commedia Dr CharlesEliotNorton throws this footnote at Par
viii 116(Per l'uomo in terra se non fosse cive?)"For the fact is
evident that man is by nature a social animal,and cannot attain
his true end except as a member of a community"

quand a l'undersigned,everything(at least in my less misguided moments)becomes luckily not what but who

— Marion sends love!

saw a silent bluejay l'autre jour;he sends you his swoopingest

* *Enclosure missing.*
† *William Yandell Elliot edited at Harvard a magazine called* Confluence.

200 / *TO ALLEN TATE*

Silver Lake, N.H.
21 juillet '52

Dear Allen—

hearty thanks for a cheering letter!

am naturally relived to find you're kiteing all over uncreation*
&(I trust)drowning,with each more merriest stroke of the dipsomaniacal fiddlebow,a premeditatedly proletarian exeagle's infradiplomatic ultrascream;keep it up

both Marion & myself heard [Djuna Barnes] solemnly aver assert state declaim emit & otherwise testify that she sank the very next day after lunching with Doubtless(Ole Mars)Thomas. Never mistrust a falling woman

please salute Caroline on our behalf;& add that I attribute the prevalent malady known as balding to a foreconscious subexpectation of the vengeful Redman's velocitous return

* *Tate was on a cultural mission to India which EEC had declined to undertake.*

[Silver Lake, N.H.]
August 9 1952

cher enf pro—

* * * if anything could please Marion & me more than your
letter,anything would be Anne's.   To imagine she's in Pyrenées!
Why,am even reminded of Oloron-Ste-Marie—& that's a deep
remind—also recall how Dos & I once finally found a snowy
col & overandoveringly rolled down into the valley where(for
minutes)nobody believed we'd come from that mountain's
further side

wrote Trilling & received one of the most charming letters any
man ever wrote.   Here's trusting les traductions will soon see
radiance

* EEC's French translator, author of a study of his work published in Paris in the Poètes
d'aujourd'hui series (1966). Lionel Trilling had agreed to select a group of poems for
Grossman to translate.

202 / TO EZRA POUND

6 Wyman Road
Cambridge, Mass.
October 24 1952

& right ye were,Ezree meee by,to communicate the Williams-
iana * which arrived this day,forwarded from nh:& gladdened
my spouse&self

now this dame "Cummins" has(as you doubtless know)been after
eec for yarz;so am selfishly-delighted she's attacking someone
else(poor shawn shay)

but regret to learn our laymyspiritatherfeetfull acquaintance
has injured his Amongmanyothers,undistinguished cote(with
a circumflex).   What was he up or down or sideways or neither
to,pray?

am in good hands here,belonging to 1 "John Finley"; † pro-
fessing Greek,extolling Humanities,&(tactfully not when I'm
around;however)praising O'Possumtotheskies.   A nice—the
JF—fellow.   Has already preserved me from well nigh not
numerable "social" phenomena:&(this in thine oreille)will,
j'espère,make possible a big escape to ny circa Xmas!

we live in a little house,far from seive lies ation;& a big BLUE-
JAY seems to be our chief mascot—a stalwart rascal,whose
Hue give me Joy unmitigated;& who fears no crow or gull ex-
tant.   I've already remembered him to you

Marion sends love to yourself & Dorothy!   Please keep many
fingers crossed(on my nonworthy bewhole)from 8 to 9 PM
this coming Tuesday,28th October;my 1st "Norton lecture"
— oop thih rubbles

l'enfant prodigue

° *A clipping from the* Washington Times Herald, *dated October 20, 1952, reporting
an attack by a certain Virginia Kent Cummins on the Library of Congress for having
appointed William Carlos Williams consultant in poetry. Williams' verse, Mrs. Cummins said, was "the very voice of Communism."*
† *Professor of Classics at Harvard, where Cummings in 1952–53 delivered the Charles
Eliot Norton Lectures, published as* i:6 Nonlectures (*Cambridge, Mass., 1953*).

203 / TO EZRA POUND

6 Wyman Road
Cambridge 38, Mass.
February 9 '53

Dear Ezra—

if by chance I understand your latest(to Marion)favor's preem-
eer paragraph,it emanates at least gross misrepresentation.
Master Mullins'° most recent appearance coincided with the
presence of a singularly honest Greek sculptor [Michael Le-
kakis] to whom he(Mullins)originally introduced us;plus a
Greek poet,friend of le dit sculptor,who emitted more aliveness per cubic moment than a dozen thousand million Mul-
linss would during several linear centuries.   Moreover said

Mullins brought along a not invited demiyouth which kept its eyes open but couldn't say boo

as for "a GOOD poEM",our unhero modestly declines what Doubtless Thomas once pontifically entitled the gambit. Neither does "Blackstone" [R. P. Blackmur?] cause requisite thrills hereabouts;though he well may amid "the healthy young" (whoever they aren't). But re your "aint steerable" tribute anent myself,I thank you heartily:& hope to prove worthy thereof ad infin

our bluejay sends love

° *Eustace Mullins, author of* This Difficult Individual, Ezra Pound (*New York, 1961*).

204 / *TO AN UNKNOWN CORRESPONDENT*

6 Wyman Road
Cambridge 38, Mass.
February 17 '53

Dear Miss _____

if the Ringling circus arrives next spring,watch very carefully the "aerial acrobats" or flying-trapeze-artists. When a group comes running out,its members look alike;but as they climb higher & higher(to their positions)they become more & more distinct & individualized,& finally attain eachness. Then the miraculous "act" begins—one eachness or is combining with another in midair to make an are—& finally these unbelievable creatures drop amazingly into great nets,& thence reach the earth:alive;mortals who have become im-mortal

6 Wyman Road
Cambridge 38, Mass.
February 19 '53

Dear Mr _____

thanks for the letter of February 14. It was an astonishing valentine! Being neither a scholar nor a critic,I don't read manuscripts or give advice. But in your case let me make a suggestion

why not learn to write English? It's one of the more beautiful languages. And(like any language)it has a grammar,syntax, etc:which can be learned. Nobody can teach you to write poetry,but only you can learn the language through which you hope to become a poet

trying to write poetry before you've learned all there is to learn about writing is like tackling the integral calculus without understanding arithmetic. It's even more like trying to build yourself a house from the ridgepole down;instead of laying the foundations first & then erecting a structure on them,story by story

there must be someone at your college who teaches English Composition. If you take this letter to him,he'll be glad(I'm sure)to help you

6 Wyman Road
Cambridge 38, Mass.
March 27 '53

Dear Elizabeth

know all men by these presents that you seem to have slowed my dogs down:an extraordinary achievement for which I thank you heartily. Heaven preserve us from bitches! Your description thereof reminds me of a magnificent passage in Rabelais ending with the immortal(per Urquart)words "in which a duck might swim".   Look it up,by all means,if you're unfamiliar with it

concerning all&any soidisant witchhunts,what-may-be-called-my-position couldn't be clearer.   (1)With every serious anarchist who ever lived,I assume that "all governments are founded on force".   (2)As a possibly not quite nonintelligent human being,I'm aware that socalled Macarthyism didn't drop unmotivated from the sky—that(on the contrary)it came as a direct result of exactly what it decries:namely,procommunist-&-how-activities throughout the USA,sponsored by Mrs FD Roosevelt & her messianicallyminded partner plus a conglomeration of worthy pals:furthermore,having kept my ears & eyes open,I am unaware that 'tis thanks to the indoctrinatory efforts of this gruesome gang of dogooders that Russia is a worldpower & the Korean War murders God knows how many innocent Koreans—not to say guilty Americans—daily.   (3)In 1931 I went to Russia,& what I found may be refound by anybody capable of reading a book called Eimi.   Since(grâce à mass "education"—the "bread&circusses" of contemporary Caesarhood)almost nobody can read pratically anything,let me add that I wouldn't like "communism" if "communism" were good.   (4)My contempt for selfstyled Americans who don't dare stand up on their hind feet & thunder "sure,I was a communist—so were Frank & Eleanor:what about that?" has been&(I trust)will remain unlimited.   O,"the"(as you were wont to remark)"strength of weakness"!   * * *

207 / TO JOHN FINLEY

4 Patchin Place
May 7 1953

Dear John—

* * * at any rate nycity's village seems marvellously sweet. Not only is The Great Tree(at washington square's nw corner) in towering total leaf—my human friends like Mr & Mrs flowerfolk Psomas("these little roses are for the madam")& master-

ofthestationary I.Schwartz("in fewchuh yuhshudbe kefful uv
those barbarus intellegchewlz")& the Cake Lady("h-o-w deoo
d-e-w?")are flourishing;only my beloved icecoalwoodman-
extraordinary Domenico DePaolo remains nonencountered,&
have already glimpsed his caravansery's handpainted("ZOOM
. . . DOOM")rearend. Such are my fullprofessors — under them
comes e.g. our manhating Jewish butcher,who wears a beret
because "eyekin taykid"(namely ridicule)& recently scared me
by dropping his guard to greet "Professor Cummings" & boasting he'd followed the latter's career "in the London Times";or a
biggesteyed softestvoiced delicatessantattendant who today observed,when I confessed an attempt to tell college kids of my
boyhood world,"it's hard to pass these things on"(adding gently)
"as Paul Valéry says,culture is mortal"

if one must inhabit an unworld . . . Can scarcely wait to smell
New Hampshire!

208 / *TO HILDEGARDE WATSON*

Silver Lake, N.H.
August 25 '53

Dear Hildegarde —

✳ ✳ ✳ Paideia's author is amazing — gentle,modest,sensi-
tive,quiet,&(unbelievably;since he's an "intellectual" par excellence)intelligent. Marion & I met him twice:the earlier time,
chez violent Professor Perry Miller & his lively wife Betty,at
Cambridge,he(the worldrenowned Werner Jaeger)gently &
almost humbly helped me off with my overcoat e'er I could possibly stop him! Did you realize that this supreme authority on
Greek culture never actually saw Greece till a year or two ago?
✳ ✳ ✳

4 Patchin Place
November 23 1953

Dear Dr Hoffmann —

thank you most kindly for lending me The Soul Of Man Under Socialism;which am mailing back tomorrow

as you know by i [:*six nonlectures*] (page 4)"The hellless hell of compulsory heaven-on-earth emphatically isn't my pail of blueberries." Why? Because,for me,that supposedly brandnew soidisant world is an all too familiar unworld—the essentially escapist unworld of a socalled future life,immemorially postulated by conventional religions—& whether this wholly & enchantingly real(to a true believer in it)unworld is an unworld of "angels" & "saints" or of "science" & "socialism",whether it happens to be located in some imaginary "heaven" or on some equally(to say the least)imaginary "earth",makes not one particle of difference,I feel,so far as its fundamental invalidity is concerned

what I feel to be valid for me is(you no doubt realize)what certain great mystics have named "eternity":meaning,not time-ad-infinitum,but time-lessness;or(in my own words,page 79)not "measurable when" but "illimitable now"—& I need scarcely add that,if nobody alive were "a mystic" except myself,if nobody else asserted the truth of what(lacking a better phrase)I call "selftranscendence or growing",this purely personal & entirely human experience(it's no mere concept,let me assure you!) would be precisely as valid as if it were shared by two million or two billion trillion human beings

does which fact make our nonhero a selfish person? Not if you agree—as I most heartily agree—with our friend OW's definition on page 77 of his essay:Selfishness is not living as one wishes to live,it is asking others to live as one wishes to live (the italics are his). You may be certain that I gave you & your wife my book not as a proselytizer,which I am not;but as an artist,which I proudly & humbly hope I am * * *

° The dermatologist who treated EEC while he was at Harvard, spring 1953.

4 Patchin Place
January 15 1954

Dear Jack —

hail

Louis Aragon(who wrote Le Front Rouge)was,in the goodold-
days of Paris,a lively if very occasional pal of mine. By the time
I'd decided to visit Russia,he'd become a fanatical communist;
via one remarkably goodlooking Russian girl(Elsa Triolet)whom
he'd married,& whose homemade jewelry he enthusiastically
peddled. Between them,A & she wrote a letter — very valuable,
as it proved,from my point of view — introducing me to her sister
in Moscow("Madame Potiphar")& presented my departing self
with an extraordinary assortment of capitalist gifts which I
duly delivered:receiving an extremely enlightening experience
in exchange(Eimi, pp 61–72). Later,while still in Moscow,I was
asked per the socalled Revolutionary Literature Bureau to translate Aragon's "hymn of hate";& set about this task with emo-
tions accurately indicated at the bottom of p 137 & the top of
p 138. My candid opinion,plus a brief analysis,of A's opus occurs on pp 142–143. Nor does immodesty forbid me to add
that subsequently — while reviewing some book of mine,probably
Eimi — a poetess named Babette Deutsch referred to our nonhero's far from painless(vide p 175)effort as,if am not mistaken,a "chivalrous gesture" * * *

* *Sweeney, the critic and Harvard librarian, had asked EEC how he had come to translate, in 1931, Aragon's revolutionary poem.*

211 / TO DWIGHT MACDONALD

4 Patchin Place
January 26 1954

Dear Mr Macdonald —

* * * a day or twain after "The Bible in Modern Undress"
appeared,Marion(who reads widely as well as profoundly)

brought me a copy of a magazine called The New Yorker;& suggested that I(who seldom adventure The Police Gazette) should painstakingly peruse your article. Having done so with joy & amazement,I immediately sought & found the nearest Western Union office(at 14th Street & 7th Avenue)where I dispatched this(if memory serves)brief telegram:Dwight Macdonald,c/o The New Yorker,25 West 43rd Street,New York City— HEARTY CONGRATULATIONS RE YOUR ESSAY AND DEEP THANKS TO THE NEW YORKER FOR PRINTING IT

encore merci!

212 / TO ELISABETH KAISER-BRAEM *

4 Patchin Place
March 9, 1954

Dear Frau Kaiser-Braem—

* * * you write me that,of all books which you & your husband have translated,mine proves the most difficult. This I consider a great compliment;as also the statement that you sense "no distance" between translator & author(not to mention your husband's suspicion that my style affects your stories)& hope you'll believe I'm most thankful that The Enormous Room is in sympathetic hands

your few questions are easily answered. French soldiers(& gendarmes)during World War One wore metal helmets called casques,which we of the ambulance playfully nicknamed "tinderbies"—derbies,because their shape suggested what Americans call a derby hat(the English bowler:French chapeau melon) & tin,because we doubted their ability to deflect bullets. "Bratwurst" should undoubtedly be "Brachwurst"(you can easily see that I'm no linguist). My dictionary announces that "Kriss" (with a double s)"Kringle" is Saint Nicholas or Santa Claus;from the German Christkindl or Christkinde a diminutive form of Christkind. "William S. Hart" was a vastly popular—with boys especially—hero of our early Westerns:i.e. melodramatic movies featuring terrific battles between noble & wicked hardriding sharpshooting supercowboys

am glad you've encountered some of my poems in German translation,but more glad you prefer the originals;feeling(as I do)that poetry in & of itself must remain untranslatable. As for my pictures,they are little known:possibly because an artist who truly "pushes abstraction beyond the abstract" returns to Nature; & this I long ago did,whereas contemporary America wallows in "nonrepresentational" "art"

° *Whose friendship with EEC began after she and her husband, Helmuth M. Braem, had translated* The Enormous Room.

---

213 / TO HIS SISTER

4 Patchin Place
March 21 1954

Dear Elizabeth,—

* * * one thing only amazes me re "McCarthy":assuming he's all his archenemies claim(i.e. Satan personified)why,pray, does none of them ever realize that he wouldn't exist for a moment if Mrs&MrsFDR(doubtless with "the best of intentions") hadn't spent decades persuading All Good Americans that a supergang of hyperthugs—openly & avowedly dedicated to the proposition that freedom of anything is nothing at all—were just the lovingest & loveliest infraangels this side of Nonexistence. Nobody can tell our nonhero anything about witchhunts, for the good&sufficient reason that he's been soundly witchhunted ever since a "bloodless(!)revolution" began revolving. Nor am I surprised to learn that everybody out-your-way seems "to be getting more and more afraid to call his soul his own"—it took at least all my senseofhumor to counteract my own little soulbeating during the last twentyorwhatever years of Religion-Is-A-Crutch "liberal" dogmatism. As for believing "in a lot of unbelievable things":de gustibus non. From my standpoint, anybody who believes in unsocalled "socialism" makes a believer in the Divinity look like the rankest of amateurs. But I feel sure you're more than right in admiring the Friends,given all their limitations:& heartily second your JohnFox reaction to what les kumrads entitle The Bourgeoisie * * *·

214 / TO J. SIBLEY WATSON

[4 Patchin Place?]
April 17 1954

Dear Sibley—

delighted 7 is welcome. Having been nearly floored by 12 last summer,your ignorant correspondent took refuge in both read-able & illuminating "Psychological Reflections;A Jung Anthol-ogy"(Bollingen Series XXXI). 16 surprisingly arrived this morning. En passant:I owe the marvellous translation of a LaoTsze ˙ sequence—Eimi p 419—to "Psychological Types"; whose probably first American edition our nonhero sampled via the sole practicing native Jungian of my then or thereafter acquaintance. (Shamelessly enough,I didn't return the volume more than generously loaned;& guiltily sometimes wonder if its rightful proprietor was subsequently crucified or merely tarred& feathered). Marion,who thanks you heartily for your latest message,once boldly affirmed that stupidity is a vice:I'll timidly risk the suggestion that any "good Freudian" who doubts that "science" is "self-superceeding" should contrast the "Religion" chapter of Ernest Jones' "What Is Psychoanalysis?"(International Universities Press NY)with Sigmund Freud's "The Future Of An Illusion",which(ilyaunefois)my beloved friend Fritz Wittels nicknamed "The Illusion Of A Future"

215 / TO EZRA POUND

Silver Lake, N.H.
June 24 1954

Multitudinous Monolith—
bonjour!

am more than happy to hear from your sundrily divers selves,& kindestly thank whom-or-which for their most gracious invitation to sputter freely in linguadante.* How any mere mortal may im-or-possibly conceive 50(let alone 500)paroles anent some at least 5thrate political whorehouse while battling(1)prehistoric floods followed by a millenial heatwave (2)a prodigious pest of actually omnivorous(they eat even the pineneedles)caterpillars & (3)a gory galaxy of blockbusting mosquitoes plus brutally bloody-ing blackflies plusorminus aptly entitled via the vernacular "no-see-'ems"(smaller than a pinpoint but with a burn like a whitehot needle)remains a shallwesay ponderable question. Meantime please rest assured that this infrahero won't willingly accept publication per The socalled New Yorker—I politely refused to send them poems long ago—albeit(to give the D his d)one Mr (now departed)Ross certainly did instigate organize & achieve a civic superservice not to mention ultraconstructive reform con-sisting of the total removal from NewYorkCity's GrandCentral station of a mis(by nobody-unless-yourself-knows-whom)begot-ten concatention of hideous deafening & otherwise entirely de-moralizing hypergigantic talkie(sic)advertisements

e'er quitting sieveliesashun,Marionetmoi dined munificently chez Useless Mullins;who inhabits a towering eastside slumsky-scraper which has many more stairs tobeclimbed than Bunker HillMonument but oddly enough is worth the ennui(aside from Eustace Muggings louis-maim). A charming fellow-mortal: whose epitaph re thyself makes(in my humble opinion)him al-ready deathless

well now about DEBT † unquote,I overtly admit that the only debts harbouring some slightest interest for the sioux seen yea are those of a purely personal nature ie which can never be paid

                                        —hoping you are secretly the same;& with great love from the Lady!

* Pound relayed to Cummings an invitation to write 500 words on the state of the U.S.A for an Italian periodical. Cummings refused.
† Pound had written "can you conceive of any greater degree of imbecility than that of a man who cannot recognize the difference between interest-bearing & non-interest-bearing debt?" Marion Cummings informs us that "as C. had no debts—had in fact a horror of debts, this didn't bother him."

[Silver Lake, N.H.]
June 27, 1954

Dear D. J.

   * * * 3 cheers for Aloysius Fitzgerald
       who,being nine-eighths unapperald,
       went strolling the Strand
       with his pr-ck in his h-nd;
       proclaiming The End Of The Werald

                                —sois sage

217 / TO HIS JAPANESE TRANSLATOR

Silver Lake, N.H.
June 28 1954

Dear Mr Ishibashi—

       On the back of this sheet I've made a
       few notes which may help you with
       XAIPE
          —here's hoping!

poem 57) ["(im)c-a-t-(mo)"]

I am looking at a relaxed "c-a-t";a creature motionlessly alive—
"(im)(mo)b,i;l:e"

suddenly,for no apparent reason,the animal executes a series
of crazily acrobatic antics—"Fall(-)leAps!flOat(-)tumblIsh?-
drIft(-)whirlF(U1)(1Y) &&&"

after which,he wanders away looking exactly as if nothing had
ever happened . . . whereas,for me,the whole universe has
turned upside-down in a few moments

<u>poem 58</u> ["after screamgroa"]

a farmer is sharpening a bush-scythe on a grindstone;& the circumference of the slowly revolving stone responds,with a noise
between a scream & a groan,to the steady pressure of the steel
scytheblade

moving the blade away from the stone(which then merely idles,
making a grunt-squeaking sound as it revolves faster & freely)
he tries the muddied blade here-&-there with one thick thumb—
i.e. his "what:of.thumb" "stutt(er(s" along the steel,feeling
how sharp it is

Pretty Good("pud-dih-gud")he grunts:& slides the steel several
times briefly against the edge of the always revolving stone;
which answers each time with a scream-groaning noise different
from that produced by steady pressure

218 / *TO DAVID LOUGÉE**

Silver Lake, N.H.
July 14 '54

Dear David—

* * * Marion left last Friday for Hartford,to see her sick
father;& returned Monday to find me slightly shellshocked
after the worst(here,since we're now enjoying a thunder-
shower,I knock on wood)"electrical storm" of my extensive re-
membrance:a circular one,which went over & over Joy Farm
from 4:30 Sunday afternoon till 1:30 Monday morning. As I
was dining on the West porch,the metal cover of our telephone
fusebox(about 20 feet away)blew off with a tremendous bang—
semidazed,I jumped into the kitchen—there stood Elizabeth
Flaherty,our staunch handmaiden(fresh from the Aran Islands
near Eire's Western coast)very erect,with her palms joined in
prayer. She had seen "a big splash"(of light)at the kitchen's
far end where the 'phone is(perhaps 6 yards from herself)& I
promptly explained its cause. A little later another crash arrived;& this time "a big splash" occurred in the very sink. Wonderful girl—cheerfully(as usual)finishing her chores she went

right to bed & fell fast asleep.   As for Captain Nemo,only once
did he make the mistake of reclining in his bedroom;just outside
which ran the 'phone wire—otherwise I miserably meandered
downstairs&up,simultaneously lamenting arthritis & trying to
decide which fraction of my lifework chiefly deserved a rescue
(supposing the ship was abandonable).   At midnight we
mounted our White Horse;& he galloped(or gallopped?)us
back into our longlost senseofhumor:then came silence:yes,a
blessed stillness for which am everlastingly thankful

you'll be amazed to learn that electricity(the manufactured
variety)will presently be installed here,enabling Marion to have
a real "dark room" for photographic purposes & me to find
needles in haymows.   Pray with us that the Reverend Maginnis
—our only near neighbour—doesn't utilize this instrument of socalled civilization for radioactive méchancetés!   If so,some-
body'll perhaps wake up dead & here's hoping it won't be I.
"They" tell me "they"'ll rig a switch so the householder can
turn off the current during Jovian outbursts . . . & "they"'d
better * * *

* The poet, formerly with Caedmon records.

219 / TO ELISABETH AND HELMUTH BRAEM

Silver Lake, N.H.
August 7 1954

Highly
Respected
Translators—

to answer the questions in your July 15th letter *
    (1)p 193:"the Mecca of respectability,the Great White
    Throne of purity,Three rings Three" is a quotation from
    a spieler describing a circus.   The spieler's job is to stand
    outside the circustent & praise what's inside until his hear-
    ers' curiosity overcomes their timidity & they buy their
    tickets & enter.   What's inside is neither hyperrespectable
    nor superpure—hence his first & second phrases are
    strictly hyperbolic—but "Three rings Three" is perfectly

accurate;since the American circus has three rings,in which equestrians or acrobats or trained animals perform simultaneously.   Even so,Count Bragard was(to my feeling)a mixture of exaggerated fake-respectability & authentic human-complexity

(2)yes;I'd rather have the honest word "fuck" printed As Is

(3)don't bother to send your translation before printing: I trust you completely

(4)as Marion long ago wrote you,the publishers may use her photograph of me & pay her whatever they like

(5)I supposed "Sunday is a dreadful day"(page 176)to be lifted from Ezra Pound's immortal parody of the English poet Housman;but,finding that the original runs

> "London is a woeful place,
> Shropshire is much pleasanter
> Then let us smile a little space
> Upon fond nature's morbid grace. ·
>   Oh,Woe,woe,woe,etcetera . . ."

realize that I parodied my old friend the parodist

am naturally pleased to learn the "the German press is very interested";& more than glad that Slater Brown's book [*The Burning Wheel*] will be translated this autumn   *   *   *

---

* *The page numbers that follow are those of The Modern Library edition (New York, 1934) of* The Enormous Room.

220 / TO CHARLEEN SWANZEY

Silver Lake, N.H.
August 16 '54

Dear Charleen—

re "criticism",see page 7 of i(six nonlectures);& let me add that, from my point of view,noone who hopes to write poetry should attempt what used to be called free verse until she or he has mastered the conventional forms mentioned on pages 29–30

[Silver Lake, N.H.]
September 17 '54

Dear Bernice —

I left NYC believing that HarcourtBrace would publish,as one book,the complete texts of all my so-far-published booksof- poems — minus everything in "Collected" Poems except its "new poems" — from Tulips and Chimneys('23)to XAIPE('50):our volume to be naturally entitled poems 1923–1950. When Mr G [Robert Giroux] of HB had suggested "1923–1954" I'd said no: since poems published in magazines after '50,as well as before '23,were not included;hence raising '50 to '54 would mean(if we were honest)lowering '23 to heaven knows what,& including more poems than we had room for. Apparently he grasped this obvious point — yet I seem to remember changing "54" to "50" on the contract before signing it

early in July HB sent me a batch of proof;urging haste. I has- tened,returned the batch with corrections,heard nothing for weeks,& finally wrote asking what was wrong? "Catherine Car- ver" replied;regretting the delay,stating that Mr G was on vaca- tion,sending more proof,& urging more haste. Marion & I worked our hardest;but missed many errors(in the text itself — not the fault of the HB printer!):so that I was often forced to make re-corrections — concerning which CC couldn't have been more generously understanding

just as both she & I supposed that all necessary corrections had been achieved(& the undersigned had most kindly thanked her for her patience & courtesy)he discovered,to my horror,further boners;not the least of which was "54" instead of "50" on our title page. — whose general appearance had so pleased me that I stupidly hadn't noticed the substitution. I caught it,however, when a proof of the otherwise excellent jacket arrived;& man- aged — between two hurricanes — to send off a telegram saying PLEASE HOLD EVERYTHING STOP MORE CORREC- TIONS ARE ON THE WAY. Then I forwarded a list of the new corrections airmail-specialdelivery,not omitting "50" on jacket & title page

days passed:& neither my telegram nor my letter was acknowl-
edged.   Although the text-errors troubled me greatly,I was even
more upset by "54".   But what to do?   Telephoning seemed impossible;moreover I daily expected a letter or wire.   At last,this
morning,I decided to make sure there'd been no mistake chez
les Brandts;& succeeded in shouting at your aimiable secretary.
Though she could scarcely hear me,I could hear her fairly well;
&(to my amazement)learned that the contract now read "Poems
1923–1954"

any radiance which you can toss on this painful situation will be
appreciated

222 / TO OMAR POUND

[4 Patchin Place]
November 8 1954

Dear Omar—

Joy is by far the rarest thing,in or out of every world:& to yourself I owe a pair of nearly simultaneous Joys—one,reading your
letter;& the other,meeting your father(or,as a timidly manmade
world would assert,father-in-law)*to be.   Please accept on both
counts my most sincere & heartiest congratulations

concerning the man I met,let me say this & this only:I can
imagine no human being who would more gladly give you just
the affectionate understanding which you,as a human being,
desire & deserve.   Then let me add:bravissimo!

with regard to the subject of your letter:our nonhero has a
single statement to make;not a generality,but a function of his
own particular experience—women are always right

by this,I emphatically don't imply the merely logical or prag-
matical or legal or whatever "right" which men(who are essentially cowards)have invented to cover a multitude of wrongs.
I do imply Something equally at right angles to "right" &

222 / TO OMAR POUND

"wrong";Something which is to "right" & "wrong" as Joy is to "pleasure" & "pain",or as Truth is to "fact" & "fiction"

today's "fact" is tomorrow's "fiction" — Copernicus super-cedes Ptolemy — & only perhaps a billion fools confuse the transient with the timeless. "Pleasure" & "pain" are heads & tails of the same coin:"pain" equals un-"pleasure","pleasure" equals un-"pain". But Joy isn't un-anything;Joy IS

precisely so,while soidisant men are content to simply exist in the silly finite tiny trivial realm of either-or which their coward-ice has evolved & their arrogance has entitled "reality",women (totally & mysteriously)ARE

this is what I imply;& can only imply,since the thing in itself (like all Good True & Beautiful things)eludes description,being strictly immeasurable. Women ARE,not because or although or for any selfstyled reason,but like Birth & Life & Death. They ARE like feeling & like breathing;like a bud exploding & a leaf spiralling:like the stars setting & the sun rising,& the moon closing & the moon opening ✳ ✳ ✳

* *Pound's son Omar had recently married Elizabeth Parkin, of Montreal.*

223 / *TO HIS SISTER*

[4 Patchin Place]
December 7(?) [1954]

Dear Elizabeth —

"thank God!" Marion(seeing your letter)exclaimed this morn-ing. And rightly. For,having just received a doublebarrelled "critical" brushoff,our strictly irrational nonhero — who went to bed last night as cheerful as 3 crickets — was buzzing like 16 whitearsedhornets in a paperbag. * I say irrational,since what could be more obvious than that nobody(in any freedom of speech-loving heavenonearth)must or can decry socalled criti-cism without causing every extant American soidisant critic to render the quoter's existence improbable thanks kindly for the tip re Vanishing Prairie. It's not often that my consort lures me to a movie;but perhaps she'll succeed this time . . . though the name Disney(I confess)harbours horrifying connotations ✱ ✱ ✱

everybody doubtless possesses his or her own variety of stage-fright#. What I generally experience before a reading is a conglomeration of anxieties involving bellyache,hearttrouble, arthritis,diarrhoea,&(temporary)blindness. But feel I'm some-how gradually evolving;despite selfpity narcissism an inferiority complex & possibly several other psychic ailments:all,I heartily believe,justified . . . if you,like me,don't fancy disrobing before perfect strangers. Not that simple people don't simply adore to do exactly that,at the least opportunity

[EEC's note] Max Eastman told me that once he felt divided-in-vertical-halves;& later a female spectator assured him she saw his aureole

✱ Poems 1923–1954 *had been published in October.*

224 / *TO HILDEGARDE WATSON*

[4 Patchin Place?]
December 8 '54

Dear Hildegarde —

hail!

there've been far(from our nonhero's standpoint)better read-ings than his latest YM&YWHA one;so,although your presence would certainly have more than cheered him,he's nearly(but not quite)glad you were elsewhere. First:I'd arranged my little act as two wholes,8–40 to 9–10 & 9–20 to 9–50,separated(& united)by an intermission — but,at 9 o'clock,all "standees" had to be given the seats of all ticketowners who by that time hadn't appeared;which quite-beyond-question-good deed demolished my earlier whole. Second:the "mike" (peculiarly costly,I was assured)proved as stiff as a new mule;which rendered acrobatics impossible — with a flexible(electronically)instrument I could

have roared as softly as a seashell or noiselessly dropped a demi-
whisper into the very last row of the balcony. Perhaps worst:my
audience seemed only about half as alive as the equivalent group
of 4 years ago;possibly because their seats are now roughly
twice as expensive. You would,however,have enjoyed the enthusiasm—& laughed heartily had you somehow spotted a bevy
of scared officials whisking(for I'd previously stipulated No
Autographs)our exspeaker out&downthrough a secretback-
entrance after 1 encore * * *

1955–1962

4 Patchin Place
January 22 '55

Dear Ez—

if am not most grossly mistaken,'twas
David called Thoreau observed he had
never met—or hoped to meet—a man worse
than himself

talents differ:if heroical thine be cursing
swine & ringing nex,our tolerant unhero
may only re-remark(vide 6 nonlectures page
70)that "hatred bounces"

item— 1 Sam XVII—something informs me
that Joy is the name of a brook from which
(as the adult hyperogre of philistinism
superstrutted)a mere child chose him five
smooth stones

226 / *TO AN UNIDENTIFIED ENGLISH CORRESPONDENT*

4 Patchin Place
April 5 1955

Dear Mr Goodchild—

your more than kind letter cheers me:many thanks

a recent book of mine,called i:six nonlectures,is now(my agent
says)on sale at the London branch of the Oxford University
Press;& if you & your friends should do me the honour to read
this book,you'd speedily understand why it "seems almost impossible to obtain" my work in England. Here in America,
also,the partisans of collectivism who control book-distribution
& book-reviewing both hate & fear those dangerous(since human)values for which I am humbly proud to stand

concerning the "small 'I' ":did it never strike you as significant that,of all God's children,only English & Americans apotheosize their egos by capitalizing a pronoun whose equivalent is in French "je",in German "ich",& in Italian "io"?

227 / *TO WILLIAM SLATER BROWN*

4 Patchin Place
April 5 '55

Dear "B" —

this is to say,as simply as possible,what I tried to say under The Great Tree:* for Christ's sake,<u>write</u> your Mexican blowup, strictly As Is & from start to finish

you know me far too well to suspect I fancy myself as a do-gooder. May God forbid. I'm speaking to you as what I de-voutly hope I am — an artist — which doesn't imply that Heaven knows how many poor mortals mightn't be worlds richer for sharing in such a perfectly amazing tragicomedy

of course you'd be doing a great & fundamentally(to use ex-actly your own word)MORAL deed if you'd <u>write</u> the terrifying saga of your whole fabulous experiment with selfobliteration — you called it,I remember,"a kind of suicide" — but maybe that's asking too much

I wish I could help you to do either,or both,these things;if only because you could & did help me inestimably when I was strug-gling with TheER:but what I'm asking of you — to re-create a <u>spiritual</u> imprisonment — would have to be done by yourself alone

better than I or anyone else you must(in your heart)feel how generous a doing this would be;since nobody except yourself knows what you've suffered,& because au fond you're one of the most generous human beings alive

---

* *Brown and EEC had met by chance under the big tree at the northeast corner of Wash-ington Square, where Brown told him the story of his Mexican "blowup," a temporary collapse into drink. Brown thought the experience too unexceptional and did not write the book.*

4 Patchin Place
April 8 1955

Dear Hildegarde—

* * * must confess I attribute my physical ills to socalled nervous tension:et pourquoi pas? If any quite unmitigatedly perverse human being insists on deliberately insulting the powersthatseem—instead of(come toutlemonde)dutifully soft-soaping same—what can he expect? Certainly not something which happened yesterday; when a pretty young girl handed me a bunch of daffodills,saying "you don't know who I am but I just wanted to give you these"

Silver Lake, N.H.
June 4 1955

Dear NF—

* * * obsoletely enough,this correspondent regards so-called publicity as a loathesome disease:hence am healthily against the See How He Does It aspect of contemporary vivisec-tion;&,let me needlessly add,I never gave any collegiate library a "preliminary draft" or other "manuscript". (Furthermore— strictly entre ourselves—have at various times had the honour of turning down e.g. a "profile" per TheNewYorker;a Life Goes To A Garret type of hullaballoo via MesserLuce's mur-murdons;& a 500$ sampleofradioactivity specifying 20 minutes of chatter plus 10 of questionanswering). Marion,however, once cornered a jumble of variants which preceded a poem who didn't win some prize emitted by Karl The Kultured [Karl Shapiro, then editor of *Poetry*]:& she'll gladly lend you her chaos if you'll solemnly promise to keep it completely (SIC) to yourself * * *

Silver Lake, N.H.
August 26 1955

Dear Hildegarde —

* * * this summer has been unique:no rain,tropical heat,&
then a downpour;but luckily not a deluge nor yet a hurricane
(only the other day Marion said "I wonder how Hildegarde's
house is" meaning Northbridge). Now NH has shifted into a
cooler key;autumnal,excellent for hardworkoutdoors;but un-
easy on arthritic folk. I celebrated by almost pulling myself
apart in our East field;from which had attempted — on both
knees,with a dull hatchet — to chop an army of meadowsweet.
The bushes grow in clumps,& bear a lovely white wonderfully
fragrant flower(spiraea,"spire")but hereabouts are aptly if
brutally named ironroot. For to really attack a clump of waist-
high bushes is to find roots running ad infinitum underground
— often appearing on the surface as other clumps — & soon the
attacker becomes crazed by mere innumerability & rushes at it
headlong:to his sorrow. You may ask "why not leave the
bushes alone?" Alas,they'd soon swallow our whole field,&
then we couldn't stroll there(as already we can't stroll in front
of the house). Ploughing might seem a solution:but with the
breaking of the tough topsoil,any number of pines would leap
into existence & create a forest in no time unless perpetually
weeded out. So am hoping I'll soon recover my strength & be
able to assume the hatchet once more * * *

231 / TO ELISABETH KAISER-BRAEM

4 Patchin Place
January 10 1956

Dear Friend —

* * * Am honoured that Marion's alltooflattering photograph adorns your "bookshelf"(which is what a "mantlepiece"
sooner or later becomes,chez nous). The "outbreak about
PARIS" strikes "Mister Nonhero" as quite eminently under-

standable—& why not?   Years after La Ferté,he had a flic on either arm dragging him up the Rue de l'Hirondelle to a poste de police where le dit nh was officially registered as a "pisseur américain";& it took Paul Morand(then luckily associated with the Quai d'Orsay)to prevent me from being expulsé forevermore!* * * *

* *For a full account of this incident, which occurred in 1923, see Charles Norman,* The Magic-Maker *(New York, 1958), 192ff.*

232 / *TO SUSAN F. COPLEY*

4 Patchin Place
January 26 1956

Dear Miss Copley—

not being a socalled critic,I don't expect a poem to be the same for any two people;or even for one person twice.   But perhaps I can give you some notion of how the poem [*Poems, 1923–1954,* 406] you're concerned with feels to me now

   all a mirror says is <u>Hello</u>:nothing more.   It's a young girl who,looking in it & seeing her reflection,asks <u>Who</u>(can this be)?   When the mirror doesn't answer,the impatient girl concludes <u>I</u>(the person looking in the mirror)<u>must be You</u> (the person whom I see in the mirror);or,how-I-look is who-I-am;or,things are what they seem;or,only the-surface-of-life is what-really-matters.   This is absolutely untrue.   But since light doesn't lie,the girl's mirror hasn't deceived her— she's fooling herself

   all a gun means is <u>Bang</u>:nothing more.   But a man who <u>means No</u>(because he's full-of-hate)<u>seeing something yes</u> (something loving or beautiful or alive)<u>will grin with pain,</u> and curse the living something;and kill it,if possible,with a gun.   If the something is a someone,in a socalled war,the killer will suppose he's triumphed over an "enemy".   He doesn't realize that <u>true wars are never won</u>;since they are inward,not outward,and necessitate facing one's self.

4 Patchin Place
March 11 1956

Dear KB — *

such a charmingly cheering hyperepistle as thine our nonhero
has rarely if ever experienced. In reply let him(quite entr'ourselves)observe that I unquestionably am the infraultrafabulous
preprotofascistic Ogre of the Cowcatchus,who devours pink
prosemites for breakfast & yellow liberals at lunch & black de-
mocrats with his dinner. Good Freudians were quick to suggest that my superego suffers from subneolithic trends;while
middleoftheroad Marxists are not slow to accuse me of sinister&
dextrous deviation. Possibly needless to add,I have been found
guilty of the misdemeanor known as lace-majesty(or making
light of Einstein)& convicted of the crime entitled happy-us-
coppers(or openly avowing a predilection for David at the expense of Goliath)but nevertheless beg to remain

---

* *A reply to a letter from Burke introducing a friend and adding: "Perhaps I should also
introduce the introducer. I am the fellow who, during Roosevelt's first term, was already
regretting the demise of The Dial and who now sometimes dreams that it has somehow
been going on all these years, without letting us know. I am the fellow whose voice carries,
but not much weight. I am the fellow who invented the slogan for Brotherhood Week: My
brother can beat your brother. I crossed a four-year locust with a seven-year locust, and to
my surprise got a twenty-eight-year locust (though I could probably have figured that out
for myself beforehand if I hadn't flunked mathematics)."*

234 / TO EZRA POUND

4 Patchin Place
May 16 '56

Dear Ezra —

am thankful Marion&I left America when we did(SaintPat'sDay)
even though coldcoldcold has driven us home again six weeks
later

Venice,city of silence & poetry,is murdered by motorboats
(gently remarked our gondolier;as he cleverly-outofexistence

-wiped an oversize wave)& that evening,off in some(far from anything known)dark square,we heard canned cries:& beheld at least four people staring at a tumbledown house whence television emanated

you're hunted from morning to midnight through Firenze by every notimaginable species of motorbicycle—the speedfiends ride their roaring machines at 40–50mph & l'on dit there are three times as many accidents as in NewYorkCity. (I saw somebody almost killed twice in five seconds). As for proud poor Roma,she long ago ceased to exist . . . except here and there . . . thanks to the wasps

but,O my friend!Italia somehow is still Herself:& always miraculous

235 / TO HILDEGARDE WATSON

Silver Lake, N.H.
July 1 1956

Dear Hildegarde—

* * * since arriving,Marion&I've been almost steadily toiling to keep our habitat livable. As you'll remember:it's a huge hilltop summerhouse through which any breeze blows in 50odd directions. We block off most of the rooms;& belabor the remaining 3 with electric & kerosene heaters,plus woodfires. When the roof leaks,beds are moved. If one of us collapses,the other plays nurse. Now & then a Real Hot Spell comes;& our inmost hearts thank Heaven

to cheer myself when I don't(as Lachaise would say)"feel to do" either painting or writing(& this <u>when</u> was perhaps what Yeats meant by declaring that ThePowersThatBe give their favorite protagonist such a destiny . . . or temperament . . . as will cause him every suffering "short of despair")I look through notebooks(whereof 200&some already exist)or rather their typed— for I rarely can read my own script—contents. Here's a passage from nb 93(A.D. '47)

"Hildegarde & Miss" sic "Selden(en route in Mrs L's car,H driving,from Maine to Mass)arrive. And H tells me of a revelation she had 'the Devil is my ally!' i.e. all fear is an ignorance of the truth that what we call 'suffering' or 'pain' or 'sorrow'(or 'evil')is a great gift . . . to him who can receive it — & he,she says,am I!"

or again('48,nb 105)

"& perhaps the New World's nearness makes revenge every-where obsolete? who knows?

"when Hildegarde & I were talking,a few days ago,as she chose a picture(for Chicago)I heard her telling me — 'if you turn the other cheek truly',something happens which makes you invulnerable & your wouldbe foe powerless:she knows this is so;she is sure"

I wonder what "(for Chicago)" signifies?

well,my dear,the typewriter's full of junebugs & I feel worlds better than when I began this letter;such is your PowerForGood

236 / TO DAVID DIAMOND

Silver Lake, N.H.
August 2 '56

Dear D —

of your multiple Florentine more-than-kindnesses to me & Marion,the one which this correspondent will probably always first remember concerns Michelangelo's version of your heroic namesake:& 'twill be a long time before I can't see the three of us floating like newborn spirits in the presence of that particular miracle

regarding anti-miscalled "semitism"(or as mon ami DJGrossman asked,how about the Arabs?)our nonhero's stance couldn't be more difinite. Anti- & pro- "semitism",he feels,are tails & heads of one&thesame coin;which coin,pour moi,most emphat-ically isn't legal-tender. Why? Because "all groups,gangs,and collectivities — no matter how apparently disparate — are funda-mentally alike"(i, page 31)& what matters to me is UNIQUE-NESS. Thank God,there's only one Michelangelo! * * *

Silver Lake, N.H.
August 12 1956

Dear Hildegarde —

am greatly cheered because a not mistakably intellectual chip-
munk has caused-to-disappear all the peanuts I put out for him
ce matin except one,whose solitary presence says "don't forget
me!" & I don't. The causer is extremely shy,remarkably un-
hurried,cares almost nothing for mere food,& frequently leaves
the ground to explore our largest grapevine. His completely
different predecessor was utterly & entirely "enchanting"(to
use Marion's beautiful word) — lovely,eager,velocitous,trusting,
a perfect poem of a creature. One day(after dancing all over
our hearts)this miraculous atom of gaiety vanished;& for a
long long time we could scarcely hold up our heads. I'd seen a
damned yellow cat lurking in the grass behind our barn,& several times shot at him with a pistol(the thirtyeight Remington
automatic which SW discovered in Jersey,decades ago)but always missed — finally Billy James lent me his Winchester rifle . . .
whereupon satan disappeared   *   *   *

4 Patchin Place
October 20 '56

Dear Howard —

hail rain & snow!

am more than sorry to hear of your various disappointments;&
can well understand how they'd depress even somebody as
lively as thou. Only to think of all the crooks thugs punks
twerps & downright shits that "make good" in a socalled world
which suddenly ups & gives Lottie's boyfriend(not to mention
Howie&christine's father)the brushoff,must set your hands
afisting. Or perhaps I should say "must have set" — since you
may have found any sort of a job by now. If you haven't,con-

sider me:broke or semibroke all my life,but still in possession
of the "divine"(as Herr Schopenhauer calls it)part of man:a
sense of humor . . . thank Heaven!   And kindly don't toss me
away with "O but you & I are different"—of course we're different;if we weren't we wouldn't be alive,we'd simply UNbe:
which is exactly what(I confess)the abovementioned world now
& then seems to try extremely hard to make us.   Yet,between
ourselves,I rather doubt if it'll succeed

more & more,our nonhero's astonished by something the supra
philosopher puts right into the proverbial pigeonhole by remarking "no man can see over his own head".   Thus,if a person's utterly selfish—disregarding other people's feelings at
least 96pc of the time without so much as suspecting how they
(naturally)resent such maltreatment—he's nearly sure,sooner
or later,to complain of a raw deal from his contemporaries.   Or
to take a real demonstration of the S dictum:not long ago this
very correspondent actually caught himself bewailing the per-
fectly(sic)inexplicable fact that a horde of "critical" racket-
eers,which I'd socked as violently & as frequently as possible
during some 2 or 3 decades;came down on me all together with
every weapon known to "civilized" stinkers.   Can you imagine
any human creature quite so dumb?   And am not exaggerating!   Luckily my beloved s-of-h came to my assistance   *   *   *

239 / TO HIS SISTER

4 Patchin Place
mardi soir [1956]

Dear Elizabeth—

*   *   *   will you now kindly solve me a trivial problem which
quite baffles my ignorance?   A recent poem comprises this
image
> "then down the sky of an afternoon
>   came slowly a wrinkled crone" *

who's(of course)the waning moon.   All I ask is,whether or not
an astronomer would accept this image of mine;i.e. whether or
not,at any time of year,a person in(say)Paris or NewYork could

soberly see a waning moon descending the afternoon sky. If not,shall have to change my poem in deference to science
* * *

° *These lines were evidently never published in this form.*

240 / *TO ELISABETH KAISER-BRAEM*

4 Patchin Place
November 26 1956

Dear Garance —

* * * having glimpsed Wien & Berlin after WWOne,can imagine how Germany reacted to the Hungarian horror. But doubt if any European can conceive the reaction of an American born & bred. Picture "God's country"(alias earth's richest nation) — the sworn enemy of brute force,the foremost friend of democratic freedom,perpetually dedicated to an unconditional defence of all oppressed peoples &(with this sacred mission in view)armed to the hyperangelic teeth with every not imaginable implement of supersatanic destruction — urging(via night&day broadcasts)the socalled satellite nations to revolt from colossal Russia;&,when diminutive Hungary miraculously did so,lauding Hungarian heroism to the skies & offering the gallant Hungarian people millions of dollars & promising the immediate dispatch of all kinds of desperately needed materials . . . until Moscow,enraged,hurled her whole hugeness ABSOLUTELY UNOPPOSED against that handful of patriots;& began blowing their cities & their women & their hopes & their children to hell . . . whereupon the never defeated United States Of America shrugged her peaceloving shoulders & murmured "too bad"

when "America" cheered wildly for Finland while secretly selling hightest gasoline to Russia so Its tanks could murder Finns,I ceased to be — in the only true sense,that is spiritually — an "American". If my bookofpoems ever comes,look at p 390 (iv),& 393(vii)& 396(xiii) . . . proving that PearlHarbor didn't fool someone . . . not to mention 357(poem 11),lest anyone suppose that the man who wrote Him Act II Scene 8(Mussolini-as-Caesar & the homos)was a "fascist"

there are notafew Americans who feel as I do—& as Marion does—but they(we)are,thanks to "democracy",helpless as far as "action" goes.   Comme disait Saint-Exupéry:when one person oppresses many people,everybody cries "tyranny!" but tyranny occurs just as truly whenever many people oppress one single individual . . . & nobody even whispers

241 / *TO CHARLES NORMAN*

4 Patchin Place
samedi [1957]

Dear Charles—

thanks kindly for the carbon of your anti"calligramme" paragraphs.*   I enjoy their tone in general,& in particular the metaphor "walls his building with music";but something puzzles me.   Take this succession—
   1) "lines based on structural elements that were independent of the metric measure."
   2) "lines which are his steel and concrete"(as his walls are music)
   3) "structural elements on the printed page which act as doors and passageways to ultimate effects."
Frankly:our unhero is confused

perhaps you could show,via quotations from his work,just what "structural elements" are;that would be a great help

& please let me make something onceforall clear:from my standpoint,not EEC but EP is the authentic "innovator";the true trailblazer of an epoch;"this selfstyled world's greatest and most generous literary figure"—nor shall I ever forget the thrill I experienced on first reading "The Return"

* *In Norman's* Ezra Pound (*New York, 1960*), *then in preparation.*

4 Patchin Place
December 11 1957

Dear Hildegarde —

how marvellous that you should love the Hanrahan volume* as
Marion & I do! 'Twas she who remarked that,since we "luckily"
had a couple of copies,you ought to have one of them;& she herself found the extra copy in a NY bookstore whose owner never
heard of Yeats. As for your praise of a tout petit éléphant — my
heart is happy!

Oscar Wilde was the man who called The Crucifixion Of The
Outcast the greatest shortstory ever written. What never fails
to amaze me here(as well as,for that matter,everywhere in the
book)is Y's equal understanding of perfectly opposed viewpoints
— collective & individual,systematic & spontaneous,rational &
instinctive. Needless to add,I'm deeply moved(& entirely delighted)that you thought of me in connection with such a reck-
less & passionate & otherwise crazy human creature as the glee-
man(who so beautifully illustrates Libra,in Marion's sense of
"either away up or away down"). Always the nobleness of those
wonderful words
          "I have drawn the sword,and told the truth,
             and lived my vision,and am content"
lifts me from undeath into Aliveness ✳ ✳ ✳

* W. B. Yeats, Stories of Red Hanrahan.

Silver Lake, N.H.
August 18 '58

Gentlemen —

so you think Ezra Pound needs rehabilitating? Allow me to
disagree. If the man has sinned,nothing you can say or do will

make him sinless — and if you're trying to render the poet socially respectable,that's an insult;because no poet worth his salt ever has given or ever will give a hangnail for social respectability. In this UNworld of "ours",lots of UNpoets and plenty of UNcountries(UNamerica,for example)need rehabilitating the very worst way. But whoever or whatever he may be,Ezra Pound most emphatically isn't UNanyone or UNanything

° *Representing a Swiss group who invited EEC to contribute a statement to a publication urging the rehabilitation of Ezra Pound.*

244 / TO M. R. WERNER

Silver Lake, N.H.
September 2 '58

My dear Baron —

lest your serenest altitude commit the mental misdemeanor of permanently reproaching itself with anything remotely suggestive of tardiness re the acknowledgement of our unhero's diminutive cadeau,he has delayed MORE THAN a month ere even attempting to thank you for a(cheering)^n epistle dated "Saturday July 26"

let me respectfully append that am delighted to learn that one Timothy,child of an ancient pal & fellow-admirer of KK [Krazy Kat],possessed the good sense to commission a portrait of GVillage at the hands of him whose wallop to NYU(appearing in wasn't it the V"Voice"?)I haven't forgotten. Nothing,of course, can or should be done about the aforesaid walloper's chevaline propensities;although 'tis more than likely that,if he didn't regularly or irregularly vent his passionate predelictions via "the track",enormous public benefits might result:e.g. the assassination of Commissar M-s-s in boiling blood. The way you now feel toward Mr JFDulles,mon cher Baron,delicately reminds me of thy former tributes to H-rb-rt H--v-r

but to descend to the domestic:your humble servitor is(as ever)a slave to hummingbirds;& am proud to observe that,despite the fact that late August & early September mean generally speaking hornets & particularly yellowjackets—which ubiquitous scions of Satan continuously rob my beloved protagonists of their daily or rather hourly sugarwater—one oiseau mouche still does me the signal honour to persist in battling what may feebly be described as the menace of innumerability. Aside from this joyous companion,am frequently attended by those staunch guardians of the rural peace entitled robins:who,at the most not expected moments,invite me to repel sundry & various quardrupedal invaders;not excluding a female fox or vixen whose contempt for my unmarksmanship couldn't be less oc-cultly manifested * * *

Silver Lake, N.H.
September 21 '58

Dear Mina—

<u>congratulations</u> re M Chabrier! And I hope to(some day)at-least-glimpse your 9yearopus. Having myself no capacity for scholarship,can't help feeling tiptoeish toward such achieve-ments;but what(as you would eloquently declare)etcetera. Any-how "only" as Count H Keyserling long since percisely observed "the saint can do nothing"

your portrait of 1917 "radical" you-descending-the-staircase(no offense:ye olde armory showe happened around '13)would al-most make me doubtful of "America" 's future if I didn't agree with G Herriman's KK that "it's what's behind me that I am". Ah,well:you should have seen Private-but-not-1st-class EEC staggering under a 50lb pack while feebly waving a 10lb rifle comma on the point of "embarking" for Oh-verr they-yerr when (blessed be his name)Guillaume R Hoist "broke" the "false armistice"—whereupon "Camp Devens" disintegrated fromtop-tobottom & toola mond below the rank of zekun-looee began drilling absolutelyalldaylong(except for a halfhour "lunch")in staked-out-very-carefully-indeed squares,1 to a "squad",each measuring 10 feet by 10 feet . . . this being(British)"General Hunt" 's system for rejuvenating senescent "moe-ral" however,I suspect that the oddest thing of all was a 3day "hike" con "fullequipment"(decreed by the General of "our" Division in the exact middle of the "Spanish Flu" epidemic)during which spell it continuously rained,& ⅓ of my fellow-fantassins died; partly of course because sick soldiers were immediately stripped & stuffed into cotton pyjamas & laid in the open air under sheets sans blankets,or so a youth who miraculously survived the "hospital" assured your h s

246 / *TO ROBERT GRAVES*

4 Patchin Place
October 31 '58

RG—

the effect of your Sunday Times benison is what collegiates used to call terrif.* Even Mad Jack Kelly(who once spanned the Atlantic Ocean with a slooprigged catboat but now collects abandoned dogs in Greenwich Village)cried his approval this morning. As for our unhero,I marvel equally at your generosity & your tact

* *Robert Graves, "Corn Can Sparkle Like a Star,"* New York Times Book Review *(October 26, 1958). A review of* 95 Poems.

247 / *TO LETA HANNAN*

4 Patchin Place
October 31 1958

Dear Leta Hannan—

the poem you mention should not be difficult for anyone who's ever been at a real(flesh&blood)Circus & seen its <u>aerial acrobats</u>

these extraordinary creatures appear together on the tanbark as mere "mortals"(like you or me)but then "climbing" up high "into eachness begin" their amazing "trapeze" act—becoming "things"-which-"swing" & turning "somersaults" & "swoop"ing far away only to "exquisite"ly "return"—& afterward "drop" into a net "fall"ing with "dreamlike" grace . . . transformed from "mortals" into "im"mortals because they risked their lives to create something beautiful. Finally they all disappear into the place from which they appeared;just as the last syllable "(im" of my poem goes back to the first word "mortals)"

incidentally you will find this poem on page 385 of a book called Poems 1923–1954:& here's wishing you good luck

248 / TO CHARLES NORMAN

4 Patchin Place
January 21 '59

Dear Charles—

re the "book on Pound":Bonne Chance

our first(since you ask)meeting occurred,if am not very greatly mistaken,about the time he began writing The Dial's Paris Letter. I was dodging deadly bores in a demimaisonpublique near Place Saint Michel,when Scofield Thayer visited Paris. At his rue de Rivoli hostelry Thayer introduced me to Pound;who accompanied our unhero to the Place aforesaid—where(having respectfully wished him a good night)I circuitously resumed my refuge. During our whole promenade Ezra was more than wonderfully entertaining:he was magically gentle,as only a great man can be toward some shyest child

249 / TO HILDEGARDE WATSON

4 Patchin Place
January 25 '59

Dear Hildegarde—

* * * haven't read the book about DT, *of whom I really saw very little(we never "read" or "recorded" together)perhaps

because at our first meeting I recognized his kinship with a
former friend of mine—a true poet,generous & brave,gifted
with immense vitality & complete honesty:who(in his unimagin-
ably perverse way)was going at deadly speed to a doom from
which noone could even begin to save him. I.e. Hart Crane &
Dylan Thomas struck me as two perfectly authentic variations of
the Poète Maudit theme:Crane being far-&-away the more vivid
phenomenon ⁎ ⁎ ⁎

° *John Malcolm Brinnin*, Dylan Thomas in America (*New York, 1957*).

250 / TO FRANCES AMES RANDALL

4 Patchin Place
Feb. 3 [1959?]

Dear Mrs Randall—

⁎ ⁎ ⁎ all poem 19 [*95 Poems*] wants to do is to create a
picture of a bee,unmoving,in the last blossom of a rosebush.
Taken alone,the parentheses read "bee in the only rose". Without parentheses,the poem asks "unmoving are you asleep". Put
these elements together & they make "bee in the only rose(unmoving)are you asleep?"

if you'll let me know which of the other poems seem least com-
prehensible,I'll gladly furnish explanations;which are certainly
harmless,as long as a person doesn't mistake the explanation
for the poem

251 / TO HIS SISTER

4 Patchin Place
February 11 '59

Dear Elizabeth—

⁎ ⁎ ⁎ did you ever read Out Of Africa(or Seven Gothic
Tales,or Winter's Tales)by the unique Danish writer Isak Dinesen? If not,do. She's visiting America—even "Life"(!)mag ran

an article about her with photos which didn't do the lady justice. Amazing person:extremely old,ghost-frail;a gallant aris-
tocrat born&bred,&(like all aristocrats)sans any trace of snob-
bery. And what Spirit! Apropos of her latest book,which(her
cool voice remarked at a recent party in her honour)she dic-
tated feeling sure she'd die—"and so I learned that,if you have
no faith,if you are quite without hope,and if you do just a very
little,and then a little more,and again still more,it will all of itself become something". Tonight Marion & I are going to
hear her <u>tell</u> a story(for one hour!)at the ex-YM,now YM&YW
if you please,HA uptown * * *

252 / TO FRANCIS STEEGMULLER

4 Patchin Place
March 5 '59

Dear Steegmuller—

greetings

seem to remember asserting that all my booksofpoems after
the original T&C manuscript—published as Tulips & Chimneys,AND,XLI Poems—start with autumn(downgoing,de-
spair)& pass through winter(mystery,dream)& stop in spring(up-
coming,joy). But as I glance over the index of Poems '23–'54,
find few hints of this progression;beyond a tendency to begin
dirty(world:sordid,satires)& end clean(earth:lyrical,lovepoems).
95 Poems is,of course,an obvious example of the seasonal metaphor—1,a falling leaf;41,snow;73,nature(wholeness innocence
eachness beauty the transcending of time&space)awakened.
"Metaphor" of what? Perhaps of whatever one frequently
meets via my old friend S.FosterDamon's William Blake/His
Philosophy And Symbols;e.g.(p 225)"They" the angels "descend on the material side . . . and ascend on the spiritual;this
is . . . a representation of the greatest Christian mystery,a statement of the secret which every mystic tries to tell" * * *

4 Patchin Place
March 7 '59

Dear Mr Faulkner—

your good letter has arrived. The praise of "my father moved
through dooms of love" [*Poems 1923–1954*, 373–375] is praise
indeed! Am glad you enjoy the Caedmon record,& especially
glad you feel truth under the words of my poems. (Could someone receive a deeper compliment?) If you happen to meet a
copy of i:six nonlectures,please turn to page 113

that philosophy "student" who objected to essence must be
stupider(if possible)than most,since the great American philosopher George Santayana—whom I read & re-read when an
UNworld threatens to get me down—makes essence the basis of
his whole life . . . but probably no "American" institution of
non-learning has yet heard of Santayana. Quite incidentally:
if you haven't encountered The Idea Of Christ In The Gospels
you've a marvellous experience ahead. I'll wager one page of
this cancels more than all teachers of the-religion-of-irreligion
ever even dreamed of unteaching! * * *

thank you kindly for the charming poem. I shouldn't call it
a sonnet,because for me "sonnet" implies a poem of 14 iambic
pentameters,none of them unrhymed. But I very much like
the feeling of the poem;& hope—ars longa,vita brevis—you
won't stop writing * * *

° *The photographer.*

Silver Lake, N.H.
September 7 '59

Dear Nancy—

yesterday being a new moon, nh has just passed from unending-
fully pouring rainRainRAIN into beautiful sunlight;as if to
celebrate which miracle,your August 30th letter arrives

probably I know how you feel about having nearly nobody read your book,since(except for my father & mother;& a few faithful girlfriends)almost nobody has ever shown the slightest interest in my drawing & painting—the "almost" refers to ST & les Watsons. But if our nonhero has been not really impatient for 60some years,perhaps you can keep relatively calm for(say)10 or 15? Anyhow:from my standpoint the only thing—if you're some sort of artist—is to work a little harder than you can at being who you are:while if you're an unartist(i.e. aren't)nothing but big&quick recognition matters * * *

255 / TO HOWARD NELSON

4 Patchin Place
November 25 '59

Dear Howard—

this is a personal letter. By that I mean it's just between you & me,& cannot be quoted

I've enjoyed reading your "British Isles" ms very much,in spite of its obvious faults. These(as far as I'm concerned)are of 3 sorts:bad grammar,inaccuracy,& bad taste

if you seriously want to write a language,you must first of all learn the grammer of the language. Somewhere there's a book called somebody's Handbook of English Usage(or some such)— & you've got to find that book out & master(sic)its contents:a tough job,if the author's worth his salt. Then,my friend,you'll know why

> Called the Boar in <u>Great Expectations</u>,Pip noted that the owner . . . (p 116)

is WRONG,whereas

> Pip noted that the owner of this hostelry(called "the Boar" in <u>Great Expectations</u> . . .

is RIGHT;& why an UNsentence like

> If it is a meal-time,why not the Lord Warden Hotel . . . for its associations with Dickens,who stopped here in 1856,and with his <u>The Tale of Two Cities</u>,called the Royal George in that novel. (p 125)

would make any honest workman blushallover;in contrast with e.g.

> If it is meal time,we may lunch or dine at the Lord Warden Hotel;which appears as "the Royal George" in A Tale of Two Cities by Dickens,who stopped here in 1856.

A(not The)Tale. Here are just a few other inaccuracies:
> p 76(Lear) — "round" should be "yond"
> 74(Chaucer) — "soot" & "root" should be "sote" & "rote"
> 28(Cynara) — delete "own"
> 41 — "I could not love thee" is by Lovelace(vs Waller)

not to mention sloppinesses such as "imprompty"(181)"Marine" (196)& "described"("it" omitted)"in"(77)

good taste,literarily speaking,is nothing but good manners in writing;& I doubt if anyone can learn good manners of any kind after 9 months. But I'm sure even Joe Blow would squirm to read

> When the former died in Venice,there was not enough room . . . for him to lie next to his hypochondriac wife,so they pickled him . . . (p 3)

for whatever you may think of Browning's poetry,he happened to be a poet;& so — unless you happen to be a barbarian — he's entitled to your respect,as is also the woman who was the love of his life

a possibly even more brutal example of bad taste occurs on p 9. I don't know what the "However,it is hoped . . . it is quoted here" UNsentence is trying to mean;but that's for the Handbook. My point is this:having given your reader one of the noblest(& greatest)poems ever written,you immediately follow this with a mere biographical item — Boswell amusing himself by screwing a whore on Westminster bridge — which is eminently noteworthy(though too crude for your public,perhaps)but which becomes merely vulgar through juxtaposition with Wordsworth's sonnet;while that poem's beauty is smudged by the nextness of obscenity. If the B item can pass muster,insert it much later — reminding your reader that W bridge has been already mentioned "in another connection"

so much for faults

now ViVa your forthright stance re "progress"(p 53) & idiocy
("you will look in vain for writers" p 3)& sexual timidity(the
Burton passages p 60)—I,too,love Lorna Doone & like John
Gilpin & stand up for Swinburne: & I particularly enjoy the
quotation re Rossetti(p 37),the reference to Blake(p 142),
Moore's indignation(p 5),the origin of Debussy's Cathédrale
(p. 188),& any number of other touches including the "blowing-
stone"(p 212). If this weren't so,I should never have bothered
to write at such length

256 / TO EVA HESSE*

4 Patchin Place
December 31 '59

Dear Eva Hesse—

* * * concerning Science & myself . . . it might be said that
S exploits nature;but that I love nature(i, p 32)& loathe exploita-
tion(103)—that,like Death,S is fundamentally a depersonalizing
leveller(47)whereas I stand for individuality or personal unique-
ness as against sameness or standardization(31–32)—that,so far
as I'm concerned,mystery is the root & blossom of eternal
verities(11,43,82,110)while,from a scientific standpoint,eternal
verities are nonsense & mystery is something to be abolished at
any cost—that for me nothing impersonal or measurable mat-
ters(68,110)but for science measurability & impersonality are
everything—that artists(poets, painters, etc)are human beings
(69)whereas scientists are inhuman manipulators of becoming—
& finally,that to know anything equals(by my values)to be merely
undead;whereas "to feel something is to be alive"(68)

in SantaClaus(as in EIMI)"a spirit descends to ascend"—i,p 110.
 As the play opens,SC is "sick at heart";but still himself.
Listening to Death,he becomes un-himself. At Scene 2,he has
turned into a propagandist for the merely knowledgeable(scien-
tific)unworld:a swindler,a wheelminesalesman.
 This swindler bets a member(Voice)of his moronic audience
(Mob)the sum of one dollar that Voice won't spend 500$ on a
share of wheelmine stock. When Voice produces 500$,SC

promptly takes it but hands Voice the dollar he "won";thus impressing Mob's other morons with a show of honesty & fairplay.

In Scene 3 the wheelmine boomerangs—whereupon SC, abandoned by his betrayer(Death)& faced with a now murderous Mob,becomes himself again. Paralleling the cynical-ironical long speech of Scene 2(i, pp 105–6)we have a long speech of agonized sincerity(i, pp 106–7). At its conclusion,SC appeals to a little girl—who,he feels,will identify him because he's no longer Death's tool & "nobody who lives can fool a child".

The identification results in Death's death & the uniting of SC(through Child)with Woman

please believe that I'd rather no play of mine was translated or produced than that a single element of one of my plays was even slightly modified via translation or production. For me "How could Death die?" couldn't be more significant:revealing,as it does,the ὕβρις which is Death's essence. And an actress who couldn't make Woman's "weeping"—however stylized—more dramatically authentic than any "stiff upper lip"ness would(from my standpoint)be no actress at all.

° *Translator of a number of EEC's works into German. The page numbers in parentheses refer to* i: six nonlectures.

257 / *TO HILDEGARDE WATSON*

> 4 Patchin Place
> January 30 '60

Dear Hildegarde—

you certainly are a very great & generous dear,to tell me about your early morning reading. I had no notion that any poem of mine could affect someone—even a most sensitive someone—so vividly:& even now am amazed that the fortunate poem should be <u>somewhere i have never travelled</u> [*Poems 1923–1954*, 263]. Indeed this correspondent can't help suspecting yourself of what the psychoanalysts call "projecting"(himself being,just entre nous,a staunch projector). Well do I remember taking AJ ("Freddy")Ayer—the foremost "logical positivist" quote-philosopher-unquote extant—for a promenade near Joy Farm;

during which stroll,my guest observed(probably anent some entirely spontaneous tribute to Nature which had escaped me)
"you're almost an animist,aren't you."   Quick-as-a-flash—with-
outthinkingatall—I deeply surprised myself by replying " 'almost'? I AM an animist" thereby placing our nonhero precisely
on a par with the least enlightened of coalblackAfricansavages
. . . but don't tell your Handsome Coloured Help,or they'll
never speak to me again

258 / TO ELISABETH KAISER-BRAEM

Silver Lake, N.H.
June 9 '60

Dear Garance—

* * * Miss GS [Gertrude Stein] (since you ask)somehow
never even slightly intrigued me,so it's far from odd we didn't
collide. I did once glimpse an immense shelike It rolling along
Boulevard Montparnasse on top of a microscopic automobile;&
thought "that must be Gertrude Stein". And once,en route to
France,I tried to read a hugely fat hyperopus stuffed-to-burst-
ing with repetitions & labelled The Making Of Americans;
finally quitting at page thirtysomething. But,to the lady's
eternal credit be it said:she stood up for Pétain(in a small &
real book called Wars I Have Known)while all her fellow-choi-
si(e)s were howling for his lifeblood * * *

259 / TO AN UNIDENTIFIED CORRESPONDENT

[4 Patchin Place]
July 4 '60

Dear Miss Lawrence—

re your letter of June 24th:not all of my poems are to be read
aloud—some,like the 3 you mention,are to be seen & not heard.
As for their meaning—I can only tell you what they mean to
me

to me,the 1st(short)poem [*Poems, 1923–1954*, 393] suggests a socalled public figure i.e. windbag. He rises to applause ("applaws")& after a pause—indicated by the(vertical)linespace— begins his speech with the words <u>fellow citizens</u>(" 'fell/ow/sit/ isn'ts' ")after which(again a linespace)comes a pause("(a paw s") during which I note that his hands resemble a pair of paws ("(a paw s")

the 2nd poem [p. 459] tells me in its own vivid way that an <u>immobile</u> cat suddenly puts on an acrobatic act:& <u>fall-leaps,</u> <u>becomingdrift-whirl-fully</u> <u>float-tumblish;</u>& then <u>wanders away,</u> <u>exactly as if nothing had ever happened</u>

via the 3rd poem [*95 Poems* #68]: what at first impresses me as merely a pair of wideopen eyes
 "the(oo)is"
becomes an intense stare
 "lOOk"
of alive eyes-which-say-yes
 "(aliv/e)e/yes"
belonging to a child who is(reminds me of)myself
 "are(chIld)and"
who's gone
 "wh(g/o/ne)/o"
leaving me with a memory of his eyes
 "o . . . o"
&,by becoming was instead of is(i.e. disappearing)at the same time becoming-intensely(the am of)myself
 "w(A)a(M)s" * * *

260 / TO HIS DAUGHTER

[4 Patchin Place]
January 15 '61

Dear Nancy—

the lucky recipients of your double letter are much more than grateful. They're delighted. As for the poem:I particularly enjoy "fused roof-tones flower" & "sky-riding/into the towering dark". Thank you again! (Hymettos has of course had favorable overtones ever since Kevin & Ioanna entertained Marion & me. there)

yes "it" 's a mustache;& my consort believes that a mustached passport-photo taken in Paris re WW1 is now hiding in NH. On verra

perhaps nobody remembers till 5. Perhaps some day you'll remember the time [in Paris] I was allowed to take you for one whole hour to some sort of little foire — where we rode a variety of tremendous animals including chevaux de bois;& the heartily handsome manageress handsomely & heartily congratulated me on you, as only une française would or could. Being myself nearly sans time-sense(except as rhythm)I can only guess when certain still-vivid childhood experiences may have occurred. But shall never forget how my staunch(then as now) friend Sibley Watson, by way of comforting our unhappy non-hero, gently reminded him that the greatly(to me)wise Freud says a child's self("psyche")is already formed at whatever age you were when we lost each other

rather imagine "Mlle Chevassus" floated somewhere in the background of a decorous visit I once made to a Mr & Mrs Macdermot; during which you were somewhat(it seemed to me)ostentatiously invited by the former to sing. Your pluck was wonderful! You hated being made to showoff, but your singing teacher's reputation was at stake & you didn't hate me; so you sang. Long before, your mother had assured you your father was dead(or a little bird?)but you sang your best. The song was enchanting — "tiens!me voilà:c'est polichinelle,mesdames" — & you sang it not only correctly but beautifully

everybody thanks you, the world thanks you, for Ioanna's remark(in Greek!)about the extraordinary intelligence of Santa Claus. Am sorry Elizabeth's rag-prone; but the-young-lady-daughter of an English friend of ours went through a period (or phase)which makes E's seem ornamental — & completely recovered. And I was a bad boy ilyaunefois

concerning Rilke — ever since Hildegarde Watson introduced us(i page 7)have slowly, as always with what I love, been studying his poems; but though I've read the Panther in German as well as translation,don't feel I ever quite understood it. Should appreciate a literal(if such a thing's possible)rendering;when you've nothing better to do

speaking of building & cutting & blasting & chopping(not to mention Fraternité or nettles)Marion was told the other day that we'd have to move,since 4 PP will be "renovated" next June;i.e. turned into a flock of 1room-with-toilet-&-kitchen "apartments";all for the sake of $$. So she—je suis faible dans la vie,as Cézanne said;before calling for an axe & chopping down his own front door because he'd locked himself out & 2 strange females were lurking nearby—finally got to see our regular lawyer;but he was(though friendly)too busy to help her. She's at present trying to locate an elusive ex-alcoholic avocat who prevented someone we know from being evicted on a charge of not paying rent;the point being,that the wouldbe evictress was that alcoholic wouldbe-lady who wishes to throw us away after decades of faithful rentpaying. Of course,by "renovating",the wouldbe would make a handsome profit;since we're paying relatively très peu

261 / *TO CAROL POULIN*

4 Patchin Place
July 8 '61

Dear Miss Poulin—

thanks for your letter of
July 3rd. I enclose a
paraphrase of the poem you
mention,which may possibly
help you

a paraphrase of poem 7, pages 282–283 of <u>Poems '23–'54</u>

the poem's 1st line(which is also,semiparenthetically,its title) tells you that this is a sonnet whose subject is:how to run the world

a sonnet has 2 parts,the octave(lines 1–8)& the sestet(lines 9–14)

A . . . the way to run the world is always not to(try to)run it;
B . . . the apparently real world being actually an illusion
C . . . that is,something negative or can't or which isn't solid
therefore,instead of worrying about worldly things,
D . . . drink &
E . . . eat of her — the earth's — voice in whose silence is the music
of spring
F . . . remembering that to feel is an opening,but to understand
is a shutting,experience
G . . . never be guilty of selfpity;if you once had a little but now
have less,forget the earlier time gladly;& when you have least,
remember gladly the time when you had most
H . . . treat your true(highest)self as something sacred — never
flaunt it in public,like a flag,for everyone to see

Sestet

lines 9 10 11 say that the subject of the sonnet's 2nd part is
     not "flesh is grass"(i.e. living is dying)as the Bible tells you,
but dying is living("grass is flesh")
     or: what's important isn't conforming(washing,not-being-
dirty)but self-expression(swimming)
     or: it isn't sleeping that matters,but dreaming;it isn't know-
ing,but guessing

L . . . I owe death one life,the mortal part of me,& bequeath all
the(immortal)rest of myself to these children;whom I see building,out of snow,the figure of a man who'll melt away in the rain
(becoming a rainman)

262 / *TO HILDEGARDE WATSON*

Silver Lake, N.H.
July 22 '61

Dear Hildegarde —

we've had a sad experience,of which I feel free to tell you because you're our most wonderful friend. Every year since a

birdhouse was installed—up on a pole some hundred yards from our own house,& so placed that Marion can see it from her bedroom—swallows have come;& raised their families:& delighted us with their faultless acrobatic flying & rippling brooklike voices.   But these were treeswallows,smaller & less brilliantly coloured than the barnswallows of my childhood;& I couldn't help hoping that some day a pair of gaudy-elegant "swallowtailed" barnswallows would return to an old nest,still standing far up under the barn roof

last autumn,at Marion's suggestion,I asked a firstrate carpenter (whose nothingifnotNewEngland name is Hidden)to make me a real—with a North light—studio in the barn.   And this summer, shortly before our treeswallows had departed,a pair of barnswallows arrived;establishing themselves after a few days in the old nest.   Presently three buffoonlike heads,absurdly masked with enormous lightcoloured bills,appeared over the nest's rim —30 feet from the barnfloor—& all day long the parents of these diminutive clowns magnificently swooped through height,capturing insects for their offspring:unless Hidden or his helper Nickerson or I came anywhere near the nest,when we were fiercely belaboured with wings & cries

meantime Septemberish wetcold changed to stifling heat,& I began worrying about the fledglings;since that nest—crammed with recklessly(by now)lurching & vividly squirming birds— must be fearfully hot:& only last year,during a heatwave,I'd seen three young barnswallows lying dead below a nest built in (of all places)the Madison railroad station.   Marion was as worried as I;& eventually we rigged a kind of net just above the floor under the nest:but without avail.   Three birds fell,in the course of a week;& only one lived a few minutes

now the father&motherbirds are gone,& our hearts feel as empty as our skies

4 Patchin Place
February 19 '62

Dear Mary—

am glad the letter-before-this pleased you,& more than glad my poems cheer you! By all means translate the CPs & Is5 introductions,if so doing renders life even slightly more pleasant. Our NewEnglandly adolescent nonhero had many a deep libidinous thrill from our family's Old Testament—since you mention "The Good Book"—& one of his favorite shortstories (which must surely be one of the greatest in the world)was & always will remain Naaman(II Kings 5)

some years back,I caught a prize which led to reciting poems outdoors of a torrid summer evening at the Boston Public Garden(extremely difficult feat both celestially & collectively on account of planes & dogfights). Afterward,the Harvard Poet in charge of literary festivities suggested I designate my successor; whereupon I promptly named Robinson Jeffers,affirming that his neglect by UNamerican "critics" was immensely scandalous. This greatly embarassed the HPicolf,since RJ happened to be his cousin;but all's-well-that-etc:for Marianne Moore—whose work,incidentally, I also admire—got the job * * *

I've already mentioned Boston—this highly respectable & incredibly corrupt town's oldest & lowest burleskshowtheatre(near Scollay Square,where sailors materialize from the nearby Charlestown navyyard)was for decades affectionately entitled "the Old Howard"(it occurred on Howard Street)by its faithful patrons;not excluding nonstudious students,e.g. EEC . . . who enchantedly watched "humanity" As Is "unflinchingly applaud all songs" carefully sandwiched between smut & sex "containing the words country home and mother"

please thank your gallant publisher for courteously agreeing re my "royalty". And I'll ask Marion about photographsof-paintings. With love to the red squirrel as well as to EP°°

** [EEC's note] "The poet is no tender slip of fairy stock, who requires peculiar institutions and edicts for his defence,but the toughest son of earth and of Heaven,and by his greater strength and endurance his fainting companions will recognize the God in him. It is the worshippers of beauty,after all,who have done the real pioneer work of the world."
                    Henry David Thoreau
                    (A Week On The Concord And Merrimack Rivers)
                    1849

* *Ezra Pound's daughter, who had written to say, among other things, that she was translating into Italian some poems of Robinson Jeffers.*

264 / TO ROBERT WAGNER, MAYOR OF NEW YORK CITY*

[4 Patchin Place]
March 6, 1962

To a human being,nothing is so important as privacy—since without privacy,individuals cannot exist:and only individuals are human. I am unspeakably thankful that the privacy of 4 Patchin Place will be respected;and shall do my best to prove worthy of this courtesy.

E.E.Cummings
March 6 1962

* *Mayor Wagner intervened to save Patchin Place from "renovation."*

265 / TO MATTI MEGED*

[4 Patchin Place]
May 13 [1962]

Dear Matti Meged—

just finished revising captions for a book of 50 Photographs †
by Marion(they're superb!)which may appear this autumn;&
can now thank you,at least partially,for your fine MayDay letter.
One of Marion's portraits,by the by,is of a dark dashingly hand-

some acquaintance of ours;& I call this picture COUGAR (meaning NorthAmerican mountainlion)under which title my caption reads

"One Law for the Lion & Ox is Oppression.

(Blake)"

on behalf of her&myselves,have turned down "The President and Mrs. Kennedy" 's "black tie" invitation ("not transferable"!!!) to dine at "The White House" with,as it turned out,70some crooks punks & preknowbellists;as well as a more recent request by The Minister Of The Interior that we celebrate Henry David Thoreau's birth or death or both in company with another select bevy including(you'll be astonished to learn)"two con-temporary friends of Thoreau" viz "Chief Justice Black and Robert Frost"! But lest thou shouldst suspect me of snobbism, know that(con spouse)I appeared not long since at City Hall (NY)& was copiously snapshotted with-&-without Mayor Wagner . . . this being the price we paid,M&I,for not being thrown out of our 35year residence at 4 Patchin;after a lawsuit lasting about a year

am delighted to find that those"Poetry"poems had the good luck to encounter yourself.‡ And here's hoping that what you call "an independent world,consistent of spiritual elements only and resistable to all destruction" may remain the undersigned's solace,challenge,home,unknownness,& shieldspearsword while his earthly life lasts! That such a world needs no excuse for itself is(of course)always being rediscovered:less than a year ago,Marion brought a "remaindered"(i.e. financially worthless) volume wherein I met these wonderful words,translated from the Greek of Plato's Republic:

"it"(the Ideal State)"is laid up in heaven as a pattern for him who wills to see,and seeing to found a city in himself. Whether it exists anywhere or ever will exist is no matter. His conduct will be an expression of the laws of that city alone,and of no other."

what can mere "use" say to the truth underlying those noble words—the truth which you yourself call "man's own and true domain"? How infinitely morethanright you are in feeling that, instead of "detach"ing you from life,"it teaches me to attend

only to this domain,where the word 'life' is still meaningful,
intense,has a chance of growth and victory"!

—bravissimo!

° *Israeli writer and teacher.*
† Adventures in Value (*New York, 1962*).
‡ *A total of seven poems, all reprinted in* 73 Poems, *had appeared in two recent issues of*
Poetry (*October, 1961; March, 1962*).

INDEX

Abbott, Beatrice, 217
Academy of American Poets fellowship, 213, 214n.
Acrobats, EEC admires, 156, 221, 258–259
Active Anthology (Pound, ed.), 138 and n.
Adventures in Value (Marion Cummings), 274, 276n.
Agamemnon (Aeschylus), 165
Agassiz, Louis, 205–206
Agassiz Museum, Harvard, 205
Aiken, Conrad, 139
Alcázar Castle, Segovia, EEC visits, 76
America, 63, 214
    EEC critical of, 19, 70, 87, 149, 157, 178, 184, 223, 253–254, 256
    militancy of, 19, 33, 34, 39
American Museum of Natural History, N.Y.C., 129–131, 204, 205
Americans, abroad, 25, 79, 122
    EEC on, 28, 32, 128, 223, 237, 244
    militancy of, 47, 53
Ames, Dick, 127
& [AND], (Cummings), 115, 261
Anderson, John, 133
Andover boys, EEC on, 19, 20, 21, 22
Andrews, Kevin, 269
Andrews, Mrs. Kevin. *See* Cummings, Nancy
"Andy" (ambulance corps), 27–28
Angleton, James, 150n., 158
    letters to, 149, 157
Angleton, Mrs. James (Cicely), letter to, 180
Aragon, Louis, 226
    "Le Front Rouge," 226 and n.
Aragon, Mrs. Louis (Elsa Triolet), 226
Arizona, trip to, 170
Armory Show, N.Y.C. (1913), 257
Army, EEC's dislike of. *See* War
Ayer, A. J., 178, 266–267
    letters to, 186, 194

Bach, Johann S., 180
Baker, Professor, 17

Dulles, John Foster, 256
Dylan Thomas in America (Brinnin), 260n.

Eastman, Max, 134, 161, 213, 238
Eastman, Mrs. Max (Eliena), letter to, 191
Echo, 162
Editions De La Revue Fontaine, 201
Editors, EEC and, 136–137, 215, 235–236
    letters to, 87, 187
Eimi (Cummings), 122, 123, 128, 139, 212, 223, 226, 229, 265
Einstein, Albert, 194, 248
Elephants as symbols to EEC, 5, 159, 205, 214
Eliot, T. S., xv, xviii, 69, 93, 115, 177, 178, 191, 218, 221
Elliot, William Yandell, 217, 218n.
Emerson, Ralph Waldo, 103
England (Albion), 139, 142, 243
Englishmen, EEC on, 25, 244
Enormous Room, The (Cummings), 63–64, 72n., 73, 83, 87–88 and n., 89,
    102, 115, 136, 137n., 165, 227–228 and n., 234n., 244
Esquire, 138 and n.
Europe, 178
    trip to, 212, 213
Ezra Pound (Norman), 254 and n., 259

Facsimiles of letters, 6, 35
Farley, James, 132
Fascism, EEC on, 214, 254
Faulkner, Douglas, 262n.
    letter to, 262
Fieldbook of Wild Birds and Their Music (Mathew), 206
Finland, 253
Finley, John, 220 and n.
    letter to, 223
Fitzgerald, M. Eleanor, 133
Fiume, Italy, 69, 104
Flaherty, Elizabeth, 232–233
Florence, Italy (Firenze), trip to, 249
Ford, Ford Madox, 104
XLI Poems (Cummings), 115, 261
Fox, Douglas, 155 and n., 163
Fox, John, 229
France, 87, 89, 100, 127, 214
    during World War I, 23, 27, 29, 30, 31, 32, 34, 39, 40, 50, 56,
      72, 73, 157

Vassar College, reading at, 208–209
Venice, Italy, 89
     trip to, 248–249
Village Voice, 256
Vision, A (Yeats), 148
Vogue (French), 123, 126

Wagner, Robert, 274n., 275
     letter to, 274
Wahl, Jean, 201
Walton, Elise Cavanna, 217n.
     letter to, 217
War, dislike of army, 49–56, 72, 157–158, 257–258
       EEC against, 14–15, 34, 38–39, 53–54, 160, 165–166, 208, 247.
        See also Korean War; World War I
Ward, Mrs. Samuel, 151
Wars I Have Known (Stein), 267
Washington Times Herald, 220n.
Watson, Mrs. (mother of J. S. Watson), 68
Watson, James Sibley, xviii, 33, 52, 59, 63, 68, 69, 71, 79, 110, 111, 128,
       133, 151, 185n., 188, 195, 207, 251, 263, 269
     letters to, 147–148, 202, 229
Watson, Mrs. James S. (Hildegarde), xviii, 68, 185n., 263, 269
     letters to, 127, 150, 166, 172, 179, 182, 185, 188, 195, 203, 207,
       208, 211, 224, 238, 245, 246, 249, 255, 259, 266, 271
Watson, Jeanne, 185 and n.
Watts, Mr., 177
Webster, Massachusetts, 26, 29, 45, 59
Week on the Concord and Merrimack Rivers, A (Thoreau), 274
Weiner, Mr., 36
Weiss, Theodore, 169, 170n.
Werner, M. R., 112, 116, 121, 125, 171, 214
     letters to, 160, 165, 256
What Is Psychoanalysis? (Jones), 229
Whitman, Walt, 72
Whittier, John Greenleaf, quoted, 62
Wilde, Oscar, 225, 255
Wiley (secretary to American ambassador), 45
William Blake: His Philosophy and Symbols (Damon), 261
Williams, Talcott, 19
Williams, William Carlos, 214, 219, 220n.
     letter to, 149
Willkie, Wendell, 158
Willkie, Mrs. Wendell, 177
Wilson, Arthur, 13–14 and n., 15, 33, 39, 92